Ahmed Abdalla was born in Egypt in 1950. He graduated from Cairo University in 1973 with a degree in political science, and received a Ph.D. from Cambridge University, England, in 1984. During his student years in Egypt, he was president of the Higher National Committee of Cairo University Students, which led the student uprising of January 1972, and he was a leading defendant in the 1973 trials of student activists.

AL SAQI
BOOKS

Ahmed Abdalla

Al Saqi Books

Distributed by Zed Books

The Student Movement and National Politics in Egypt

1923–1973

British Library Cataloguing in Publication Data

Abdalla, Ahmed
   The student movement and national politics
   in Egypt.
   1. Education, Higher——Political aspects——
   Egypt——History——20th century
   I. Title
   378.62   LA1648

   ISBN 0-86356-117-9
   ISBN 0-86356-027-X Pbk

   First published 1985
   © Ahmed Abdalla, 1985

   Al Saqi Books, 26 Westbourne Grove, London W2

   Typeset by P.R.G. Graphics Ltd., Redhill, Surrey.

   Printed in Great Britain by
   The Thetford Press Ltd
   Thetford, Norfolk.

Contents

Tables

Abbreviations

ASU	Arab Socialist Union
CAPMS	Central Agency for Public Mobilization and Statistics
ECS	Executive Committee of Students
EMNL	Egyptian Movement for National Liberation
GUS	General Union of Students
HADITU	Democratic Movement for National Liberation
HECS	Higher Executive Committee of Students
HNCCUS	Higher National Committee of Cairo University Students
MCS	Mixed Committee of Students
MP	Member of Parliament
NCs	National Committees of students
NCS	Nationalist Committee of Students
NCWS	National Committee of Workers and Students
PCNCS	Preparatory Committee for the National Committee of Students
PLO	Palestine Liberation Organization
RCC	Revolutionary Command Council
SSPR	Society of the Supporters of the Palestinian Revolution
SYO	Socialist Youth Organization
UN	United Nations
US	United States of America
USSR	Union of Soviet Socialist Republics
YMMA	Young Muslim Men's Association

To the People of *Masr al-Qadeema*
(Old Cairo)
the illiterate who gave me knowledge;
the poor who enriched my conscience.

إهداء ..

إلى أهـــالى مصـــرالقـديــمة ..
الأميــين الــذيـن عـلـمـونى ..
والفقــراء الــذيـن أغنــوا ضـميرى.

Preface

The research carried out to produce this book was no easy task for someone who started from scratch, in both the academic and the financial sense. The long years involved were but a reflection of the rocky start. Throughout these years I received assistance and support from many people who were duly mentioned in the preface to my doctoral dissertation, which represents the core of this book.

I am particularly indebted to those who helped me in the academic arena: Mahmoud Abd al-Fadil, John Dunn, Roger Owen, Samir Radwan and Aniel Seal.

People whose moral and material support was crucial to the accomplishment of this work are my wife Ebtehal Rashad who carried the burden with me most of the way, and Haj Abd al-Latif al-Kaumy who assisted me materially on rainy days and led the campaign of encouragement amongst my neighbours and friends in our Cairo district of Ain al-Sera.

I am also indebted to Dr Ibrahim Saad al-Din Abdalla and other colleagues at the Arab Planning Institute in Kuwait where I worked for a while, to a number of Cambridge neighbours, friends and colleagues who contributed both directly and indirectly to the accomplishment of this work, and to those Egyptian friends who helped me in various ways.

In writing this book, I have consulted a wide range of references in the two areas of student politics and Egypt's modern history. An important primary source of information is represented by interviews with activists of the student movement in Egypt during the period under investigation. I succeeded in winning the co-operation of a number of them, who gave valuable historical testimonies. Scattered throughout the world, it was not always easy to gain access to these former activists, and some of those I managed to reach unfortunately refused to co-operate, giving various excuses or at times no reason at all.

A number of original documents which I obtained as a student activist myself in Egypt in the 1970s provided another important source of information. Since many of these are now reprinted in book form, they are referred to in the endnotes.

Finally, I hope this work will be of academic value to those who study Egyptian politics, and student politics in general. As to those Egyptian students who represent the subject matter of the book, I hope it may contribute to their understanding of the very sphere in which they act, thus helping them to build the future of their country with a clearer vision of their role in it. The research which led to my writing the book has cost me many years of separation from those to whom it is dedicated; I hope they will forgive the separation and accept the dedication.

Ahmed Abdalla
Cambridge, September 1984

Part One

1923–52

1

Independent Egypt's Political System

The direct consequence of the Revolution of 1919, when a wave of armed revolts and strikes followed Britain's rejection of requests by Egyptian nationalists, led by Saad Zaghlul Pasha, that a delegation (*Wafd*) be permitted to present Egypt's plea for independence directly to London and then to the Paris Peace Conference, was that in February 1922 Britain felt compelled to announce its recognition of Egypt as an independent constitutional monarchy. Despite this Declaration, however, major sectors were reserved for British control: defence, the security of communications, and a continuation of the Capitulations system, whereby foreign nationals in Egypt and Sudan were exempted from taxation and had the right to be tried in their own courts. In view of these restrictions, many nationalists regarded the Declaration as granting Egypt only nominal independence, terming the situation 'a legal farce, a sop thrown to them to keep them quiet'.[1] It failed in any sense to realize the 1919 Revolution's demand for complete independence and merely allowed Egyptian representative institutions a measure of power-sharing with the British authorities.

While the British saw the Declaration as a means of consolidating their precarious position in Egypt, the new arrangement was viewed by the country's first constitutional government, dominated by the Wafd leadership, as only a first step towards complete independence. These disparate interpretations ensured that 'nominal independence' would prove both unstable and contentious. In practice, the Declaration augmented rather than diminished British difficulties: it provided grounds for Egyptians to denounce Britain's efforts to defend its interests in Egypt as blatant interference in the affairs of an independent country.

Britain continued to employ strong diplomatic pressure to

influence every aspect of political decision-making in Egypt. Nor did it hesitate to call on military force to impose its will on the supposedly independent government of the country. Between the Declaration of 1922 and the Anglo-Egyptian Treaty of Independence of 1936 Britain came close to resorting to military force on three separate occasions: after the assassination of Sir Lee Stack, the Sirdar of Sudan, in November 1924; over the Egyptianization of positions of command in the Egyptian army in May 1927; and over the excessively 'liberal' bill for the regulation of public assemblies proposed to the Egyptian parliament in March 1928. As Saad Zaghlul, the leader of the nationalist movement, said a few years after the Declaration of independence, 'Our big mistake was that we thought we were really independent.'[2]

Egypt's nominal independence took the form of a constitutional monarchy, where the two main poles of the political system were the Palace on the one hand and the core of the nationalist movement, the Wafd party, on the other. The persistence of British power added a third element. The power struggle between those three components shaped Egyptian politics for three decades. Within this framework, nationalist forces continued their struggle to transform Egypt's nominal independence into genuine independence, while Britain remained eager to legalize its presence in the country. Accordingly, repeated negotiations over this issue in the late 1920s and early 1930s all ended in failure.

With the emergence of Fascism in Europe and the intensification of the nationalist movement in Egypt itself, Britain became even more eager to bring the issue to a satisfactory conclusion.[3] Thus the Treaty of 1936 came into being. The treaty was regarded as a major success for British diplomacy: after fifty-four years Britain had finally established a legal title to its occupation of Egypt. Despite the advantages of the treaty for the Egyptian side (the abolition of Capitulations, an independent army, membership of the League of Nations, and so on), the general feeling among more educated Egyptians was somewhat ambivalent because the treaty allowed a British military presence to continue. Hence 'nominal' independence came a step closer towards becoming 'partial' independence in practice. As with the 1922 Declaration, Egyptian nationalists saw the Treaty of 1936 as another step towards complete independence.

The treaty did not fundamentally alter the three-cornered political system. The British continued the role they had played since the first constitutional government took office in 1924: holding the balance between the Wafd majority and the autocratic inclinations of the Palace. Although the Wafd aimed to stabilize the constitutional life of the country, through neutralizing the British and consequently hampering the autocracy of the Palace, the treaty did not help it to achieve this aim. Britain remained the principal force in the political system: in foreign affairs it favoured the Wafd, which, with its stable government, was a more reliable partner; in internal affairs it favoured the Palace, hoping thereby to offset the populist policies of the Wafd and to avoid alienating the Palace.

Thus both before and after the Treaty of 1936, Egyptian politicians remained convinced of three constants in British policy towards Egypt. First, Britain supported the Palace. Second, Britain's primary commitment was to the defence of its own interests; any concern with those of Egypt was purely incidental. Third, an Egyptian cabinet survived for only as long as the British Resident, or later the British ambassador, permitted.

Hence Egyptian politicians of all shades acknowledged the influence of the British Embassy in Cairo. Sir Miles Lampson, later Lord Killearn, played the role of virtually an uncrowned King of Egypt. Only when Lampson left Egypt in 1946, after twelve years of service, did King Farouq start to feel truly a king. Despite their hatred of the British presence in their country, ordinary Egyptians were obliged to swallow British interference in Egyptian affairs when it was the only alternative to suppressing the autocratic leanings of the Palace and restoring constitutional rule, as happened in 1926, 1934 and again in 1942.[4] When British tanks installed a Wafd government in 1942, Lampson was greeted by an Egyptian crowd wishing him long life and bearing him on its shoulders.

During the Second World War, the British had an even bigger say in Egypt's economic and political affairs. In the course of their retreat before Rommel's attack, they even considered flooding the Nile Delta to halt his progress if necessary.[5] Egypt's contribution to the Allied war effort was enormous.[6] When the war ended, many Egyptians expected Britain to show its gratitude by withdrawing its troops and thus setting the seal on the country's independence. On 14 June 1945 Captain J.S. May reported the reaction of the Egyptian crowd watching the parade of British troops celebrating their King's birthday:

* There was a great deal of anti-British feeling amongst the crowd.

* Egyptians were surprised that there were so many troops still left in Egypt.

* Hope that this would be last parade of the British was heard to be expressed by several onlookers.

* Remarks overheard included: 'We shall do the same to them as the Syrians have to the French.'

* Remarks passed by illiterate natives included: 'Why is there no Egyptian flag? Why should we allow them to do this? – this is our country.'

* Better educated Egyptians remarked: 'They can celebrate their King's Birthday in their own country', 'Why are all these troops still in Egypt when the war in Europe is over?', 'The day is not very far away when we shall win our real independence.'

* Two young Egyptian students said that the parade was organised to intimidate the Egyptians.[7]

Lord Killearn's comment speaks for itself: 'Not one word of gratitude was heard in regard to the role played by the British troops in general, and by those on parade in particular, in saving Egypt from extinction at the hands of Rommel and Mussolini.'[8] The British remained oblivious to Egyptian nationalist demands until the Wafd government unilaterally abrogated the treaty in October 1951 and guerrilla warfare broke out against the British troops in the Suez Canal Zone, paving the way for the army seizure of power in July 1952, which destroyed the entire political system in which the British were operating.

The Egyptian monarch for the first few years of constitutional government was King Fouad. He had been brought up in a despotic environment and was a great admirer of machiavellianism. He resented the Constitution of 1923, and indeed believed that without British insistence there would have been no constitution. While it was being drawn up, he confided to one of his aides that 'if this constitution was meant to be Bolshevik he would claim Lenin's powers, and if it was meant to be democratic he would claim the powers of the American president'.[9]

The Constitution of 1923 allowed the King very wide powers — the absolute right to dissolve parliament and dismiss cabinets; the right of amnesty and reprieve; and the right to appoint army officers, diplomats, the Shaikh of al-Azhar and two-fifths of the Senate. Fouad did not hesitate to use his powers to the full and encouraged his supporters to establish royalist political parties: in 1925 al-Ittihad (the Union) was founded, and then in 1930 al-Shaab (the People). His power rested in the permanency of his position, a fact appreciated by both the British and the Wafd. He frequently attempted to reduce parliament to a consultative body and cabinets in his reign never fell through a vote of no confidence or served out a term of office; they were dismissed at royal will. Parliaments never lasted for their full term of four years but were invariably dissolved by decree. The average life of a cabinet was eighteen months and during the ten-year period from 1926 to 1936 parliament sat for a total of only thirty-two months. In addition, King Fouad was known to have a weak character[10] and was notoriously corrupt.[11]

When Fouad died in April 1936 his son Farouq, after a brief period under a Regency Counsel, ascended the throne in July 1937. The political pattern established under Fouad persisted in the new regime. The powerful chief of the Royal Cabinet, Ahmad Hasanain Pasha, confided to a journalist friend:

> Tell your Wafdist friends that if His Majesty had to depose the government or dissolve the parliament once, he will indulge in it for good . . . I advise them to be gentle and mild with him . . . They should understand his feeling as a young man who might be sneered at by his princely relatives if he showed weakness before the Wafd . . . If he follows the course of his father he will never stop, for he is young, obstinate and proud of his people's love for him.[12]

Farouq's policies were attributed by many commentators to his taste for pleasure in his private life and to the despotic exercise of his will in public life. According to a minister of the period, Farouq was 'a victim of mental unsoundness, unstable family life, the breeding of a father who in effect hated the Egyptians, lack of education, bad advisers, and accession to the throne at a young age.'[13] But this is a necessarily partial verdict: the basic responsibility plainly lay with the system which gave free rein to such inclinations.

The Treaty of 1936 settled the issue of Anglo-Egyptian relations for a while, and the internal power struggle between the Palace and the Wafd intensified. The young King bolstered his popular image by presenting himself as a devout and energetic figure. He managed to rally the support of the al-Azhar shaikhs, powerful independent politicians like Ali Maher Pasha and emerging extra-parliamentary groups such as Young Egypt and the Muslim Brotherhood. In this way he reinforced his own position in relation to the Wafd and made himself, as he saw it, much less dependent upon the British than his father had been. In the early part of the Second World War he showed pro-Axis leanings, to the fury of the British: in February 1942 British tanks surrounded the Royal Palace and Farouq was forced to order the formation of a Wafd government, a gesture that enhanced his popularity as a symbol of national resistance.

Farouq did everything in his power to consolidate his own position and undermine that of the Wafd. He started by appointing an opponent of the Wafd, Ali Maher Pasha, as the chief of his Royal Cabinet. Ali Maher transformed the Palace-Wafd struggle from the language of memoranda and articles into the language of demonstrations and street clashes between supporters of the two camps. Farouq's fifteen-year reign witnessed no fewer than twenty-four cabinets.[14] He widened the inclusion of non-partisan politicians, known as the independents, in cabinets most of which acted as pliant instruments of the Palace. He strengthened his grip on al-Azhar and found among its *ulama* those ready to offer theological sanctions for his actions. He interfered directly in elections, making it possible for his supporters to raise electioneering slogans such as: 'Elect the candidate of the Palace' and 'Do not elect so-and-so . . . Our beloved King is angry with him.' He did not hesitate to dismiss the Wafd government in 1944, giving the following perfunctory explanation:

> Since I am anxious to see my country ruled by a democratic government which works for its good and implements its constitution, establishes equality between all Egyptians in rights and obligations, and provides food and clothing to the people, We decided to depose you from office.[15]

When he met the members of a Senate committee he told them bluntly, 'It is not enough that the nation confides in you . . . the King's confidence should go with it.'[16]

Farouq also took great pleasure in interfering in the daily running of the executive. He infiltrated government offices through agents who leaked detailed information to him. At his trial following the downfall of the monarchy the King's press consultant, Karim Thabit, testified:

> The King knew everything . . . He was consulted in everything . . . His permission was required for everything, by all governments . . . Nothing could be done without his approval . . . Not just the major affairs which he was entitled to know, but also the minor ones like appointing a municipal director, giving fifteen days leave to the Egyptian consul in Liverpool to see his ill mother, changing the winter uniform of army and police men into the summer uniform . . . etc. Since the time of King Fouad, between 1924 and 1952, the agenda of the cabinet was checked first by the King to recommend the items which he wanted and defer the ones he did not want. This happened in all reigns whether of the majority or of the minority governments.[17]

The Egyptian monarchy, accordingly, was far from constitutional. Parliament never attained sufficient weight to control or even to challenge the monarch, and the executive administration remained a façade behind which virtually dictatorial powers were exercised. As al-Tabi put it, 'A supreme order neatly written on a piece of paper and signed by the Master of the country was sufficient to paralyse the constitution and dismiss the government which people elected, for no reason but a royal whim.'[18] In addition, the Palace had its own unaccountable police force and an extra-parliamentary secret apparatus known as the Iron Guard, created to intimidate its enemies. It is hardly surprising that the monarchy should in the end have lost the support of its own ultimate guarantee, the army, and become the principal target for the young officers who seized power in July 1952. Even the British began to view with concern the excesses of the monarch. As Lord Killearn reported:

> Prince Mohamed Aly called on me in Alexandria this morning and said he wished to speak seriously on a very grave matter . . . The vagaries of King Farouk were becoming altogether too much; and in the interest of the country one of two things should be done: (1) either he should go, or (2) the laws of the country should be so tightened up as to exercise a real check upon the Royal vagaries. Egypt was ruled by a crazy youth *who must* be restrained . . .

I told His Royal Highness that he must know that this teasing situation was continuously in our minds. But clearly we did not wish to provoke any more internal crises in Egypt: nonetheless I would confess, in strictest confidence, that I often wondered more and more how we could carry on with this irresponsible youth . . .

At the same time we were not in the habit of crossing our bridges until we came to them. And I could not foretell in advance how we should react in the event of a major constitutional clash. But my own present feeling was that, admirable though it was in *theory* to keep out of Egyptian internal politics and leave the King and his Prime Minister to fight it out together, yet the more I pondered upon it the less easy did it seem in *practice* for us to do so. If, for example, Nahas Pasha went to King Farouk and insisted (as on the face of it he had every right to insist, as a Constitutional Prime Minister) upon His Majesty comporting himself both with greater correctitude towards the elected Government of his country and also with decorum more befitting a Monarch (and incidentally the Head of the Moslem faith in Egypt . . . [19]

The Wafd (the Delegation) was established in the heat of the Revolution of 1919 to represent the Egyptian nation in its bid for independence from British rule. It was not initially a political party in the conventional sense of the word.[20] Its leader, Saad Zaghlul Pasha, said, 'Those who say that we are a party aiming at independence imply that there is another party among the people which does not aim at independence.'[21] The doctrine of the Wafd maintained that it was the 'unchanging guardian of the public interest'.[22] Its vision of independent Egypt was conceived in liberal terms: an Egypt where Muslims and Copts were united in the sacred bond of national loyalty, where government was constitutional, individual rights were respected, women were free and national education was universal. This vision, however, was not born with the Wafd but took shape gradually in the course of its struggle.

By 1924 'neither in act nor statement was the Wafd liberal nationalist, but in fact mostly as a result of a pursuit of a pragmatic policy of political agitation it had indigenised the imported ideology of liberal nationalism'.[23] The Wafd party which took power in 1924 was in no sense a typical parliamentary party. In the first parliament of 1924, where the Wafd had a majority of 195 seats out of 214 (well over 90 per cent), Zaghlul used his majority to bar the journalists of the opposition Constitutional Liberal party (al-Ahrar) from attending the inauguration of parliament and shortly afterwards stripped its leader of his parliamentary seat. Between 1926 and 1928, however, the Wafd became more willing to co-exist with other parties.

The transformation of the Wafd into a parliamentary political party was facilitated by a number of practical steps. First, it contested the elections of 1924 on the basis of the Constitution of 1923, formulated by a committee in which the Wafd was not represented and which Zaghlul denounced as a 'committee of gangsters'.[24] Second, Zaghlul himself assumed the premiership after the Wafd's victory. His assumption of office, rather than leaving this to one of his lieutenants, sobered his attitudes, transforming him from nationalist leader into party president. Third, Zaghlul's first cabinet included a number of ministers who were neither Wafdist nor militant nationalists. Finally, the assassination of Sir Lee Stack in the same year brought the humiliating downfall of Zaghlul's government under British pressure, and provided a further impetus to the Wafd's transformation into a fully parliamentary political party.

As a political party, the Wafd became the guardian of the constitution—the constitution of the 'committee of gangsters' became the Constitution of the Nation. Apart from amending the Election Act, to widen its franchise, the Wafd majority in parliaments of the period did not amend the constitution itself but defended it as it stood. The scant respect shown by the Palace for constitutional life further encouraged the adherence of the Wafd to the constitution.

Moreover, the constitutional question occupied the Wafd's attention beyond its former concern with Anglo-Egyptian relations. Depriving the Wafd of power seemed an effective means of forcing it to compromise with Britain and divert its attention to its own internal opposition. By the mid-1930s an exhausted Wafd had to content itself with whatever it could get out of the British, as indeed happened in the Treaty of 1936, labelled by the Wafd as 'the Treaty of Honour and Independence'. A speech by its secretary-general Makram Ubaid Pasha during the Palace–Sidqi regime (1930–33), which abolished the Constitution of 1923 and introduced a more royalist one, indicates the Wafd's new appeal:

How do other countries get rid of unpopular Governments? By a parliamentary vote. In Egypt today parliament is a tool of the Government and contains no representatives of the people because the Opposition took no part in the elections. What other course is open to the nation to effect the desired change of Government? Revolt. But with the British troops in Egypt revolt is impossible, for, on the pretext of protecting foreign lives and interests, these troops would be rushed to assist the Government at the first sign of trouble.[25]

The Wafd's inability to lead its mass following to an enforcement of constitutional rule since the early part of the liberal era was observed by a foreign commentator of the period:

It seems that though the great majority of voters remain faithful to the Wafd, Egyptians are becoming wearied of an agitation which has been so active for ten years . . . The defenders of the Constitution could hardly count on a popular insurrection to bring them back to power.[26]

The Wafd learned an important lesson from the repressive Sidqi regime: never willingly to give up governmental power. Thus a greater element of unscrupulousness entered Egyptian politics, so that any means justified the need to seize and retain power. In its short spells of office, a total of six years, two months and twenty-nine days over three decades of parliamentary democracy, the Wafd did not always respect its principles and corruption, embezzlement, and favouritism were prevalent under its rule. When its opponents started to adopt semi-Fascist techniques of political agitation (the Green Shirts of Young Egypt, the Palace-sponsored street clashes with supporters of the Wafd, and so on), the Wafd retaliated by establishing its own paramilitary Blue Shirts (1935–38).[27]

The Wafd government of 1942–44 ruled the country along dictatorial lines. Although this style of rule was prompted by the state of war, it weakened the image of the Wafd as representative of the nation and guardian of the constitution and increased public dissatisfaction with the constitutional system as a whole. As one political party among others, the Wafd's goal was simply to replace its rivals as the majority party and its success, accordingly, held little promise of radical change.

There were several reasons for this decline. The signature of the Treaty of 1936 lessened the intensity of the national issue, in which the Wafd had been protagonist, and brought to the fore-front, the country's internal problems. The Wafd's popularity, accordingly, came to depend more on its ability to rule the country effectively and to handle its social problems success-fully. Although the Wafd's record in this respect was more tan-gible than that of its opponents, it remained generally one of failure in view of the grave social problems faced by most Egyptians.

The resurgence of the nationalist movement, however, allowed the Wafd to retain its leading position and secure alle-giance of the vast majority of the population. On the other hand, the party's championing of constitutional rule secured for it a measure of popularity, since most Egyptians enjoyed greater political freedom under a Wafd government.

The general decline in the position of the Wafd was noted by Sir Walter Smart of the British Embassy in Cairo:

> When it fell from power in 1944, it was generally agreed that its majority in the country had been considerably reduced but even then it was calculated that in ideally free elections it could probably count on a 60% majority.[28]

In the elections of January 1950, however, the Wafd won 228 out of 319 parliamentary seats, with an electoral turnout (61 per cent)[29] slightly higher than that of the previous elections (54 per cent).[30] The failure of the minority governments to match even the poor record of the Wafd was an important factor in the Wafd's retaining its majority. The Palace's attacks against it were even more crucial in this respect:

> The Palace's resolve to keep the Party out of office proved to be a blessing in disguise for the latter. For it enabled the Wafd to evade the responsibility of solving the post-War problems in Egypt which it would not have been able to solve without a radical change in its outlook.[31]

As a party, the Wafd was poorly organized. The parliamentary party remained the only organized link between the leadership and its mass following. According to Salah Issa, 'the Wafd was a broad banner hovering over a crowd which it had no interest in organizing'.[32] Some critics have even contended that it was not a party at all,[33] but others, more plausibly, treat it as a Congress-type of party with a large membership and a loose organization.[34] Its leading echelons were appointed by the higher level of leadership rather than elected by the grass roots.

The uneven course of solving the national problem, together with the diverse social interests and the aggravation of Egypt's social and economic problems, had an impact on the heterogeneous Wafd. It suffered, but survived, a number of splits. As early as 1921–22 a group of its leading figures seceded from it while negotiating with Britain to establish their own Constitutional Liberal party (al-Ahrar), thus setting the scene for a multi-party system in Egypt. They succeeded in reaching agreement with Britain and formulated the Constitution of 1923. Although this group had formed the core of the original delegation which became the nucleus of the Wafd, the vast majority of Egyptians followed the Wafd of Zaghlul Pasha, since the Constitutional Liberals were seen as defenders of landed interests who had been alarmed by the extensive sabotage committed in the *jacquerie* of 1919.

Another secession occurred in 1937 and led to the formation of the Saadist party, led by popular ex-Wafdist leaders of urban business-class background. It came at a time when the Wafd's status as representative of national unity was fading after the signature of the Treaty of 1936. But by allying themselves to the Palace and by their repressive measures after taking office, the Saadists themselves repaired the damage which they had inflicted on the Wafd's popularity.

For the same reason, the secession of the Wafdist Bloc in 1942–43, led by the Wafd's secretary-general Makram Ubaid Pasha,[35] proved an abortive threat. Its 'psychological' impact, however, was of paramount importance in increasing public mistrust of the Wafd because of the details of its corruption which Makram Ubaid published in his 'Black Book', irrespective of whether his allegations were true.

These dissensions in the higher ranks of the Wafd were less important than those which affected its main following. They took two forms. The first was the alienation of an increasing proportion of both actual and potential supporters of the Wafd in the ranks of the politically most active sector of the population, the urban middle class and the intelligentsia, which had now begun to find new platforms for political expression. The second was a sharpening of divisions within the ranks of the Wafd itself.

Towards the end of the Second World War the party activists had begun to polarize into right and left groupings, each of which maintained distinct views on nationalist issues, relations with the Palace, and social and economic policy. Post-war repression forced the two camps to stand together. The right[36] continued to dominate the party's leadership, confining prominent leftist figures like Dr Muhammad Mandour and Dr Aziz Fahmi to a subordinate level. When the Wafd took office in 1950 the polarization was virtually complete on both party and cabinet levels. There were at least three groups within the cabinet and they did not hesitate to publicize their wranglings over policy and personality issues. By 1950 the Wafd had become such a heterogeneous organization that it bore little resemblance to the policy and outlook of the party which formed its first government in 1924. Its internal divisions persisted until the army takeover of power in July 1952, when the party proved quite unable to resist its dissolution by the new regime.

The Palace was the stumbling block in the Wafd's attempts to establish a steady constitutional life in Egyptian politics. From the very beginning the Wafd believed in the sovereignty of the nation and aimed at a constitutional monarchy, which clashed with the autocratic tendencies of King Fouad. Without reaching a pact with the monarch or taking part in the formulation of the constitution, the Wafd envisaged a constitutional pattern which would better the prospects of a constitutional monarchy. The two sides first clashed openly in 1924, when the government of Zaghlul Pasha confronted King Fouad over the issues of his right to appoint members to the Senate, to grant decorations, to appoint Palace personnel and to communicate with foreign states and Egyptian diplomatic missions abroad. The cabinet insisted that this should all be carried out through the government. After legal arbitration and Zaghlul's threatened resignation, Fouad was forced to give way but he soon restored his position after the downfall of the government in the same year.

Under the leadership of Nahhas Pasha, the Wafd tried to pilot through parliament bills designed to prevent the violation of the constitution by the King. The Wafd government, however, never finalized such bills. In practice, the Wafd leadership chose to compromise with the King. While continuing to fight for the curtailment of his powers, it declared its loyalty to the throne[37] and 'never envisaged the feasibility of forming a Republic of Egypt as it took monarchy for granted'.[38]

The Wafd leaders assumed that the death of King Fouad in 1936 would improve their prospects. They made no effort to protect themselves against recruitment to positions within the Palace during the Regency Counsel period. Makram Ubaid confided to the leading Palace official Ahmad Hasanain that the party 'had buried the past with the death of King Fouad, that it anticipated more favourable opportunities under Farouq and that the Wafd government had rejected a proposal to raise the age of accession to the throne from eighteen to twenty-five years'.[39]

In Farouq's reign, however, things turned sour for the Wafd and the party's position suffered a dramatic decline. The young and energetic King enjoyed a measure of popularity in the early part of his reign. He succeeded in undermining the Wafd's position in that Nahhas Pasha was unable in the 1930s to challenge the power of the King as Zaghlul had done in the 1920s. Both the King's constitutional powers and his autocratic tendencies remained unchanged save for periods when the British chose to check his powers and exercise their own.

The Wafd government imposed by the British in 1942 failed to seize the opportunity to undermine the powers of the King and indeed adopted a less hostile attitude towards him. In this period also the Palace instigated the secession of Makram Ubaid from the Wafd.[40]

In 1944 the Wafd was dismissed from government. It returned to power in January 1950, with the ambition of at last arresting the decline of the entire political system after years of repressive rule, economic crises and political assassinations, and in the face of the intensification of the nationalist struggle after the army's defeat in Palestine. By this time the King's reputation stood so low that he was compelled to compromise with the Wafd to save his tottering throne. Instead of taking the opportunity to rid itself of Farouq once and for all, the Wafd adopted a policy of reconciliation with the Palace. The party's justification for this attitude was its intention of abrogating the Treaty of 1936 and its consequent desire to neutralize any possible opposition from the King. In practice, the outcome was simply to perpetuate the King's control over the Wafd and to leave him free to indulge himself as before. The Wafd's conciliatory attitude towards the King did not result in a comparable change in the latter's attitude towards the Wafd.

Responsibility for the choice of this policy lay with the Wafd's secretary-general, Fouad Sirag al-Din Pasha, who believed that while popular support was sufficient to bring the party to power, it could not for long sustain it in power in the face of royal opposition. Sirag al-Din was widely criticized for turning a blind eye to the King's excesses.[41] An important concession made by the Wafd, in response to royal pressure, was to introduce a series of laws restricting press coverage of Palace affairs. These laws were introduced by a Wafd deputy who was in fact forced to withdraw them in the face of public outrage.[42]

The scope of the confrontation between the Wafd and the Palace was identified by al-Tabi, a Wafd sympathizer, as follows: 'The Wafd government used stubbornly to oppose the King in minor questions while giving way on serious issues.'[43] The Wafd's attitude is clearly indicated by Sirag al-Din: 'No government in the world is supposed to clash with the Head of State simply in order to flex its muscles. That is not how things work.'[44] The extreme insensitivity of the party in government to the growing public criticism of the monarchy ensured that when the latter collapsed the Wafd fell with it.

The precarious balance between the three main forces of the political system was bound to collapse sooner or later. Conditions during the Second World War made Egyptians realize that their country was no nearer to independence than at the time of its Revolution in 1919. Few Egyptians had any real sympathy with either side in a war in which, as they put it, they 'had no camel'. If they were compelled to take sides, they would choose the Germans in the hope of disrupting the British control which rendered their country's independence a mere travesty. As one politician put it, 'The people of Egypt are Germans . . . the King of Egypt is Italian . . . and the government of Egypt is English!'[45] 'We are enslaved . . . we do not even have a government that can say to the British "Goodbye Masters" and to the Germans "Willkommen Herren"!'[46] said another politician. While the Axis and the Allies clashed at al-Alamain, Egyptians discussed the quarrel between Nahhas Pasha and Makram Ubaid and joked about the British and the Germans at war.

British power in Egypt was all too clearly demonstrated in the incident of February 1942. Although this incident was prompted by the war conditions and resulted in installing a government which enjoyed the popular support of the Wafd, it became clear in the aftermath of the war that it had had a much more profound effect on the credibility of all three forces in the Egyptian political arena:

> The Wafd lost its patriotic lustre because it seized power with the backing of British bayonets, the King lost face because he succumbed to British blackmail, and the British lost whatever little trust the Egyptians still reposed in them because their action demonstrated that the independence conferred by the Treaty of 1936 was mere sham.[47]

In the years that followed the war, Egypt was seething with a frenzied political unrest. The emergence of extra-parliamentary political groups led to the intensification of the political struggle. A wave of political assassinations claimed the lives of two prime ministers; and two cabinets were forced to resign because of their inability to ensure public security. Even the staunchest defenders of the political order began to lose confidence in its merits.

The last Wafd government was summoned to act the role of saviour, to control the increasingly uncontrollable public unrest, and in the hope that it would keep the people quiet rather than lead them. Under this government both public unrest and royal misconduct intensified. The Wafd was caught in the middle, totally unable to take clear measures to tackle the problem. Confiscating newspapers and magazines did nothing to reduce the level of press agitation and the attempt to legislate tighter control of the press ended in failure. Even existing laws were less strictly enforced and citizens accused of insulting the 'Royal Entity' (the King) were usually acquitted.

Under public pressure the Wafd government abrogated the Treaty of 1936. In doing so, it declared the exhaustion of its traditional methods of national struggle and legitimized the use of force against the British which amounted to a negation of the system itself. Guerrilla attacks on British troops in the Suez Canal Zone soon followed. The government was unable to prevent these attacks or to control their repercussions, which in the urban and rural middle class—the effendis, the professionals, the impact of the guerrilla action within Egypt itself far exceeded Sirag al-Din's expectations in allowing it 'to convince the British that their base in the Canal was useless if Egypt was hostile to them'.[48]

The government began to lose control of its ultimate weapons, the police and the army. There was growing unrest among the police since the army had been used to suppress their strike for a wage increase in 1947. During the struggle in the Canal Zone they found themselves national heroes in the Zone itself, with flowers thrown at them for fighting the British, while in Cairo they acted to repress the demonstrators who instead hurled stones at them. On 26 January 1952, however, they gained a measure of sympathy when they took the side of the demonstrators a few hours before the Burning of Cairo. The previous night a squad of their colleagues had been besieged in their station by British troops in the Canal Zone and a number of them had been killed.

The army, which had once served notoriously as the protective shield of the monarchy,[49] had felt increasingly bitter after its defeat in Palestine and the scandal of the defective arms deal in which the monarch himself was implicated. Some of the younger officers took part in the armed struggle in the Canal Zone. A small and secret nucleus known as the Free Officers began to extend its influence and succeeded in distributing leaflets throughout the country. Their first open act of defiance was to reject the Palace candidate for the presidency of their club and elect their own choice. In the face of his loosening grip on both the police and the army, the minister of the interior and defence proposed the formation of an intermediate force modelled on the Italian *carabinieri*,[50] but it was too late.

In a memorandum to the King during the last Wafd government the Opposition leaders wrote:

> Your Majesty, people can not bear it for long. We fear a holocaust that will not only destroy those responsible for the country's troubles but will also subject the whole nation to moral, financial and political bankruptcy. Destructive doctrines will spread as a reaction to the prevalent epidemic of the abuse of power.[51]

The politicians' fears proved justified and on 23 July 1952 the Free Officers took power.

The Emergence of New Forces

The steady decline of Egypt's political system in the parliamentary era paved the way for the emergence of new extraparliamentary political forces. The development in size and influence of the politically active middle class offered a breeding ground for these new forces. The political role played by the middle class dates back to the time of the Revolution of 1919, which opened the way for the establishment of a liberal parliamentary system in Egypt. At that time, the urban intellectual and professional wing of the middle class, the effendis, together with its rural wing, the village notables, played an active part in the Revolution and formed its local leadership in various urban districts and rural provinces.

The very establishment of a liberal system in Egypt was largely attributed to the existence of a small, but active, middle class highly receptive to liberal ideas. In his first People's Government in 1924 Zaghlul was prudent enough to include in his cabinet two effendis, Wasef Ghali and Naguib al-Gharaballi, for the first time in the history of Egyptian cabinets. Over the three decades of the constitutional regime the local leadership of the Wafd party was drawn mainly from this social stratum, although it was not proportionately represented in its highest command. The Wafd was able to claim the allegiance of most sections of the urban and rural middle class—the effendis, the professionals, the petty bourgeois shopkeepers and merchants, the less wealthy rural notables and the Egyptian section of the nascent industrial and commercial bourgeoisie. One of the early attempts to undermine the effendis' allegiance to the Wafd was in 1928, when the government of Muhammad Mahmoud Pasha introduced regulations prohibiting government employees from taking part in political activities.

Despite its narrow economic power base, being largely a self-employed or an employed class rather than an employing class, the political influence of the middle class in a country like Egypt reflected the fact that, although numerically small, it was nevertheless the largest articulate and literate grouping in the society. In addition, the civil servants, a major component of the middle class, were close to the seat of power in both central and local government.

The expansion of Egyptian industry during the Second World War enhanced the development of the urban middle class by enlarging the local bourgeoisie and increasing the numbers of white-collar workers (see Tables 1.1 and 1.2).

Table 1.1: Urban Middle Class in Egypt, 1947

Occupation	No.	% of all middle class	% of total population gainfully occupied
Merchants	254,388	51	3.00
Chief clerks & clerks	127,876	26	1.51
Professionals[a]	94,339	19	1.11
Businessmen & agents	22,561	4	0.27
Total	499,164	100	5.89

Note: *a.* Includes actors, doctors, chemists and pharmacists, school administrators, professors, teachers, authors and editors, lawyers, engineers.

Source: Morroe Berger, 'The Middle Class in the Arab World' in Walter Laqueur, *The Middle East in Transition* (Routledge & Kegan Paul, London, 1958), p. 64.

The number of theologians, usually classified among professionals, increased merely from 53,000 in 1937 to 52,400 in 1947[52] (a 2.7 per cent increase), guaranteeing that the expansion of professional groups of the middle class was essentially secular in character. The massive increase in the number of writers and journalists was also of great political importance.

Since the 1930s a variety of reasons had led increasing numbers of middle class to express their discontent with the political system: the moral bankruptcy of a regime supposedly 'democratic' but in fact extremely 'dictatorial', as best indicated by the repressive regime of Sidqi Pasha (1930–33); the regime's evident failure in the face of the economic crisis of the 1930s, with its severe impact upon the middle class and consequent

Table 1.2: Number of Professionals in Egypt, 1937–47 (thousands)

Profession	1937	1947	% increase
Teachers (schools & universities)	35.3	52.0	47.3
Engineers	8.4	15.8	88.1
Doctors & dentists	3.7	6.3	70.3
Lawyers	3.4	4.7	38.2
Chemists & pharmacists	1.2	1.6	33.3
Writers & journalists	1.2	8.2	583.3
Total	53.2	88.6[a]	66.5

Note: *a*. The discrepancy between this figure and the figure of 94.3 in Table 1.1 is due to different statistical sources.
Source: Jean-Jacques Waardenburg, *Les Universités dans le Monde Arabe Actuel* (Mouton & Co., La Haye, 1966) vol. II, p. 81, Table 110

massive unemployment of the educated; the 1936 Treaty of Honour and Independence, brought to an end by Britain imposing a government of its own choice in 1942; Egypt's losses in the Second World War and the British refusal to respond to the aspirations of Egyptian nationalists in its aftermath; the deteriorating social and economic conditions in the country, and so on. Arnold Smith, a British scholar teaching in Egypt at the time, noted:

During the past two years, in which I have been lecturing to 3rd and 4th year students at the Egyptian University, I have become convinced that there is a widespread and growing awareness among educated youth here of the almost hopeless backwardness of the present social and economic set-up in Egypt. Students, young professional men, young army officers, etc. are becoming increasingly dissatisfied with their status quo—and who can blame them?[53]

Towards the end of the Second World War the political climate in Egypt came once more to resemble that of 1919. There was increasing middle-class activism, and extra-parliamentary organizations which had in the 1930s represented merely a vocal challenge to the regime began in the 1940s to pose a serious threat to it. The prospective political significance of the growing numbers of members of the educated middle class was clear even to the British Foreign Office:

> The Effendis (by whom I mean the educated and semi-educated products of Eastern universities and schools) seem in fact to be rapidly developing into a professional middle class destined to claim for itself a definite position in the social order of the Arab world and to play an increasingly important part in shaping the political destinies of the Middle East . . . The very fact that they are, by reason of their scholarship, breaking away from practices of their ancestors, must necessarily encourage a feeling of restlessness which is no doubt intensified by their growing realization of the social inequalities of the society in which they live and in which the remuneration for the posts and careers open to them is, in most cases, still very poor. It is not surprising that in such circumstances the great bulk of the Effendis should have a strong feeling of social grievance . . . The question of the growing importance of the Effendis and their probable future role in the Middle East would seem indeed to deserve careful examination . . . [54]

The political activism of the disenchanted elements of the middle class was channelled into the evolving extra-parliamentary groupings, of which three (the Muslim Brotherhood, Young Egypt and the Communist movement) were the main challenges faced by the regime. It was also these groupings which supplied the student movement with its active core. None of the new forces which emerged to challenge the ailing liberal system had the strength to transform the political order on its own; but their joint impact, despite their divisions, served to undermine its credibility and accelerate its eventual collapse. In the final years of the liberal regime, its challengers began to identify the consi-

derable degree of agreement on practical policies which under-
lay their ideological differences and members of the various
political groupings began to advocate the formation of a national
front. No such front was in fact formed and no clearly worked-
out organizational formula for its establishment was ever
seriously discussed. Such limited efforts at co-ordination as
were undertaken in no way justify the estimates of its success
offered by Anwar Abdel-Malek and other writers.[55] The only
organization to include most of the new forces, the Partisans of
Peace,[56] made some contribution towards the discussion of local
issues; but it was concerned essentially with an international
issue and not with the pursuit of a domestic political programme. Even the period of the Canal Zone guerrilla struggle did
not lead to the establishment of a national front. But it was not
only ideological differences that hampered the creation of such a
front. In the absence of an organized mass movement or vigorous trade unions, the new political groupings were under little
pressure from below and showed little active inclination to
attempt to seize power.

One crucial inhibiting factor was the continuing presence of
the Wafd party as the major force in the political system. Not only
did the extra-parliamentary groupings fail to agree on a homogeneous policy towards the Wafd; but the very fact that the Wafd
retained to its last languid minutes the allegiance, though no
longer the enthusiasm, of the majority of the population pre-
cluded their thinking in terms of an immediate inheritance of the
Wafd's position. Paradoxically, therefore, these groupings were
obliged to rally to the support of the Wafd whenever 'political
power' was immediately at issue, just as they had done in the
January 1950 elections which brought the Wafd to power with a
considerable majority. The prestige of the Wafd declined more
slowly than that of the other components of the regime, the
Palace and the minority parties, partly because it was the minority governments and not the Wafd itself which undertook the
task of suppressing the new political groupings. The Wafd was
thus left to assume power through parliamentary elections in
1950 and no attempt was made to exploit the temporary dissidence of 26 January 1952, the day of the Burning of Cairo, to seize
power.

Only through their links with the armed forces (the Free
Officers) did the new groupings have any real chance of over-
throwing the regime. As bearers of the rank of 'officer', these

men were the product of Egypt's second step towards independence. (After the signature of the Treaty of 1936, admission to the Military Academy was broadened to allow the entry of sons of the middle class.) Their choice of the epithet 'Free' marked the growing disenchantment of their class with the country's political failure to complete its independence and secure stable government. The incident of February 1942, in particular, had injured their national and professional pride and alienated them from the Wafd. Their defeat in Palestine and the scandal over defective arms had alienated them from the Palace. Their political awareness had been deepened by the agitation of the new political groupings, with which in some cases they enjoyed direct organizational ties. While they shared the broad political and social ideas of these groupings, they were unique in their organizational capacity to act as a single unit despite the political differences[57] within their ranks. Consequently, while they may well have been sincere in wanting to seize power on behalf of the new groupings, it is not surprising that they should ultimately have chosen to retain it for themselves.

2
Educational and Social Conditions

The System of Education

The Egyptian educational system of the liberal regime was designed to satisfy the requirements of a dominant class of large landowners, who needed to recruit government personnel and to furnish a bare minimum of education for the rural majority of the population. The newly emerging industrial bourgeoisie struggled to introduce educational changes which were a prerequisite for fulfilling its very different needs for accountants, engineers, technicians and managers. But its attitude towards the education of the urban working class (that it required merely the provision of basic literacy) had much in common with the attitude of the landowners towards the rural population. The majority governments of the Wafd, however, were more responsive to public pressure for better opportunities, and they achieved some advances in their terms of office over the three decades of liberal government.

Apparatus
An indication of educational development during the period is provided by the state budget, the main source of finance for education.

From the data given in Table 2.1, it is clear that expenditure doubled over the period of twenty-six years, while expenditure on higher education in particular more than tripled in the same period. The number of students as a proportion of the total population also increased over the same period while the number of university students rose steadily, more than doubling in the five years between 1945 and 1951. Although the numbers of girls enrolled in higher education increased, they remained massively under-represented in higher education throughout this period (Table 2.3).

Table 2.1 Expenditure on Education as Illustrated by the State
Budget, 1925/26—1951/52

Year	(1) State budget (£E)	(2) Min. of Educ. budget (£E)	(3) % (2/1)	(4) Universities budget (£E)	(5) % (4/2)
1925/26	36,288,266	2,336,477	6.4	110,287	4.70
1930/31	44,915,000	3,301,299	7.3	298,599	9.04
1935/36	32,846,000	3,350,257	10.1	578,706	17.20
1940/41	47,718,000	4,643,201	9.7	849,300	18.20
1945/46	89,968,000	11,635,657	12.9	1,455,700	12.50
1950/51	205,988,900	22,335,336	10.8	3,257,722	14.50
1951/52	231,447,300	28,030,472	12.1	3,982,462	14.20

Source: Jean-Jacques Waardenburg, *Les Universités dans Le Monde Arabe Actuel* (Mouton & Co., La Haye, 1966), vol. II, p. 120, Table 157.

Table 2.2 Student/Population Ratio in Egypt, 1925/26–1951/52

Academic year	No. of state school pupils per 1,000 inhabitants	No. of university students per 1,000 inhabitants
1925/26	15	0.24
1935/36	45	0.48
1940/41	69	0.51
1945/46	56	0.75
1950/51	55	1.54
1951/52	66	1.64

Source: Waardenburg, *Universités*, vol. II, Table 109.

The students were divided between theoretical and practical
faculties (see Table 2.4).

Table 2.3: Total Enrolment in Higher Education Institutions, 1930–52

Year	Enrolment	% girls	Year	Enrolment	% girls
1930	4,247	0.5	1945	13,927	5
1935	7,515	2.0	1950	31,744	7
1940	8,507	4.0	1952	42,494	8

Source: Waardenburg, *Universités*, vol. II, p. 78, Table 108.

Table 2.4: Number of Students in Theoretical and Practical Faculties, 1925/26–1951/52

Year	Theoretical faculties (humanities & social sciences)	Practical faculties (applied sciences)
1925/26	1,810	1,558
1930/31	2,066	2,181
1935/36	4,041	3,474
1940/41	4,544	3,963
1945/46	6,244	7,683
1950/51[a]	16,492	13,910
1951/52[a]	19,671	15,174

Note: a. Figures for these two years are different from those totalled in Table 2.3.
Source: Louis Awad, *The University and the New Society* (National House for Printing and Publication, Cairo, 1963) (in Arabic), p. 58, Table 5.

The rough numerical parity between the two branches of higher education, however, was not reflected within the general secondary schools, where greater emphasis was laid on the study of theoretical subjects. The syllabus of the last year of the general secondary school, from which students pass to the university, showed a clear concentration on theoretical subjects.

As Table 2.5 shows, the emphasis on languages was particularly heavy.[1] A student of literature had to spend 59 per cent of

Table 2.5: Programme of Studies for Orientation Year of Secondary Schools, 1945/46

Subject	Periods per week		
	Literary section	Science section	Maths section
Arabic language	6	6	6
First European language	7	6	6
Second European language	7	3	3
History	5	-	-
Geography	4	-	-
Philosophy or maths	3	-	-
Library	2	-	-
Biology	-	9	-
Chemistry	-	6	3
Physics	-	4	4
Pure & applied maths	-	-	10
Drawing or additional physics or biology	-	-	2
Total	34	34	34

Source: Roderic O. Matthews and Matta Akrawi, *Education in Arab Countries of the Near East* (American Council on Education, Washington D.C., 1950), p. 61, Table 12.

his school-time studying languages, while even students of science or mathematics had to spend 44 per cent of their school time on the same activity.

The youngest pupils were taught in two distinct types of school: primary schools in the urban areas and elementary schools in the rural areas. Although the number of elementary schools increased greatly between 1925 and 1945, they were of such poor quality and so over-crowded that the impressive statistics of rising enrolment were widely regarded as almost meaningless.

About 80 per cent of all school children attended the elementary schools, which employed some 57 per cent of the country's teachers at this level. In the primary schools, by contrast, the remaining 43 per cent of teachers taught only 20 per cent of the children in this age group. Thus the elementary school teacher had an average of forty-two pupils in a class, as compared with the primary school teacher who had fourteen. Moreover, the better-educated teachers were largely concentrated in the urban primary sector. Even after the two types of primary education were merged in 1951, the former elementary schools remained poorly equipped, especially for the study of foreign languages; in practice, the way to higher education remained blocked for their students.

In secondary education, academic schools continued to draw the great majority of the students. Following a law of 1950 which made secondary education free for all, a flood of primary school leavers jammed the academic secondary schools in the course of 1951. The secondary technical and trade schools, on the other hand, which had expanded to some extent during the 1940s, experienced a drop in enrolment. The technical schools were poorly administered, inefficient and inadequately equipped and the quality of the teaching staff was also poor. Most graduates sought not a position in industry but a clerkship in the bureaucracy.[2]

Al-Azhar remained a wholly separate educational institution with levels of education parallel to those in the secular system. The number of its pupils, however, increased relatively slowly since the turn of the century. As shown in Table 2.6, the number of al-Azhar students between 1928/29 and 1948/49 rose by about 66.5 per cent. By comparison, the number of students receiving secular state education between 1930/31 and 1950/51 increased by 183 per cent.[3]

Table 2.6: Total Enrolment in al-Azhar, Selected Years

Year	Enrolment
1898/99	8,246
1908/09	9,000
1918/19	15,826
1928/29	11,157
1938/39	13,163
1948/49	18,582

Source: Waardenburg, *Universités*, p. 121, Table 159.

In 1945/46 there were 14,402 students at al-Azhar, distributed among the different levels of education as shown in Table 2.7.

Table 2.7: Enrolment in al-Azhar Institutions, 1945/46

Division	Enrolment
Primary sections	
Secondary sections	5,729
General section	4,678
	1,422
Higher Faculties	
Faculty of Arabic	1,162
Faculty of Muslim Law	873
Faculty of Theology	538
Total	14,402

Source: Matthews and Akrawi, *Education*, p. 103.

Intellectual Trends
Until 1951 the basic feature of the educational system was the dual system of primary education. Primary schools led to an academic secondary school and thence to the university or to a white-collar job in the bureaucracy. Elementary schools, by contrast, were the sole (and very poorly equipped) schools designed to absorb the vast majority of the children of school age in the rural areas. Liberal intellectuals took a critical view of this duality in primary education:

> It has been considered undemocratic to have two systems of education, a superior and comprehensive program for those who can afford to pay a small proportion of the expenses of their education, and an inferior and dead-end program for those who cannot . . . [It] unquestionably tended to perpetuate differences between social classes by creating an intellectual elite who monopolised government positions and high income professions.[4]

Ismail al-Qabbani, a protagonist of the pedagogical school of educational reform, saw the political outcome of this discrimination as inevitable: 'It was felt that in the long run it would result in harmful social consequences because the masses would eventually become discontented with their unequal social and educational treatment.'[5]

Dualism was also apparent in the two separate educational systems—the state system of secular education and the religious education of al-Azhar. Al-Azhar remained an independent educational authority in its own right and it was only in the mid-1930s that its traditional lower education institutions, the *kuttabs*, which had survived for centuries, were transformed into schools.

In his controversial book *The Future of Culture in Egypt*, published in 1938, Dr Taha Hussein pioneered liberal criticism of this situation in an outspoken manner. He suggested that al-Azhar:

> should not be allowed to remain a state within a state, a privileged body capable of defying public authority with impunity. State supervision of Al-Azhar's primary and secondary school is vital at this stage of Egyptian history since the traditions and religious obligations of the venerable institution have made it a focus of conservatism and antiquated practices.[6]

This attitude was opposed by a number of Muslim fundamentalists. According to Hasan al-Banna, the founder of the Muslim Brotherhood, 'The division of our school system is unparalleled in the world and imposes danger on our people's unity. However, any unification attempt should be in favour of Islamic education, not the opposite.'[7]

However, Taha Hussein received support from another more liberal school of Islamic thought. Sayyid Qutb[8] supported his view that the state should supervise all kinds of education with the exception of higher education, which 'should be left independent to find freely its way to knowledge within the limits of public law'.[9] He maintained that although al-Azhar could devote itself to its purely theological faculties, 'it cannot be independent in a faculty like that of the Arabic language which produces teachers for the government schools'.[10]

On pedagogical grounds, al-Qabbani endorsed this view:

> There should be in Egypt one type of primary education and one kind of secondary education to prepare the young generation for living in Egyptian society, before preparing them to

be doctors, engineers, theologians or teachers. The place for specialization and vocational preparation is the higher institutes of learning.[11]

By contrast Ahmed Radwan expressed the more practical concerns of the emerging bourgeoisie:

> Egypt in her present stage of development does not need so many thousands of theologians and linguists. The new age needs a more diversified professional leadership—engineers, scientists, agriculturists, doctors, social scientists and humanists as well as theologians. The curriculum of schools would reflect these needs of the nation . . . [In his view] a compromise plan which would serve the interests of the country would be to confine Al-Azhar to the higher studies of religion and language.[12]

Many commentators were also concerned at the persistent failure of the educational system to adjust itself to the requirements of the labour market. There was a permanent surplus of school-leavers and graduates of certain branches of secondary and higher education.[13] Government bodies remained overstaffed with a large proportion of the graduates, as they had been since the time of Muhammad Ali. The business sector provided a very narrow labour market for educated manpower. Advocates of educational reforms attributed this problem partly to the popular prestige attached to government occupations. As Radwan noted, 'There is something unhealthy about a situation in which the youth of Egypt seek the security of government posts even when salaries are low and work is of a routine clerical type.'[14]

This distortion was further worsened by the expansion of academic secondary schools at the expense of technical secondary education. As Radwan complained, 'The nation suffers a very serious occupational maladjustment, and the most promising jobs and the most needed are these in the field of industry. But still the only true schools in the opinion of the people are the academic secondary schools.'[15] Even in the existing academic schools, subjects were treated in a highly abstract manner, bearing no relation to the students' experience outside the walls of the school: 'A student knows where iron is to be found in England, but he knows nothing about the iron of Egypt.'[16] 'Prior to the 1952 coup', as Malcolm Kerr has noted, 'the Egyptian secondary and university student learned surprisingly little in school about the political, social and economic problems of his own country.'[17]

A number of proposals were advanced for the solution of this problem. In his book *The Policy of Tomorrow*, published in 1951, Mirrit Boutros Ghali wrote:

> We must warn, and persist in warning, that the economic development of the country does not allow the absorption of these young men. It is necessary that the responsible people should acknowledge this bitter truth and then combine their efforts to see to it that advanced and specialised instruction is spread with measure and calculation, proportionately to our economic development. The means thereto must be the closing down, for a certain time, of some schools like the Junior Agricultural and Trade Colleges, some professional schools, and others which are not clearly and obviously needed. Admission to every school or college should be limited, and higher examinations made more strict, so that the cultural level of the educated be raised and the number of yearly graduates kept down.[18]

Taha Hussein, however, saw the question in a broader context: 'We shall not correct the situation if we restrict education or create a class structure or make knowledge the monopoly of a small group. We can treat it best by reforming the social system that created it.'[19] One reform which he proposed was that of the civil service itself:

> It is probably true that our civil service is overcrowded owing to faulty appointment procedures. A major overhauling of the system would lead to the elimination of many highly paid but useless positions. The resultant savings could be used to create more job opportunities for the unemployed, who would gladly work for modest salaries . . . I know of none of the Western democracies that dealt with unemployment by contracting education or restricting it to one class of people to the exclusion of all others. What they did was to make their education an education for life, to prepare the student to face the world armed with the knowledge he acquired in the school.[20]

The system of examinations, though less strict than that which Lord Cromer had imposed on Egypt, was criticized for perpetuating the antiquated teaching methods in use. As Taha Hussein put it:

> Everyone waits for the end of the year and the paper that will arrive from the school or the Ministry announcing the results. Consequently, school boys are driven to the virtual exclusion of everything else. As long as examinations are a goal, passing them will be the goal of goals.[21]

The disastrous educational consequences of this concentration were also emphasized by Radwan:

> When the teacher has to cover a long syllabus in a few months, with the understanding that an examination in the information involved is the criterion of his success, he is obliged to follow the traditional pattern of recitation. He explains the material piecemeal, and the pupils try to commit it to memory after him.[22]

The same stultifying impact was noted by Naguib al-Hilali Pasha, a former minister of education and prime minister:

> Students have resorted, or have rather been forced to resort, to memorizing even Mathematics . . . Knowledge has become deficient and vague, hardly exceeding mere definitions, classifications, technical terms, dates of events or examples given in books. The student has thus been transformed into an intelligent parrot.[23]

The administration of education remained inefficient and highly bureaucratic over the period. The Ministry of Education was criticized for concentrating executive powers and for hindering all initiative on the school level. It concerned itself with minor details at the expense of drawing up a clear educational policy.

The need to reform women's education was recognized as particularly urgent. The movement for the emancipation of women had developed in parallel with the broader nationalist movement since the active role which women had played in the Revolution of 1919. Gradually they won increasing support from large sections of the intelligentsia. Girls were admitted to the university in 1928, while by the end of the Second World War the case for giving girls equal opportunity for education was accepted by large sections of the population.

Liberal advocacy of educational reform met resistance not only from the traditionalists and Islamic fundamentalists but also from within liberal ranks—a populist section advocated the 'democracy of education' by universalizing public education and minimizing restrictions on admission to higher education, and a conservative section stressed the 'quality' of education in purely pedagogical terms. The contrast between these two currents of thought was typified by the controversy between Taha Hussein and Ismail al-Qabbani over the question of teacher training. While the former was willing to allow university graduates to become school teachers, the latter advocated that only those who had received pedagogical training in special institutes should be permitted to become teachers.

Socio-Economic Conditions

Despite the lack of statistics about the social origins of university students in Egypt from the 1920s to the 1950s, many researchers agree that the bulk of these students came from lower middle-class families in the urban areas, especially the effendis, and middle landowning families of the rural areas.[24] It is also agreed that many students lived under difficult economic conditions. Some, indeed, lived perilously near to starvation in order to complete their studies.

A.J. Craig, a British scholar who lived in Egypt for some time, reported a telling example:

In a shack built on the roof of our house there lived, throughout the winter, part of a provincial family which had come to Cairo so that the two sons may be educated. The menage consisted of the elder boy who was at Cairo University, the younger who was at a secondary school, the grandmother who had come to look after them, and their young sister who had been sent as an afterthought to run errands and spare the crone's weary legs. All of them lived on beans and bread and various scraps, financed by the distant father, a peasant working in his fields.[25]

He also noted that:

In Egypt, despite the praiseworthy efforts that are being made in the field of education, a lad must still go to school when he can, and after may not get the opportunity until he is fully grown and can leave his village for Cairo.[26]

The poor of the university, however, were not the poor of the country. Levels of student fees,[27] together with the high cost of living in urban areas, sharply restricted student numbers, confining higher educational opportunities to families with sufficient resources and placing impossible barriers in the way of the sons or daughters of the poorer rural families. Al-Azhar, however, with its theological schools and university, provided these poorer families with an alternative opportunity since it offered free tuition, board and lodging for the period of study. Its students included a large number drawn from relatively poor rural families. Egyptian students were acutely sensitive to questions of economic opportunity. For many of them, education was their only passport to a better future and they were deeply concerned with the likely effect of economic conditions upon their future prospects.

In 1936 there was a series of strikes by school and university students over employment and other related issues. On 10 November students of the Faculty of Commerce went on strike for one day and published an article in *al-Misri* newspaper entitled 'Graduates of the Faculty of Commerce and their Future'.[28] On 23 November there followed a strike in the Faculty of Law to modify the regulations governing the award of degrees. There were also demonstrations by the students of the school of arts and crafts, followed by a wave of strikes by students of other technical schools who formed a committee to contact parliament about their demands for future employment and higher education.[29]

In his report, Bashatli Effendi of the Ministry of the Interior attributed the student uprising of 1935–36 essentially to the poor employment prospects for students:

A state of discontent has for a considerable time been reigning amongst the university undergraduates, owing to the unpromising future before them. They see that a large number of students who have completed their studies at the university remain without employment, while those who were lucky enough to enter the Government Service have, in accordance with the Ministry of Finance circular of the 8th October, 1935, been engaged in an initial salary of E£8.50 per month only, a remuneration which they consider much too low in view of their 'paper' educational qualification. The same circular lays down that holders of the Egyptian baccalaureate certificate (i.e. graduates of secondary schools) are to be engaged at E£6.00 per month and graduates of the Intermediate School of Commerce at E£5.50.

A few years ago, i.e. before education was so widespread in Egypt, most of the young men educated in Government schools were absorbed into the Government Service, and the feeling still exists to a large extent that those educated by the Government should also be employed by the Government. The fact that this is no longer possible is attributed to some fault of the Government's and the existing feeling of discontent is therefore directed against the Government. In order to ease the situation as far as possible, the Ministers of Finance and Education have done their best to open new venues of employment. They have approached directors of banks and other large financial and commercial establishments recommending that graduates of Government schools and of the Egyptian University should be employed by them, but this appeal has so far met with little success, chiefly owing to the fact that the qualifications required by such establishments, e.g. initiative, savoir faire, a good knowledge of languages, chiefly French, are lacking in so far as these candidates are concerned.[30]

Foreign nationals were so widely employed in commercial and industrial firms that Egyptians had little chance of being employed in them. The government was compelled to tighten up the immigration regulations, and no foreigners were permitted to enter the country to take up employment until proof had been given that no suitable Egyptian candidate could be found.

In the post-war years further strikes were reported. In 1947, for instance, students of the industrial schools went on hunger strike for permission to pursue higher technical studies and become engineers. University tutors and school teachers joined in the agitation, demanding better salaries and job conditions.

The problem of graduate unemployment was one of the major themes throughout the controversy over educational reform. British officials in Egypt, too, showed an acute interest in the problem. As one of them put it, 'The real "effendi" problem is that of the poorly paid government officials, the commercial clerks, and the "out of work" graduates'.[31] They were also anxious about the political repercussions of the problem and, indeed, of social and economic conditions in Egypt as a whole. In a memorandum on the state of education and student unemployment in Egypt written at the request of the British Embassy, a British university teacher, Arnold Smith, noted:

> During the past two years, in which I have been lecturing to the 3rd and 4th year students at the Egyptian University, I have become convinced that there is a widespread and growing awareness among educated youth here of the almost hopeless backwardness of the present social and economic set-up in Egypt. Students, young professional men, young army officers, etc. are becoming increasingly dissatisfied with their status quo, and who can blame them? That this situation can become politically dangerous is of course obvious.

In this light Smith challenged the Embassy's hostile attitude towards the establishment of the new University of Assiut:

> Restricting higher education is a very superficial remedy to the problem of graduate unemployment. The only real solution would be energetic measures of social reform . . . The Egyptian Government should be encouraged to undertake the creation of more health centres, educational campaigns among the fellaheen, of better housing . . . etc. This would employ graduates of technical schools and would also necessitate a large number of inspectors, administrators, etc., the products of the Faculties of Arts and Commerce.[32]

The living conditions of Egyptian students and the limitations placed on their future ambitions[33] by the problem of graduate unemployment, as well as the maladies of the country's socioeconomic set-up as a whole, merely increased their activism. As Kerr put it:

> It is this explosive compound of the high aspirations and self-conscious dignity instilled by university education and the unpromising conditions of the job market that has made university students and graduates a continuing revolutionary force throughout the past half-century in Egypt.[34]

Students went on strike:

> for all kinds of reasons—for a change of Cabinet, against a
> declaration by an Egyptian or foreign minister, the high per-
> centage of failures in public examinations, the low salary
> given by the state to graduates of an institution, to express
> their joy or disappointment on all kinds of occasions—in fact,
> for every reason under the sun. The student body turns into a
> proletarian dictatorship . . .[35]

On their own, however, student grievances over the educational
and social conditions were not sufficient to explain the extent of
the activism and turbulence in this period. Nor can it adequately
be explained by purely domestic problems such as 'serious
trouble in the family budget',[36] as suggested by French commentators, or for that matter by students' lack of sports activities
as one British commentator believed.[37] The underlying cause of
the activism of Egyptian students must be sought in the framework of their country's struggle for national independence and
the conditions of its social and political development in general.

3
Student Political Activism

Uprising and Aftermath, 1935–36[1]

By the mid-1930s the liberal regime in Egypt was confronted by a discontented progeny of its own. The spread of liberal education gave students a numerical strength while the country's low level of economic development frustrated their ambitions for future careers. The rocky course of the country's constitutional life led increasing numbers of them to doubt the adequacy of its political system. The regime's inability to achieve the complete independence for which the nation had revolted in 1919 was the concrete proof of its overall failure.

The collapse of Ismail Sidqi Pasha's government (1930–33), which had replaced the Constitution of 1923 by a less 'populist' version in 1930, prepared the way for a renewed wave of political agitation aimed at restoring the original constitution. The government of Tawfiq Nassim Pasha (1934–36) was seen by many shades of Egyptian political opinion as an *ad hoc* government suited to fulfil this task. It acquired the support, or rather the passive co-operation, of the Wafd against a background of British consent. For one thing, Nassim was well disposed towards the British. More importantly, Britain was eager to clear up the disorder in Egypt in order to concentrate on the looming threat of Fascism nearer home. Nassim's government began by abolishing the Constitution of 1930 but it did not supplement this measure with the restoration of the 1923 Constitution. Instead Nassim, backed by the British, preferred to formulate a new constitution combining elements of its two predecessors.

On 9 November 1935 Sir Samuel Hoare announced in London's Guildhall that although Britain acknowledged that the Constitution of 1930 had proved 'unpopular', it viewed the Constitution of 1923 as 'unworkable'. As a result, Nassim's government, in view of its dependence on British support, was forced into a critical position in the face of public opposition to the

British attitude. In this predicament it lost the support of the Wafd and was denounced by its leaders as 'a clerical office annexed to the Residency'.[2]

Hoare's announcement changed the political atmosphere in Egypt. It came as an additional demonstration of British hegemony and infuriated the country's students; as such, it did more to prompt student reactions than was warranted by its purely constitutional implications. The students began to organize and called at the headquarters of several political parties to discuss the matter. On 13 November 1935 Zaghlul gave a public speech in which he called for non-co-operation with the British and demanded once again that the government resign. Encouraged by the Wafd declaration, the students took to the streets of Cairo. Bashatli Effendi of the Ministry of the Interior reported that:

on the 13th November about 2000 undergraduates marched from the University of Giza to Cairo in a most threatening manner . . . The students displayed a very determined, bitter, and aggressive spirit. They were much more difficult to deal with than in the past.[3]

On subsequent days demonstrations continued on a larger scale in Cairo and other cities. On 14 November a university students' demonstration in the capital, with an estimated four thousand participants, clashed with the police force, led by some British constables, at Abbas Bridge which connects the University with central Cairo. An agricultural student, Muhammad Abd al-Mageed Morsi, was shot and killed by the police. A second demonstrator, an arts student named Abd al-Hakam al-Garrahi,[4] was seriously injured and died in hospital a few days later. His funeral turned into a national demonstration:

Whenever a demonstrator dies, the great problem for the authorities is to get the funeral over with the least possible disturbance. In all cases but one the police succeeded in avoiding serious trouble. The exception was the case of Mohamed Abdel-Hakam Al-Garrahy, who died on the 19th Nov. The deceased was related to an officer of the Royal Guard. Medical students at first concealed the body in the hospital and refused to divulge its whereabouts until an assurance had been given that a public funeral would be permitted. The funeral, which took place the same evening, was very largely attended. The deceased was treated like a national hero and political leaders such as Nahas, Sidki, Mohamed Mahmoud and others, accompanied the procession part of the way.[5]

Student demonstrations and strikes evoked a sympathetic response from professional unions, newspapers, shopkeepers, teachers and even judges. To curb their spread, Nassim's government prohibited the newspapers from publishing the news of student demonstrations and called on the army to suppress them. It also closed the university on several occasions for a week at a time, and then was forced to close it indefinitely on 8 December. The previous day, several thousand students held a ceremony in the university grounds where they erected a monument (which they smuggled into the premises) in memory of their martyrs. The rector of the university, together with other professors, attended the ceremony and addressed the students. Afterwards a large number of students marched towards the capital.

The Egyptian historian Abd al-Rahman al-Rafi saw the student uprising of 1935–36 as an episode of great importance:

> The student demonstrations of November and December 1935 were sound in form and pure in purpose. They were motivated by nationalist sentiment and aimed to achieve national demands. No one prompted the students to demonstrate except their own abundant and sincere patriotism. They were crying out for independence, freedom and the constitution. Their demonstrations were neither aggressive nor subversive. They protected their ranks against the intrusion of the riff-raff. On the whole it was a glorious page in the history of youth. It was a mini revolution, an epitome of the 1919 Revolution.[6]

The immediate outcome of these student activities was the formation of a United Front of all political parties. Students played a major role in bringing this about. As contemporary political leaders noted, 'Students kept moving from one party headquarters to another, begging their leaders to unite and insisting on this demand in a spirit of anxiety for the country's destiny.'[7] In a bid to entice the Wafdist rivals into co-operating with his party, the leader of the Constitutional Liberals, Muhammad

Mahmoud Pasha, went so far as to proclaim that, 'The young men undertook their duty, they sacrificed their lives; the duty of the politicians is to respond to this voice of the nation and unite.'[8] As Bashatli Effendi reported, this plea had some success:

On the 10th Dec. a deputation of students went to see Nahas Pasha and insisted that in the interest of the country he ought to agree to co-operate with the other parties, and threatened that, if he refused to do so, they would cease to support the Wafd. The same day it was stated that Nahas Pasha had consented to the formation of the United Front, and this in spite of the fact that only a few days earlier he had been in serious disagreement with the Constitutional Liberals.[9]

In response to an appeal from the leaders of the United Front, the Palace on 12 December 1935 issued a Royal Decree restoring the Constitution of 1923. The students, however, persisted in their strikes against the British. On 17 December a number of them gathered in the Faculty of Medicine and discussed how their movement should continue. Some decided to form 'committees for national propaganda' in the provinces, although this met with little practical success. On 31 December thousands of students met the delegates of the International Conference of Surgery, held in the University Hall, with cries of 'Egypt for the Egyptians', taking particular pains to shout down the British delegates. The prime minister, on arrival, was held up by students and eventually obliged to return to the city. A number of students entered the conference hall and disturbed its session for a while.

Apart from pressing the leaders of the political parties to form the United Front, to restore constitutional rule and to pave the way for the signature of the Anglo-Egyptian Treaty of 1936, the student uprising of 1935–36 marked the emergence of the student movement as a distinctive force in Egyptian politics. In its aftermath these years came to be dubbed the 'years of youth'. They were years of youthful disenchantment with the professional politicians, towards whom the students expressed relative independence of both thought and action. In the judgement of an official of the British Residency, 'Students, who now regard themselves as responsible for national victory and [the] establishment of a united front, are not under full control of leaders and may act independently of them.'[10]

The student uprising of 1935–36 marked the beginning of a stage in which the Wafd began to relinquish its grip upon the student body and the latter joined the emerging extra-parliamentary organizations in increasing numbers. The role of the activists of Young Egypt during the period shows this particularly clearly.[11] In a bid to restore its student following, the Wafd was forced to adopt the approach of its rivals, organizing the students on semi-Fascist lines[12] in the Blue Shirts. From 1935–36 onwards different student groupings and rival camps within the student movement began to appear and continued to polarize ever more dramatically in the years that followed the Second World War.

Factions and Currents

The Wafdist Students

The history of student activism under the banner of the Wafd dates back to the time of the 1919 Revolution. The Revolution, which broke out spontaneously, was sparked off at the Law School of Cairo University. It gradually acquired a measure of organization around a nucleus in the Higher Schools Club, founded before the First World War as a social and cultural forum for students and graduates. The secretary of the Wafd's Central Committee, Abd al-Rahman Fahmi, relied on students to convey and execute his directives in different parts of the country. In one leaflet he assured them that 'it is upon you, students, that your nation and the Wafd depend'.[13] Students also formed the majority of cell members of the Wafd's Secret Apparatus led by Fahmi himself. When Zaghlul returned from exile, he found that the Wafdist students had already established an Executive Committee to organize their activities in various cities and provinces. He endorsed this development and allowed the committee to meet twice a week in his own residence, *Beit al-Umma* (House of the Nation), promising to put its leader Hasan Yassin on the Wafd's slate as a candidate in the parliamentary elections. Yassin did eventually win a seat in parliament and became the first student to be elected as an MP.

In the first parliamentary elections of 1923, a Wafdist Student Electioneering Committee was formed, consisting of fifty-two students who in turn elected ten of their number to form the Students' Executive Committee. Zaghlul praised the students' efforts in explaining the complexities of the electoral system and guiding the voters, especially in the rural areas. From that time onwards the students came to be known as the 'Army of the Wafd'.

Student participation in the Wafd's political activities was a permanent source of annoyance for the minority governments opposed to the Wafd. During the constitutional crisis of 1928, the Wafd mobilized its student committees to organize anti-government protests. Those sections of the press hostile to the Wafd denounced them as 'Soviet committees, not student committees'.[14] In the same year, the minority government of Muhammad Mahmoud Pasha issued the Public Act for the Maintenance of Order in Educational Institutions, prohibiting students from engaging in political activity and from membership of political parties.

By the mid-1930s, however, many students had lost their enthusiasm for the Wafd, and other political factions began to win the support of a considerable proportion[15] of students. The first non-Wafdist political grouping to win significant student support was the emerging Young Egypt Society. Although the golden age of the Wafd's hold over students in the 1920s, when it virtually monopolized their allegiance, had come to an end, the Wafdists remained the largest grouping in the student body. As a British Embassy official noted, 'Although other parties can cause some trouble, it is only the Wafd who can create really serious disturbance.'[16]

The year 1937 was marked by clashes between Wafdist and anti-Wafdist students over the issue of the teaching of religion and the segregation of the sexes in the university. The Wafd government of the time used force against student demonstrations, dissolved the Students' Executive Committee and implemented the Public Act for the Maintenance of Order in Educational Institutions which it had considered void when in opposition.[17]

In a bid to assert its authority over the turbulent young men, and in response to the challenge posed by the para-military Green Shirts of Young Egypt, the Wafd leadership encouraged the formation of its own Blue Shirts.[18] According to the British ambassador:

The Wafd's decision to foster this movement is, no doubt, partly due to their alarm at the progress which the minority parties have made in enlisting the support of the students and even in organising them on semi-Fascist lines.[19]

The British felt uneasy about this development. As Anthony Eden wrote to Lampson:

> You should urge him [Nahhas Pasha] with all the emphasis at your command to undertake early measures to control the movement, to limit its activities and if possible to guide them into harmless channels. The matter is one of the greatest importance for the future of Egypt.[20]

Shortly before the creation of the Blue Shirt squads (composed mainly of students), the party set up the Wafdist Youth Committees, consisting mainly of young workers in urban areas. These committees were combined into a General Union, which adopted a hostile attitude towards the Blue Shirts. The latent hostility between the two groups came into the open when they clashed in public. This, together with British pressure, prompted the Wafd leadership to take direct control of the Blue Shirts until the squads were dismantled in 1938.

In a number of incidents, the Wafdist students' clashes echoed the struggle between different factions within the Wafd itself. When al-Nokrashi Pasha and Dr Ahmad Maher tried to obtain the ministerial portfolios of Defence and Education, Zaghlul accused them of trying to impose their hold on the army and the students. In 1942 the emerging leader of the Wafd's right wing, Fouad Sirag al-Din Pasha, tried to instal his brother as leader of the Wafdist students.[21] Although the attempt failed, its result was to divide the Wafdist students into rival camps, a situation they described as 'the battle of the Wafd against the Wafd'.[22] This rivalry helped to create a radical faction of the Wafdist students and the party's conference of 1943 marked the growing influence of the young Wafdists.

Subsequently a separate forum, the Wafdist Vanguard, was created by the radical elements within the party. It consisted mainly of students and intellectuals eager to formulate a radical programme to solve Egypt's grave social problems. They became ever more conscious of the international context of Egypt's national predicament and of increasing US involvement in the Middle East. The Vanguard had considerable support among the students and was represented on their Executive Committee.

The incident of February 1942 did nothing to enhance the Wafd's appeal to students. By the end of the Second World War:

> its position in the universities and schools had been very much weakened by successful palace propaganda on nationalist lines and based largely on indictments of the Wafd as responsible for the British intervention in 1942 and as a corrupt body.[23]

The Wafdist students, however, proved more sensitive than the rest of the party to the social problems of their country and tried their best, especially through their organ *The League of Wafdist Youth*, to prompt their party to address these problems seriously. In practice, however, they failed to alter its traditional policies and tactics, which reflected the vested social interests of the Wafd leadership rather than the pressures of the party's young men.

The Muslim Brotherhood

Hasan al-Banna considered students as the 'striking force' of his organization. He therefore devoted particular attention to them, meeting with a different group for the whole night every week and covering the Brotherhood's entire student membership in rotation during the course of the year. His relationship with many of the students was that of a combined God and father figure. He maintained personal contact with them and knew in detail about their interests and activities and even their personal lives. He was particularly concerned about their academic progress and encouraged them to devote themselves to their studies at the time of their examinations. Student members of the Brotherhood were organized in 'families' which met regularly every week in the house of one of them to study an Islamic educative syllabus specially designed to suit their age group and educational level. Most of them, if not all, were also members of the Brotherhood's Rover Scouts.[24]

In the early years, the Muslim Brotherhood did not recruit a large number of students. Shortly before the Second World War, its student membership amounted to some five hundred, mostly from al-Azhar.[25] When a dispute broke out in 1937 between students of Arabic at al-Azhar and their counterparts in the Faculty of Dar al-Uloum at the secular university, the Brotherhood favoured the students of al-Azhar. As a result they succeeded in attracting a number of al-Azhar students, as well as several of its ulama, to attend the organization's meetings.

After the incident of February 1942, the Brotherhood made every effort to absorb those students who were disappointed by the Wafd's attitude. Its magazine gave more space to student affairs and a regular talk for students was arranged every Thursday. After the end of the Second World War, the Brotherhood continued to interest itself actively in the student body, creating a special section for them at its headquarters and designing a series of lectures for student audiences. Students were also encouraged to write about aspects of Islam related to their education and about other Islamic subjects. A liaison officer was chosen from the students of each faculty, and their student committees were supervised by one of the Brotherhood's leaders.

As a result of these efforts, the Muslim Brotherhood succeeded in enlisting the support of increasing numbers of students. As Sir Walter Smith of the British Embassy noted in 1946, 'The rise of the Moslem Brethren has weakened the Wafd, particularly in the University and Schools, where they have recently become stronger than the Wafd as an element of disorder.'[26] The Brotherhood's infiltration of the secular university overshadowed even their earlier success at al-Azhar.[27] It created what was seen as a wholly new phenomenon—Islam of the effendis.[28] This, however, was a political achievement which proved to be of very little intellectual significance:

> They stated in their books and speeches many times that their movement was conservative and traditional, not philosophical. Accordingly they avoided involving themselves in those problems so deeply concerning the minds of the educated . . . This is not contradicted by the participation of a number of the educated—university students and men of religion and law—in their movement. This participation is attributable to concord of political doctrine and not to concord of religious thought.[29]

The Brotherhood became increasingly active in the post-war student movement[30] and any adequate account of the Egyptian student movement at this time must identify and acknowledge the role played within it by their student members. While the Brotherhood considers itself to have been the 'predominant force'[31] in the student movement in this period, it would be more accurate to see it as merely one of the major forces, since it had to compete for student allegiance with the large body of the Wafdist students. Moreover, the proportion of Muslim Brethren in the student body as a whole remains uncertain, since some of them kept their ties with the organization a secret even from their own families. Some estimates, however, give at least an approximate idea as to this proportion:

—By the end of the war, the number of Rover Scouts, mainly students, was estimated at between twenty thousand[32] and forty-five thousand.[33]
—After the Brotherhood's activities were banned in December 1948, the number of its activists dismissed from secondary schools and universities amounted to one thousand.[34]
—At the outbreak of the Revolution of 1952, one of their leaders claimed that the Brotherhood 'made up 30 per cent of the student body'.[35]

The Brotherhood's appeal among the student body can be inferred from the fact that it was able to sweep the board in the Student Union elections at Cairo University in November 1951, winning the following proportions of the contested seats:

11/11 in the Student Union of the Faculty of Agriculture
11/11 in the Student Union of the Faculty of Science
7/10 in the Student Union of the Faculty of Engineering
11/16 in the Student Union of the Faculty of Arts
9/10 in the Student Union of the Faculty of Law
9/13 in the Student Union of the Faculty of Commerce.[36]

Their election victory in the Faculty of Law was particularly significant since this faculty was known to be the stronghold of the Wafdist students. The extent of their triumph in this particular year, however, was largely due to their initiative in providing students with military training to take part in the anti-British guerrilla activities in the Canal Zone, where they sacrificed their celebrated martyrs, Omar Shaheen and Ahmad al-Minayyisi.

The students of the Muslim Brotherhood were known to be highly organized.[37] Many of them gained their organizational experience through membership of the para-military Rover

Scouts, the only group to be exempted from the 1938 Act banning all para-military organizations. Some students were also members of the Society's underground Special Apparatus, a number of whom had been among the volunteers in the 1948 Palestine war.

The most prominent of the Brotherhood's student leaders was Mustafa Mumin,[38] who was an indefatigable campaigner and could always rouse the enthusiasm of a crowd (while other leaders like Hassan Hathout and Ezzeddin Ibrahim were known more as skilful organizers). Mumin is particularly remembered for transmitting the 'voice of Egypt'[39] to the UN Security Council in 1947, when he accompanied an official Egyptian delegation carrying a petition written in the blood of students demanding their country's independence. He is also remembered for his notorious speech of 1946, in which he quoted the Qur'an to prove that the prime minister Ismail Sidqi, with whom the Brethren were in accord, was as faithful as the Prophet Ismail!

The Communists

Towards the end of the Second World War the emerging Communist movement began to attempt to influence the student movement from within rather than from without. The academic year 1945/46 witnessed a high point of Communist activism among the students, especially in the Faculties of Science and Medicine in Cairo and Alexandria Universities, and in the Faculties of Commerce and Law in Cairo. The Faculty of Science in Alexandria in particular was nicknamed the 'Red Faculty'.[40]

The Communists formed an organized group within the student body. The different Communist organizations each contained a high proportion of students and maintained a separate student section. The organizations which were most active among the students were Iskra, the Egyptian Movement for National Liberation (EMNL), and to a lesser extent the Citadel and the New Dawn groups.

The student section of Iskra had some three hundred activists, a large proportion of whom came from well-to-do families. Since it was a highly secretive organization, its student members nominally belonged to the Students of the Scientific Research House, a cultural club established by the organization in Cairo as a forum for intellectual discussion. Later they established an open student forum, the League of Egyptian Students, whose activities were led by a number of activists including Gamal

Ghali, Abd al-Monem al-Ghazali, Saad Zahran, Muhammad al-Khafeef and Gamal Shalabi.[41] Ghali represented the league at the founding conference of the International Union of Students. The league published three issues of a magazine called *Student's Voice*, in an edition of some five to six thousand copies, before the magazine was confiscated by the police. One further clandestine issue was subsequently published. The League also brought out a series of booklets, such as al-Ghazali's *We Want to Learn*, in which he criticized the government's educational policy.

The EMNL also had a relatively large student section and was active in educational institutions outside the Universities of Cairo and Alexandria, especially in al-Azhar and the independent Faculty of Fine Arts. In addition, it recruited a number of Sudanese students who were in Egypt at that time.[42] Unlike Iskra, its student membership was drawn from poor families.

The small organization of the Citadel, founded in 1942, formed a small but active nucleus of student activists at Cairo University. The influence of the New Dawn group on the student body was confined to its co-operation with the Wafdist left which dominated the Students' Executive Committee.

Towards the end of 1945 the various Communist organizations made an attempt to co-ordinate their activities among students. Regular meetings between Iskra and the EMNL were held for this purpose, an effort reflected in the prominent role played by Communist students in the uprising of 1946.

The tactics of the Communist students were often imprudently bold.[43] On one occasion a group of them went so far as to chant anti-monarchist slogans over Cairo Radio during its regular broadcasting of the chimes of the university clock. They also went to some lengths to encourage female students to take part in political activities.[44] Their fortunes reflected the ups and downs of the Communist movement in the country at large, and their tactics were often subject to vigorous doctrinal squabbles in the wider Communist movement. In October 1945 the EMNL expected a student revolt on the first day of the academic year and distributed a leaflet calling on policemen not to suppress their fellow-citizens. When demonstrations failed to break out that day (they eventually occurred four months later), this misjudgement led one faction within the movement to secede and establish a new organization of its own.

Student members in both Iskra and the EMNL pressed their

leaders to unite.[45] When this union eventually materialized, students took an active part in the new Democratic Movement for National Liberation (HADITU), and edited the student section of its *al-Jamaheer* (The Masses). They also played an important role in the movement's subsequent ideological conflicts and organizational split. Curiel's draft of the Plan of National Democratic Forces maintained that students could play as much of a revolutionary role as the working class in the national struggle and the transformation to socialism. One of HADITU's leaders later admitted:

> I was so convinced of the importance of the role of the students in semi-colonized countries that I considered workers in Egypt different from the ones Marx had talked about. I looked instead to students as the main political force.[46]

The recurrence of divisions within the movement, together with its unpopular stand on the 1948 war in Palestine, caused its influence within the student movement to decline from 1948 to 1950.[47] With the revival of the nationalist movement in the early 1950s, however, it started to regain its strength. In April 1951 HADITU attempted to establish a Democratic Union of Students, forming a Preparatory Committee and launching a campaign in its magazines *al-Malayeen* and *al-Wageb*. A meeting, under the title of the 'Conference of the Charter', was held at Cairo University with the active participation of HADITU, advancing a number of nationalist demands and calling for the formation of national charter committees to campaign for them. After the abrogation of the Anglo-Egyptian Treaty of 1936 Communist students joined in the anti-British guerrilla warfare in the Canal Zone. Some of the army officers who led the Revolution of 1952 were introduced to the clandestine Communist movement through their links with the university as external students.[48]

Young Egypt

Young Egypt was the first national political organization to be established and led by students and young graduates. Its principal political message concerned the role which the young generation must play in restoring the country's glory and achieving its independence. In his memoirs, Ahmad Hussein dates his group's first attempt to take part in student activities to 1930, when his colleague Fathi Radwan was put forward as a candidate for the Student Union elections in the Faculty of Law. Their campaign at the time was:

> something unfamiliar to students . . . There was no mention in it of the Wafd and Nahhas Pasha or of Muhammad Mahmoud Pasha and his treaty, or even of the constitution and its implementation . . . It was all about the glory of Egypt and its restoration.[49]

When Ahmad Hussein and his colleagues inaugurated the Piastre Plan in support of local industry, they were accused by the Wafd of diverting the students' attention from politics. The Wafdist students in various schools 'energetically prevented fellow students volunteering as flag-sellers in the plan'.[50]

When Young Egypt was formally created in 1933, however, it was a straightforward political organization. In a very short period of time it succeeded in attracting a number of students from the university, government and private schools, and al-Azhar. In 1934 students formed 40.8 per cent of its membership and it rapidly became a potential focus for rallying Egyptian youth. As a British official serving in Egypt at the time noted, 'This budding organisation has already incurred the enmity of the Wafd, who naturally are jealously unwilling to see the student masses escape from their influence.'[51] The Green Shirts of Young Egypt, composed mainly of students, were largely responsible for prompting the Wafd to create its own Blue Shirts.

The students of Young Egypt played a major role in the student uprising of 1935–36. The movement's earlier propaganda had helped to create the general mood of discontent which led to the uprising, seen by Ahmad Hussein as a 'triumph of the spirit of Young Egypt'.[52] The students of Young Egypt, led by Nour al-Din Tarraf,[53] Ibrahim Shukri[54] and others, were in the forefront of the student opposition to the Wafd. A report from the Ministry of the Interior noted:

> It is considered that the association of university students with members of Young Egypt in that manner is likely to result in a large number of these students joining the membership of the society.[55]

Student members of Young Egypt participated indirectly in Ahmad Hussein's first international campaign. Students from the Faculty of Medicine printed a fifty-page booklet of photographs of those who had been killed and wounded in the riots. A copy was dispatched by the organization to its president in London for use in anti-British propaganda.

In 1937 Young Egypt candidates successfully contested the Student Union elections and won a majority both in the Wafd's stronghold of the Faculty of Law and in the Faculty of Arts. But their victory was short-lived, as the Wafd regained its supremacy in the following year.

After the suppression of Young Egypt in 1941, its few reported activities were mainly confined to the student body. A memorandum[56] submitted to the British Embassy by the Special Branch reported that members of Young Egypt at al-Azhar had distributed a pamphlet entitled *To Azharite Young Men*, accusing Nahhas Pasha of ruling the country as a dictator and calling for the release of Ahmad Hussein and others from prison. The released members of Young Egypt whom the Special Branch considered 'dangerous to public security' were two lawyers, a printer and six university students.

After the Second World War, Ahmad Hussein resumed his activities on his release from detention, focusing his attention on students. A Cairo police report to the Embassy noted that his speeches were becoming 'more clearly anti-British' and that he was calling 'for students to double their efforts and get ready for the school-year'.[57] In an article entitled 'Revolution . . . Revolution', Ahmad Hussein proclaimed that:

> Revolution is coming, no doubt. We shall see in November or December when the universities reopen and masses of students representing their nation regather . . . It is the army of students that will spark the revolution, as they always have throughout the history of Egypt.[58]

The students of Young Egypt played a prominent role in daubing the walls of major cities with dissident slogans.[59] They also participated in the xenophobic campaign of public burnings of books written in European languages. Their student organization, although still fairly small, was capable of causing a disproportionate level of disturbances. By the mid-1940s Young Egypt had largely lost touch with the mainstream of the student movement and it was not until the late 1940s and early 1950s, when it became the Socialist Party, that it regained some strength. But at no point was it a negligible force within the student movement.

Other Groupings
The fact that the university formed the bastion both for the emergent extra-parliamentary political forces and for the Wafd does not mean that other anti-Wafdist parliamentary parties had no representation within the student movement. Although the other major parliamentary parties came into being as a result of splits within the Wafd leadership, these splits had little effect on the party's mass following. Much the same was true among students. While many of them joined the new extra-parliamentary organizations, relatively few deserted the Wafd for its parliamentary opponents.

Only a very small minority of students defected from the Wafd to join the seceding al-Ahrar (Constitutional Liberal) party in 1921–22, despite the fact that al-Ahrar's leadership included a number of prominent intellectuals and university professors, and despite the popularity of their leader Muhammad Mahmoud Pasha among some of the student activists during the uprising of 1935–36. The Wafd was still strong at this point because of its appeal as the representative of national unity before the country had attained even nominal independence. The Saadist defection of 1937–38 (see p.12) seems to have attracted more deserters, perhaps because its leadership was drawn from the urban middle class. While the Constitutional Liberals were seen as representatives of large landowners, it was easier for the Saadists to influence members of their own class, including students. In addition, the Saadist grouping was led by popular former leaders of the Wafd who kept their links with the activists of the student movement.

The defection of 1942–43 which created the Wafdist Bloc may have attracted a few defectors owing to the personal influence of its leader, the secretary-general of the Wafd, Makram Ubaid Pasha.

The only parliamentary party which did not owe its existence to a secession from the Wafd was the Nationalist Party, which had been in existence before the Wafd's foundation. The role of the Nationalist Party within the student movement mirrored the party's steady decline. Although its vocal and intransigent nationalism[60] attracted a number of students, some of them female,[61] it never achieved a wide membership within the student body. Its influence was somewhat stronger than this might suggest, however, because of the uncompromising vigour of its nationalism.[62] Because of the party's hostility to the Wafd and its relative lack of interest in parliament, it formed part of the anti-Wafdist camp within the student movement.

There were also numerous other minor groups within the universities. Some were organized on political lines,[63] while others catered for a variety of interests (religious,[64] artistic, sporting, and so on). There were also a number of regional associations, such as those of students from Upper Egypt and from the Delta province of al-Munufiyya. All played a political role subsidiary to one or other of the principal factions within the student movement.

There were, in addition, two further distinctive groups within the student movement—the students of the secondary schools and the students of al-Azhar. These were not themselves specifically political groupings, but since they were infiltrated by all the political factions they served as a recruiting ground for both the main camps of the student movement.

It was secondary school students who initiated student political activism in Egypt. According to von Grunebaum:

Pupils in the secondary schools often started rows long before the founding of the university; the first large riot of this sort of which I have knowledge was the demolishing of the building used by the editorial staff of the newspaper Al-Muqattam, carried out by students under the direction of the nationalist leader Mustafa Kamil (1874–1908) in 1893.[65]

Secondary school students also supported the Nationalist Party campaign for the establishment of a parliament in Egypt at the turn of the century. When the British unilaterally declared Egypt a protectorate in 1914, 'every school in the country was transformed into a centre of anti-British propaganda'.[66]

Secondary schools also became centres of party politics. Schools like al-Khediviya and Khedive Ismail were renowned as centres of student activism in Cairo. One educationist complained:

Things are turned upside down as school pupils began forcibly to control many school activities, as a result of the infiltration of party politics. The voice of the pupils became louder than that of the teachers and headmasters![67]

Students from the secondary schools represented the main recruiting ground for the Wafd outside the universities. The enthusiasm of these students for the Wafd party was, however, sometimes checked by the influence of their teachers and head-masters, who either had different political inclinations or chose to comply with the wishes of the party in office. The importance of the role played by the secondary school students within the student movement lay in their sheer weight of numbers, which gave an appearance of strength to those strikes and demonstrations in which they took part.[68]

The secondary school students were also important in giving the student movement a broader geographical base. While university students were concentrated in Cairo and Alexandria, the secondary school students were scattered throughout the country.[69] In 1947 the British consular agent in Fayyoum reported to the Embassy that, 'All demonstrations that have occurred in Fayoum have been caused solely by school-boys, who are totally ignorant and misguided. In demonstrating they are only imitating the students of Cairo.'[70] The consular agent in Sohag also predicted that, 'Disturbances, if any, will probably come through the school-boys, most of whom will not know why they are demonstrating.'[71]

When it was suggested that secondary school students should be given military training by the government, a certain Giles Bey advised the Embassy that, 'This idea of training students of the Secondary Schools in arms holding is rather dangerous as it prepares the minds of young students to use the arms which they will be prepared to do in critical times.'[72] A number of secondary school students did in fact take part in the guerrilla warfare in the Canal Zone and scattered groups of them attacked British soldiers in order to obtain arms.

The second distinct group within the student movement was formed by the students of the schools, institutes and faculties of al-Azhar. Al-Azhar had been infiltrated by various political parties, especially those extra-parliamentary organizations with a religious orientation: Young Egypt and the Muslim Brotherhood. But such influence was much weaker than in secular educational institutions, since al-Azhar remained essentially a bastion of religious and political conservatism.

When the Green Shirts of Young Egypt and the Blue Shirts of the Wafd tried to extend their organizations to al-Azhar, they were rebuffed by most of the students. A petition against the

Blue Shirts was even addressed to the King by the al-Azhar student body. Violent clashes between the two groups took place in October 1937, when some one thousand Azharite students attacked two encampments of the Blue Shirts in the neighbourhood of their university and burned them to the ground.

On 2 February 1942 a group of Azharite students took part in a demonstration with shouts of 'Go ahead . . . Rommel.' After the British had succeeded in installing a Wafd government two days later, some three thousand of them demonstrated in opposition. The demonstrators distributed a memorandum to foreign diplomatic missions in Cairo, to the fury of Nahhas Pasha who instructed the Shaikh of al-Azhar to calm his students down. When the Wafd government recognized the USSR in 1943 al-Azhar students demonstrated against this gesture and in January 1944 they went on strike in protest against the proposed visit of the Mufti of the USSR. Within the student movement, accordingly, the students of al-Azhar stood clearly in the camp which opposed the Wafd, openly favouring the King.

Factional Struggle

During the student uprising of 1935–36, a report by the Ministry of the Interior classified the students into two parties or sections, one consisting of supporters of the Wafd and the other of Nationalists.[73] This split within the student movement has proved to be a lasting one. In 1937 there were violent street clashes between student supporters and opponents of the Wafd. Towards the end of the Second World War student factions once again polarized around two extremes: the Wafdist students in alliance with the newly emerging Communists, and their opponents bringing the Muslim Brotherhood into a tactical alliance with Young Egypt, the Nationalist Party and other minority parties.

The leftist camp enjoyed certain elements of strength. First, the Wafd historically enjoyed great popularity, as demonstrated by its large student membership, now being reorganized under the radical leadership of Mustafa Musa. Second, the leftists had the advantage of the intellectual and organizational abilities of the Communist students, and particularly their capacity to formulate a political programme which went beyond general slogans. Third, there was a reservoir of support from a large mass of independent students who, while not identifying with specific political groupings, nevertheless sympathized with the main objectives of the Wafd. The main weaknesses of the left lay in the reluctance of the Wafd leadership to permit its students to act with any degree of independence,[74] and in the factional strife among the Communists. As a whole, the left was put on the defensive by its opponents and did not achieve the organizational coherence and discipline imposed by the leadership element among its opponents, the Muslim Brotherhood.

The main strength of these opponents lay in their being led by an extra-parliamentary organization which had the determined aim of changing the political order in the country at large. Although Young Egypt could claim to have pioneered this grouping, it was by this time clearly led, and indeed dominated, by the increasingly popular Muslim Brotherhood.[75] While the Brotherhood, Young Egypt and the Nationalist Party were in broad agreement on a variety of issues—their hostility towards the Wafd, their pan-Islamic ideals and the attitude of the first two towards the parliamentary system—the element of weakness in their camp lay in the major divisions which remained between them[76] and in their consequent competition for the allegiance of the non-Wafdist students. The Brotherhood in particular tended to act independently and without due consideration for its allies.

The two camps clashed politically and sometimes physically. The year 1946 witnessed the worst fighting between them, both inside and outside the universities.[77] The head of the Student Section in the Brotherhood at the time later defended his organization's attitude:

> We had every intention of avoiding violent confrontation. But we were attacked and had to defend ourselves . . . The proof of this is that it was the Wafd whose popularity was declining while the popularity of the Brotherhood was growing . . . Our relation with the Wafd was not one of competition for power but rather a relation between a declining force and a progressing one.[78]

It is true that the Wafd was at that time a declining force; and the Brotherhood was in general loath to engage in premature confrontation. But this scarcely absolves the Brotherhood of responsibility for such confrontations, since in the very nature of the violent street fighting it is hard reliably to distinguish aggressors from victims. On a number of occasions the Brotherhood was keen to show its numerical strength in a provocative manner.

The relationship between the Brotherhood and the Communists appears to have been the worst of all.[79] It was a confrontation between two growing forces who found no room for conciliation. Muhammad Farid Abd al-Khaleq of the Brotherhood acknowledged that, 'It was difficult to accept political co-operation with the Communists due to the differences in principle between Islamic thought and Marxist thought . . . In addition, the Communists were not honest partners in the movement as they tended to ride the wave.'[80] According to a student activist in the Brotherhood, the student movement failed in two principal respects: 'First, it welcomed opportunists, i.e. students belonging to political parties. Second, it allowed Communist infiltration of the country.'[81] Representatives of the Brotherhood stress the limited role played by their Communist counterparts: 'The leadership of all national events was Islamic . . . A handful of Communists took part just for the sake of commotion, or in order to make a political point.'[82]

The Communists in turn denounced the Muslim Brotherhood as Fascists, reactionaries, British agents, pawns of the Palace, instruments of minority governments and brokers of religion. The Communists also accused the Brethren of being terrorists and *al-Jamaheer* (the magazine of HADITU) was the first to suggest that the organization should be dissolved. Reporting the Student Union elections in Cairo University in the academic year 1947/48, a clandestine Communist bulletin described the 'Triumph of the Democratic Forces':

> The electoral battle was very hotly contested . . . The authorities expected a victory for the Fascist Moslem Brotherhood . . . The Young Fascists had based the electoral campaign on the enrolment of Egyptian students in the anti-Jewish brigades and on the exclusion of women-students from the council of the Students' Union . . . The Wafdists and the progressives based their campaign on the struggle against imperialism in general, beginning in Egypt, the payment of fees for the poorer students from the funds of the Union, and the removal of the police cordon around the University.[83]

The Brotherhood and the Communists were unquestionably the

most dynamic factions within the student movement. Had they come to terms with each other, the entire course of the movement would have changed. Although the differences of principle between the two prevented any very intimate co-operation, the main source of their antagonism was of a more practical nature.

Each group represented a new force aiming at a radical change in the political system[84] and competing primarily for the allegiance of the same sector of the population, namely the urban middle class. The common orientation of the two groups towards other forces along the political spectrum was not based on any agreement in principle. The Brotherhood did not hesitate to ally itself with even the most unpopular governments when it found this to its tactical advantage. The Communists in turn did not hesitate to ally themselves with the Wafd although the party was on the decline, was controlled substantially by landowners and remained unreceptive to the idea of introducing social reform. There was little difference between the Brotherhood and the Communists in the class composition of their membership. With the growing strength of the nationalist movement between 1950 and 1952, a large section of the Communist movement abandoned the accusation of Fascism and called for a United Front with the Muslim Brotherhood.

At a number of points in the course of their confrontation, however, the two student camps[85] maintained some open bridges between them. When the Saadist prime minister Ahmad Maher was assassinated in February 1945, activists from various student factions were arrested and subsequently met in prison, where they came to an agreement to co-ordinate their activities within the movement after their release.[86] The summer of 1945 saw a continuation of these discussions between virtually all student factions. There was at times a close rapport between the Wafdists and the Brotherhood.[87] Even between the Communists and the Brotherhood 'there were dialogues at the time when there was a call for a united front'.[88]

The principal issue which drew the two camps of the student movement together was their common stance on the question of national independence.[89] Nationalist demands such as the evacuation of British troops and the abrogation of the Treaty of 1936 were the common aims of all factions. Everybody took part in demonstrations, 'even without pre-arrangement'.[90]

Apart from this area of agreement, however, the student movement was divided on every issue and never attained organizational unity or created a unified leadership. Each of the two political groupings claimed the leadership of the movement for itself to the exclusion of the other. This rivalry dominated the activities of the movement and few of those who were then student activists show any real appreciation even in retrospect of the role played by their political opponents. As early as 1936, as Sir Miles Lampson observed, it was evident that, 'Left to themselves the students would fall out with one another and disintegrate.'[91]

4
1946: The Climax

The Second Student Uprising

In political terms the summer of 1945 was as hot as the weather itself. The Second World War had formally ended and the Egyptian nationalist movement expected a favourable British response to its demands. Nationalist activity intensified:

—The Wafd is active, especially Fouad Sirag El-Din who is in co-ordination with Young Egypt and the Moslem Brothers.
—The focus of activity is students at the university and schools, in preparation for riots in October and November 1945 when the school year starts.
—The Union of the University Graduates, led by Wafdist Hussein Diab, is active.
—Speeches of Ahmed Hussein of Young Egypt are becoming more clearly anti-British with more talk about the rights of the poor. He calls for students to double their efforts and get ready for the school year.
—The Moslem Brothers are becoming very powerful and Al-Bana unveiled his face to get directly involved in politics. On the 5th of this month he met students who called for a general congress to be held on the 4th October to discuss national demands.
—The number of communist students is increasing and some are members of the Union of University Graduates and they demand complete independence and social justice. They are encouraged by press writings about Communism since the lifting of censorship. They will be active in the University.[1]

Student activists held extensive discussions in the sports hall of the Cairo Faculty of Medicine. Attendance at these meetings averaged between twenty and fifty[2] leading figures in the student movement. The topics discussed included: imperialism and national liberation; military pacts and Western proposals for the collective defence of the Middle East; and democracy and the social system.[3] Almost all student political factions were represented at these meetings. The initiative in calling them was taken by the left wing of the movement—the Wafdists, the Communists and other independent activists. Its ultimate aim was to unify the various factions behind a common programme and to prepare for the establishment of a National Committee to lead the movement.

At the beginning of the 1945/46 academic year, the leftist students called for a general conference on 7 October to discuss student attitudes towards the national problem against the background of a renewed Anglo-Egyptian exchange of memoranda. On the previous day, the Muslim Brotherhood, in the first of many such manoeuvres, held a meeting (for which they claimed an attendance of some six thousand students) which submitted a memorandum to the government in the name of 'the green land of Egypt', advancing their views on the national issue. The meeting on 7 October called for the establishment of National Committees of students (NCs) in the various faculties of the university. Representatives of the Brotherhood who attended asked the meeting to endorse the resolutions of its own meeting, but without success. The result was a breakdown in their relations with the leftist students.[4]

A few weeks later, students went on strike in solidarity with the Arab population of Palestine on the anniversary of the Balfour Declaration. A memorandum from the commandant of Cairo police to the prime minister, al-Nokrashi Pasha, reported the event as follows:

> On the 1st November the students crossed to Giza to the university where a full strike was in progress. The question of demonstrating and coming up to Cairo was discussed amongst them in the university but at about 11.05 a.m. it was decided that it was sufficient that they had declared their sympathy with Palestine and Indonesia, and that there was no need for demonstrations. They elected some groups to carry pamphlets and circulars for distribution to the Labour Syndicates, Commercial Departments, and Shops to urge them to go on strike on 2nd November in order to show their sympathy with Palestine. They then dispersed quietly.[5]

In December a meeting of representatives from both camps of the student movement was held in an attempt to unify the movement. An Executive Committee of supporters of the Wafd was elected.

On 26 January 1946, infuriated by Britain's non-committal reply to the Egyptian government's memorandum, the students closed ranks for united action. Students from the al-Azhar Arabic Faculty went on hunger strike inside the premises; the Union of University Graduates issued a statement of protest; and a series of meetings in various faculties, institutes and schools followed suit. A mass meeting was held at the headquarters of the Young Muslim Men's Association (YMMA), which passed a resolution to organize a march on 9 February, and to submit a memorandum to the Palace, calling for negotiations with Britain to be broken off, the abrogation of the 1936 Treaty and the rejection of any defence pact with Britain.[6]

The ninth of February 1946 proved to be a key day in the history of the student movement. Thousands of students from the secondary schools in Cairo flocked into the university campus, where a huge congregation of students was preparing for the march. A number of speeches were delivered and a group of students was chosen to maintain strict order during the march. The marchers[7] headed towards the city along the usual route, aiming to cross the Nile by Abbas Bridge. When they reached the bridge they found its two halves had been raised. A group of students succeeded in lowering them once more and the demonstrators began to cross. But the police[8] managed to raise the spans once again while the students were still crossing the bridge, splitting the march into two and causing panic. A number of students fell into the river. Estimates of the numbers injured vary; the most reliable appears to be that of the Egyptian historian Abd al-Rahman al-Rafi, who claims, after a thorough investigation, that eighty-four were injured but no one was actually killed.[9]

Sporadic demonstrations occurred the same day in Cairo and on the following days in Alexandria and other towns on the Delta.[10] A Sudanese student, Muhammad Ali Muhammad, was killed and his body hidden by students of the Faculty of Medicine. A day-long battle with the police took place when they attempted to prevent the holding of a large-scale funeral. The Faculty of Medicine in Cairo became the focus of attention that evening, as students held continuous meetings on its premises.

On 10 February the King went to the university, as previously arranged, to open the new student dormitory; despite his cool reception,[11] he invited student leaders to the Palace. The following day a demonstration led by Mustafa Mumin, this time under police protection, headed in the direction of the Palace. The King dissociated himself from the government action against the students and hinted at his intention to dismiss the prime minister al-Nokrashi Pasha.

On 15 February the government was replaced by one under Ismail Sidqi Pasha, an imprudent choice in the circumstances since the new prime minister, who was also head of the Federation of Industries, was hated by a wide variety of political groupings because of his notorious abrogation of the 1923 Constitution while he was premier in 1930. Immediately after Sidqi took office, the recently elected Executive Committee of Students (ECS) issued a statement:

> The reason for our struggle is still there—negotiations must be on condition that the British side issue an official declaration recognizing our natural right to total evacuation and unity of the Nile Valley . . . Our struggle and the blood we spilt for the country were not to overthrow one government and replace it by another, but for the noble purpose which we still cling to.[12]

On 17 February the Mixed Committee of Students (MCS) issued a National Charter with the following demands: first, there should be a total evacuation of British troops from all lands, waters and the air of the Nile Valley; second, the Egyptian question should be internationalized by being put before the UN Security Council; and third, the country should be liberated from economic slavery. The following day, a large demonstration of students from both Cairo University and al-Azhar went to the Palace to reaffirm their nationalist demands.[13] On their return, a further meeting was held in al-Azhar at which it was decided to form a General Union of Students (GUS).

The period 17–19 February saw for the first time a serious attempt to co-ordinate the activities of the students with those of the working class.[14] The leftist students were the principal promoters of this move and a number of them had approached a group of trade unionists immediately after the events of 9 February. They succeeded eventually in forming a common platform for both workers and students, the National Committee of

Workers and Students (NCWS), which became the most prominent of the student committees. Its members were drawn predominantly from the left, a female student, Suraya Adham, and a
worker, Hussein Qasim, being elected as its secretaries. The
Muslim Brotherhood students, together with other small groups,
declined to merge with the committee in this way. Shortly afterwards they formed a parallel committee consisting solely of
students and with a somewhat similar name, the Nationalist
Committee of Students (NCS).

The NCWS proclaimed Thursday 21 February 1946 the Day of
Evacuation and called for a general strike:

> The Egyptian trade unions and the students of the Egyptian
> universities, of Al Azhar, of the Higher Institutes, of the
> private and secondary schools, have all resolved to make
> February 21st, 1946, the Day of Evacuation, a day of strike by
> all bodies and groups of the people—
>
> A day that will make it clear to British imperialism and to
> the world that the Egyptian people has completed its prepara-
> tion for active combat until the nightmare of imperialism that
> has crushed our hearts for sixty-four years has vanished—
>
> A day that will be a document in the hands of the Egyptian
> negotiators so that they may present it to the imperialists as
> proof of the fact that the Egyptian people is resolved not to
> give up, even for a moment, the evacuation of Egypt and the
> Sudan—
>
> A day that shall be a universal awakening of the Egyptian
> people, which will thus make it plain that it will accept no
> deviation, no relinquishment of its right to independence and
> freedom—
>
> A day when public services, means of communications,
> commercial and public offices, institutions of learning, and
> factories will halt all activities throughout the country.
>
> The majesty of this day summons us all to keep our sacred
> cause from being diverted into riots, destruction, or impair-
> ment of the public safety.
>
> Let us all raise aloft the banner of our country, let us reaffirm
> our unity without divisiveness—workers and artisans,
> students, merchants and officials, our whole people standing
> solidly together to tear off the infamous badge of humiliation
> and slavery.[15]

The response was overwhelming. Massive demonstrations took place in several cities. In Cairo tens of thousands[16] of people, both students and non-students, flocked into the city centre. As Abbas Bridge was not raised on this occasion, the students were able to cross it and demonstrate in the very centre of the capital, chanting a song written for the occasion:

> O people . . . prepare to set sail in the bloody seas.
> It is no time for crying . . . It is time for sacrifices.
> Let us break off the chains of subjugation.
> Let us ensure the Evacuation takes place.[17]

When the demonstrators reached Ismailiya Square they were confronted by the British garrison and began to burn the barracks fences. In response, four British army vehicles moved towards them and a barrage of machine-gun fire opened up. According to the most reliable estimate,[18] twenty-three demonstrators were killed and some one hundred and twenty injured. This bloodshed nullified the effects of the change of government and Sidqi's success in winning over the Muslim Brotherhood.[19] The government disclaimed all responsibility and blamed students for allowing their 'peaceful demonstrations' to degenerate into violence 'because of infiltration by a mob of riff-raff . . . in which students and educated people simply disappeared from view'.[20]

On 24 February the ECS issued a statement calling for: the declaration of national mourning; support for the National Committee's call for the publication of a National Charter signed by the country's leaders, undertaking to refuse office unless the British declared that 'total evacuation' would be the basis for any further negotiation; the expulsion of British personnel from the Egyptian police; a protest against the government statement denouncing the demonstrators as a mob of riff-raff; a boycott of the English language;[21] and for newspapers to end their party polemics or face a student boycott. The NCWS in turn issued a similar statement, with the additional demand for Britain to schedule a final date for evacuation or for Egypt to refer the dispute to the UN Security Council. It also protested against the government's ban on publishing news of student activities in the press. The fourth of March was proclaimed Martyrs' Day, in memory of the students killed on 21 February, with the agreement of all factions (the ECS, the National Committee and the

NCS), possibly on the initiative of the Muslim Brotherhood.

At this point, the prime minister agreed to meet representatives of the National Committee, who asked him to allow government employees, the police and the army to join in the mourning. The prime minister refused and advised the students not to proceed with their plans lest the British intervene, but the students pressed their demands and urged him to provide them with guns if the British were really planning to intervene.

The strike in Cairo, involving the closure of shops and factories, was peaceful and highly successful.[22] In Alexandria, however, demonstrators pulled down the Union Jack flying over a residence of the British navy and attacked a British military post; 2 British soldiers and 28 Egyptians were killed and a further 342 Egyptians were injured. The killing of the soldiers led the British to send an official protest to the Egyptian government. Walter Smart of the British Embassy sent a dispatch to the Foreign Office insisting that British troops 'should have' intervened:

> No-one more than I have pleaded for recognition of Arab and Egyptian nationalist claims, which I think are highly justified, but it seems to me intolerable that we should allow Egyptians and Arabs to mishandle and flout us unjustly whenever they like to do so.[23]

The student uprising of 1946 underlined clearly the dilemma of all parties concerned with the national status of Egypt: the British, the Egyptian regime itself and the nationalist movement at large. It prompted the search for new ways to solve the problem and confirmed the importance of the student movement as a source of pressure to find a way out of the existing impasse.

Institutional Dimensions

The 1946 student uprising took place against the background of a declining liberal system. The hold of the political parties on various sectors of the population, especially the middle class, was faltering, giving way to new political forces and spontaneous outbursts of nationalist activity and enthusiasm. In 1942 a weekly magazine published the results of a questionnaire addressed to five thousand university students, asking whether the leading politicians were competent to rule the country: 74.5

per cent said that they were not, 23.5 thought that they were, with a mere 2 per cent left undecided.

Student political activism clearly reflected these attitudes and the students managed to create an organizational framework of their own outside the political parties. None of the student sections of these parties could claim the allegiance of the large mass of independent students, whether patriots, democrats or simply apathetic. This mass was influenced more by the spontaneous expression of nationalist sentiments than by organized political activity. Whenever nationalist feelings ran high enough to involve the large mass of independent students, the leaders of the different political factions found themselves compelled in haste to create a common organization to direct the uprising.

The variety of student committees created in the course of the 1946 uprising is sufficiently complicated[24] to bemuse even those who took part in the events[25] (see Table 4.1).

Table 4.1: Student Committees, 1945/46

Name of committee	Abbrev.	Date of establishment
Preparatory Committee for the National Committee of Students	PCNCS	Summer 1945
National Committees of students	NCs	7 Oct. 1945
Executive Committee of Students[a]	ECS	Dec. 1945
Higher Executive Committee of Students	HECS	Dec. 1945
Mixed Committee of Students	MCS	17 Feb. 1946
General Union of Students	GUS	18 Feb. 1946
National Committee of Workers and Students	NCWS	17–19 Feb. 1946
Nationalist Committee of Students	NCS	28 Feb. 1946

Note: *a*. Different from the standing committee of Wafdist students which had the same name.

These student committees can be grouped into three categories:

1. Committees created on the spur of the moment to serve a transient purpose, usually a single event (like the MCS) or proposed or partially implemented but never established effectively (like the GUS).
2. Committees established over a relatively longer period of time to represent the main stream of the movement. To this category belong the PCNCS, the NCs, the ECS and the NCWS.
3. Committees established in reaction to this last group (such as the HECS and the NCS).

The committees in the first category were an organizational expression of the purposes of the large mass of students without political affiliations. The second and third categories deserve greater attention.

The Preparatory Committee for the National Committee of Students (PCNCS) was formed in the summer of 1945 by leading figures in the movement. Almost all political factions were represented in the discussions that led to its creation—Wafdists, Marxists of the three Communist organizations, the Muslim Brotherhood, Young Egypt, the Nationalist party, the YMMA, Egypt's Front, students from al-Azhar, the Student Union of the secondary schools and independents. The attempt to co-ordinate the activities of different student factions in this period matched attempts to co-ordinate the Opposition forces in the country at large.

The establishment of the PCNCS was formally proclaimed at the student mass meeting of 7 October but the Muslim Brotherhood chose to desert it the same day. As a result, the committee formed a coalition mainly drawn from Wafdists, Communists (the majority) and independents. The same meeting also called for the formation of National Committees[26] in different educational institutions—faculties, institutes and schools.

The Executive Committee of Students (ECS) was the most representative of these student committees. It was drawn from the leadership of various groups and possessed a more sophisticated hierarchical structure. Students in each grade elected two of their colleagues to represent them in the Executive Committee of the educational institution and these in turn elected the ECS. The election of the ECS was held in December 1945. In it the Muslim Brotherhood was defeated by a slate of candidates drawn mainly from the Wafd.[27] At a meeting held at the Brotherhood's headquarters, they retaliated by forming the *Higher Executive Committee of Students (HECS)* and denounced the rival committee as Communist-infiltrated.[28] The HECS appears simply to have been a short-term reaction, however, and there were no subsequent reports of its activities.

The *National Committee of Workers and Students (NCWS)* was the most prominent of these committees for several reasons. Its establishment marked the culmination of several months of preparation. It acted as the focus for at least three of its predecessors. It also combined for the first time in the history of the Egyptian student movement representatives of both workers and students,[29] and it organized the strikes and demonstrations of 21 February and 4 March 1946, remaining in existence as late as July 1946.

The role played by the NCWS is a matter of controversy. Anwar Abdel-Malek has claimed that it constituted a new entity:

> created by Wafdist, nationalist, and Communist intellectuals and the trade unions: the National Committee of Workers and Students, whose direct and daily influence extended to the two universities of Cairo and Alexandria, to the students in the secondary and technical schools all over the country, to the whole of the intelligentsia, to major sections of the professions and to all Egyptian trade unions without regard to allegiance or geography . . . the coalition of the Wafdist left and the Communists brought the idea of democracy to the urban masses and gave the people a desire to take the fate of the whole country into its own hands.[30]

One activist in this period, Michel Kamel, has boasted that the NCWS 'swiftly assumed a position of indisputable leadership in the streets of Egypt'.[31]

Shohdi al-Shafi,[32] who was at the time a leading figure in the Egyptian Communist movement, shared this enthusiasm but offered a more balanced assessment. According to him, the NCWS:

> did not last for more than a few months. It was inadequate because it confined its activities to urban areas—in the ranks of students, workers, and artisans. It did not extend them to the army of the national revolution—the peasants. At the same time it was not properly organized since it did not

establish grass roots committees in factories, schools, districts . . . etc, thus remaining up in the air. It formed a nucleus for a new popular leadership, though a divided one from the very beginning.[33]

The NCWS was criticized sharply on political and organizational grounds by the Preparatory Committee for the Confederation of Egyptian Trade Unions in the magazine *New Dawn* of 14 April 1946.[34] The events of 21 February and 4 March 1946, insisted the magazine, were spontaneous rather than pre-arranged by the NCWS, which itself did no more than fix the dates on which they took place. The NCWS failed to keep pace with the current political developments of the period. It failed to declare its view of the official Egyptian delegation formed to negotiate with Britain after the events of February and March. When a Sudanese delegation arrived in Cairo, the committee did not take the opportunity to present its views on the issue of Sudan. The success of the 21 February strike was not a result of the NCWS's efforts but rather of those of a variety of democratic organizations throughout the country, especially workers' unions and student committees in Cairo and Alexandria. The committee proved incapable of carrying out its own decision to strike on 1 April 1946. For a whole month it had met at least twice a week, without coming to any practical conclusions. Its procedures at such meetings were not sufficiently democratic. The representatives of various organizations taking part in its work were obliged to present their proposals indirectly through the committee's secretariat and were not informed in advance of the meeting's agenda. The NCWS had repeatedly overlooked these organizations when taking decisions, especially as regards the decision to strike.

Instead the Preparatory Committee for the Confederation of Egyptian Trade Unions proposed a markedly different approach:

> The NCWS should confine itself to the task of general guidance. This is inevitable for a committee that has failed in the proper handling of organizational matters. This failure, however, is not attributable to any personal defects but rather to the very structure of the committee, being composed of different groupings each with its distinct history, experience, organization and connections. It is necessary for the NCWS to let these groupings strengthen their own organizations, con-

centrating its efforts instead on providing them with guidelines.[35]

This attitude was provoked by the kind of treatment received by workers in the NCWS. Some commentators have argued that the worker members of the committee were forced to play second fiddle to the students.[36] As a leading figure of the Marxist New Dawn group explained subsequently:

> At that time some people envisaged the NCWS as the Egyptian version of the Soviets. We rejected this idea for the simple reason that the committee was a long way away from the peasants . . . We saw it as an *ad hoc* committee for mobilization rather than an established organization of a united front kind.[37]

The role of the NCWS was greatly admired by the majority of the Egyptian left. Many left-wing activists saw it as the nucleus of a 'new popular leadership of the national struggle' and 'a progressive national front'. The hostility of the New Dawn group was a response to first-hand experience of the committee's functioning and to a more coherent view of the broader political context. It may have been undiplomatic to express such an attitude in public but this does not render it less cogent. The short life of the NCWS and the limited scope of its achievements themselves serve to confirm this. The NCWS's primary importance was symbolic. It did not break off all ties with the traditional forces of the parliamentary system, as indicated by the continued influence of the Wafd within it, but it anticipated the growth of radical movements both within the system, like the later Wafdist Vanguard, and outside it, like the Communist movement itself.

The last of these committees was the *Nationalist Committee of Students (NCS)*. Although it lasted for only a few days, its creation was more significant than its duration. The NCS was a committee sponsored by the government which combined the forces of the Muslim Brotherhood, as the leading group, with other smaller student groupings—Young Egypt, the socialist Peasant Party, Egypt's Front, the Nationalist Party, the Wafdist Bloc, the Saadists, the Constitutional Liberals and the Partisan Arabs.[38] When its leaders met the prime minister on 1 March he appointed the minister of education, Muhammad al-Ashmawi, as the government representative on the committee. While a black-out was imposed on the activities of the NCWS, the NCS was given wide media coverage. Clashes were reported between supporters of the two committees, especially in the industrial area of Shubra al-Khaima. A meeting of workers in private companies, dominated by the left, denounced the NCS as unrepresentative and as employing 'Fascist' tactics, while it described the NCWS as the legitimate representative of students, workers and 'employees'.[39]

The NCS was created partly because the government wanted a counterbalance to the NCWS and partly because the Muslim Brotherhood was unwilling to work under a Wafdist or leftist leadership. Zakariya Bayoumi argues that the Brotherhood was willing to close the ranks of students for united action[40] but gives no examples of sustained effort by the Brethren to achieve this end. During the preparations for the 21 February strike, however, a delegation from the NCWS went to Hasan al-Banna to ask the Brotherhood to take part. Al-Banna refused on the grounds that he was 'not ready',[41] an unconvincing claim in view of the massive presence of the Brotherhood at the demonstration of 11 February at the Palace.

Although the Brethren appear to have participated in the strike and demonstrations of 21 February, the fact remains that they did so on their own initiative and not in fulfilment of an organizational arrangement to unite the movement. Similarly, when they actively participated in the strike of 4 March, they did so in their own right and without committing themselves to any kind of procedural agreement with the NCWS. When the students of Young Egypt and the Nationalist Party pressed the Brethren to oppose Sidqi Pasha's handling of the Anglo-Egyptian negotiations, they withdrew from the committee under the pretext that it had served its purpose in organizing the 4 March strike. In doing so they left the committee, for all the attempts by other participants to sustain its existence, virtually a dead body.

When the students wrote to the prime minister on 7 February 1946, describing their reason for forming the NCs as to promote the 'conduct of a free discussion about the rights of the country away from political malice and party politics',[42] they were promising something which they could not hope to provide. They were bound to be influenced by party political activists and to succumb to the wranglings of the extra-parliamentary organizations. Although they hoisted the banner of 'national unity', students were unable to implement this slogan in the organization of their own political activities, as the 1946 uprising had proved.

Aftermath

One immediate effect of the 1946 uprising was the announcement by Clement Attlee on 8 March 1946 that British troops were to evacuate the Cairo and Delta zones and to be stationed instead at the British base in the Suez Canal area. This gesture was regarded by Egyptian nationalists, especially the left, as a triumph for their movement.

Students turned to prepare for their examinations and their political activities came to a halt, only to start up again with the beginning of the summer holidays. On 8 July the newspaper *al-Ahram* published an appeal from the NCWS calling for the Anglo-Egyptian negotiations to be broken off and the dispute to be referred to the UN Security Council. It proclaimed 11 July, the anniversary of the bombardment of Alexandria by the British in 1882, a day 'for the revival of the national struggle'. On 10 July representatives of fifteen organizations endorsed this appeal.

That same night, Sidqi Pasha pre-empted the revival of the movement by arresting some two hundred leading leftists, dissolving a number of societies—including the Union of University Graduates, the Committee for the Diffusion of Modern Culture, the Scientific Research House, the League of University Women and the Congress of Egyptian Trade Unions and closing down several magazines including *New Dawn*, *The Egyptian Wafd*, *The Front*, *The Vanguard* and *The Conscience*.

This campaign became known as the 'Destructive Principles Case' or the 'Major Case of Communism'. Sidqi sought exceptional legislation from parliament to combat Communism, quoting extensively from the leftist literature that was being diffused throughout the country:

> The government is enriching the rich and impoverishing the poor . . . the wealth of Egypt is monopolized by a handful of capitalist Pashas . . .
> These social conditions must be transformed . . .

The ruling class is an imperialist pawn . . .
Land must be allotted to small farmers and co-operatives must
be established.[43]

He also quoted a poem written by a leftist poet:[44]

Bars and jailers do not intimidate the free.
If we were sparks . . . we can be a volcano.
The dogs of our masters indulge themselves in life.
Is it not ironic that we have to struggle?
Revolution recreates . . . tears do not revive
Either we live free . . . or we die with pride.

Besides eliciting this reaction from the government itself, the
activities of the NCWS and other new organizations of the left
sharply modified the tactics and programmes of the Wafd, the
Muslim Brotherhood and other established political groups, all
of which adopted more radical social programmes and called for
economic reform.

The NCWS also had an important impact on the issue of
Sudan. Whereas before the 1946 uprising the Egyptian left had
advocated the complete unity of the Nile Valley under the
Egyptian Crown, under pressure from its Sudanese component
it began intead to call for the common struggle of the Egyptian
people and the Sudanese people against Britain.

Despite the repressive measures taken by the government, the
student movement resumed its activities with the beginning of
the academic year 1946/47. On 16 November a meeting at Cairo
University established a Student National Front and issued a
proclamation calling for the breaking off of negotiations with the
British and the abrogation of the 1936 Treaty. Throughout
November there was a wave of violent clashes between students
and the police, forcing the government to close Cairo and
Alexandria Universities on 28 November. The level of violence at
these demonstrations was unprecedented and students resorted
to acts of arson. For the first time some of them were armed with
light weapons and hand grenades.[45] Scores of students and
policemen were injured and two students were killed.

The effective failure of the final round of Anglo-Egyptian
negotiations, along with the student opposition to the Sidqi-
Bevin proposals for a new treaty (which the Egyptian poet Beram
al-Tunsi described as a 'hollow treaty that squeezes the sugar-

cane and leaves you the reed'), helped to bring down the Sidqi government. In December 1946 al-Nokrashi Pasha assumed the premiership once again, with the negotiations deadlocked and in the face of continuous student disturbances. He decided to take the dispute to the UN Security Council,[46] to little effect. Preparations for further student demonstrations were reported.[47]

Sporadic demonstrations continued for the remainder of the academic year 1946/47 and intensified at the beginning of the following academic year. The publication of news of student demonstrations was banned in response and a number of magazines were closed for violating the ban. An armoured police cordon surrounded the University of Cairo. On 27 December 1947 some two thousand students tried to make their way through the cordon but were forced back. They occupied the university administrative offices, summoning the rector, Dr Ibrahim Shawki Bey, either to dismiss the police or to resign. On 3 January 1948 the cordon was withdrawn. Strikes also broke out at the University of Cairo when the British authorities in Sudan arrested members of a Sudanese delegation on their return from Cairo. Striking students trampled on portraits of King Farouq and shouted anti-monarchist slogans. Following this, the university was closed for some time. In April students went on strike in support of policemen who were striking for an increase in their salaries.

The 1948 war in Palestine, however, sharply divided the student movement since the left refused to support a war against the Jews. The war also strengthened the position of the Muslim Brotherhood and increased the students' readiness to resort to violence.[48] Fierce fights between students and the police broke out over the Palestine truce and student activists killed the much-hated Cairo police commandant Selim Zaki with a bomb. The Muslim Brotherhood was dissolved and many of its student members, especially those who had volunteered to fight in Palestine, were arrested.

The most important effect of the 1946 student uprising and its aftermath was to keep open the issue of the archaic 1936 Treaty. Since Anglo-Egyptian negotiations remained deadlocked, and all attempts to resolve the problem through the UN Security Council had ended in failure, the only way open to the nationalist movement was to press the government to abrogate the treaty unilaterally.

Such a decision was certain to result in a bloody confrontation with Britain. Without powerful pressure from below, it is scarcely conceivable that any of the country's parliamentary political parties, who spent their entire time negotiating with Britain over the treaty, would have chosen to take such a step. The extra-parliamentary organizations, with their influence in the student movement in particular, played an important role in exerting such pressure. By 1951 these groups had begun to co-ordinate their efforts to force the Wafd government in this direction. Despite the reluctance of the Wafd leadership, it eventually yielded and on 8 October 1951 Nahhas Pasha himself announced that, 'For Egypt I signed it . . . and for Egypt I abrogate it.'[49] This decision was welcomed enthusiastically by the great majority of the Egyptian political spectrum. All eighty thousand Egyptian workers and employees withdrew from the British base in the Suez Canal Zone and guerrilla warfare against British troops in the Zone began.

October 1951 witnessed an intensification of student activism and there were at least fifteen strikes. In December thirty-nine national student committees were established in Cairo, and two large meetings were held at the headquarters of the Muslim Brotherhood and at the university. A student congress issued a National Charter calling for 'the recruitment of the people to an armed struggle'.

The university itself was turned into a military training camp in which some ten thousand students received instruction. Arms were provided by the Muslim Brotherhood and the first university fedayeen battalion left for the Canal Zone on 9 November 1951. All political factions among the students took part in the guerrilla war,[50] side by side with other participants—peasants from the Canal Zone, workers (many of whom had been formerly employed at the British base), intellectuals and a group of young officers who volunteered to instruct the fedayeen in the use of arms.

The clashes with the British army in the Canal Zone were accompanied by a wave of demonstrations throughout the country, especially in December 1951 and January 1952. The funeral on 14 January of Omar Shaheen, a student member of the Muslim Brotherhood, turned into a nationalist demonstration in which Shaheen was seen as a symbol not only of a bloody foreign occupation but also of a humiliating national betrayal. The Wafd government was criticized by the guerrillas for giving them too little assistance and attacked by Britain for encouraging the terrorists. It was finally forced to resign after declaring martial law on 26 January 1952, the day the centre of Cairo was set on fire.

The short-lived government of Ali Maher Pasha began to clear the Canal Zone of the guerrillas, an operation continued by his successor, Naguib al-Hilali Pasha, whose government was equally short-lived. Al-Hilali Pasha, however, yielded to the students' demands and permitted them to continue their military training inside the university[51] until the examination period brought renewed calm and (more decisively) the liberal regime itself finally collapsed on 23 July 1952.

The Free Officers who seized power on that day had been directly influenced by the student movement. Many of them had come to political awareness as secondary school students. There were indirect links between officers and students through the extra-parliamentary organizations, while some officers were themselves external students at the university. Their political programme had much in common with those of the student movement.

5
The Student Movement and the Political System

Students and the Monarchy

In its power struggle with the Wafd, the autocratic institution of the Palace often looked to students for support. In several instances, student demonstrations were simply a surface expression of the conflict between the Wafd and the Palace. Student supporters of the King went on strike against the Wafd governments of Zaghlul Pasha in 1924 and of Nahhas Pasha in 1930 and 1936. During the constitutional crisis of 1937 the Palace instigated anti-Wafdist demonstrations by Azharite and university students, who went to the Palace and were greeted by King Farouq himself. When the Wafd government was dismissed in 1944 the Palace exhorted students to demonstrate their joy.[1] When in 1952 the Wafdist minister of the interior, Sirag al-Din Pasha, permitted a demonstration by engineering students against the minister himself, the King saw it as simply a front for anti-monarchist demonstrations.

The Palace was particularly anxious to undermine student support for the Wafd. When the Wafd government, in a bid to win popularity among students, legislated to lower the minimum pass marks in examinations, the King refused to ratify this. The Palace devised its own means of winning over students. During the student uprising of 1935–36 a report from the Ministry of the Interior noted, 'The Parquet [i.e. the Palace] was to a large extent in sympathy with the students. In a number of cases Parquet representatives ordered the release of students without even enquiring into the accusations made against them.'[2]

Al-Azhar was the principal focus of student support for the Palace. This was not surprising, in view of its pan-Islamic ideals and its readiness to see the King as Caliph, especially after Kemal Ataturk had brought the Ottoman Caliphate to an end. The Palace also found it easy to gain the support of the relatively

impoverished student body of al-Azhar by direct financial in-
ducements. In 1938 a Wafd newspaper accused the Shaikh of
al-Azhar[3] of using the Azharite students as a political instrument
forged in the name of religion and thrust into the hands of the
Palace. Petitions detailing al-Azhar students' grievances were
frequently addressed to the King rather than to the government
and seasonal greetings, often with a political significance, were
conveyed to the King from Azharite students. In 1925 the Palace
supported al-Azhar when it resisted government attempts to
incorporate it into the structure of the Ministry of Education and
it later supported an increase in the number of al-Azhar theological institutes and the modernization of their equipment.

In 1943 the British Embassy reported that:

> There is a row on between the Azhar students and the govern-
> ment, arising out of an attempt by the former to proceed to the
> Palace some days after the event to demonstrate their loyalty
> on the occasion of King Farouk's birthday. This the govern-
> ment forbade on ground that on the actual date there had been
> no ban on anyone acting as proposed . . . Clashes with the
> Police have occurred . . . Government have ordered arrest of
> certain Azhar Sheikhs whom they hold responsible for not
> controlling the students.[4]

The King was furious at this incident and demanded that the
government explain its role and release the arrested shaikhs.[5]

The King's visit to the university amid the turmoil of February
1946 and the relatively cool reception which he received marked
a historic decline of the monarchy's role as symbol of the nation
in the eyes of the students. Student slogans such as 'Down with
the Tyrants' and 'People's Will Over All' were explicitly hostile to
the monarch. Some demonstrators even went so far as to accuse
him of being a 'King of Women' because of his notorious
amatory exploits.[6] In 1948 students trampled on the King's portrait and shouted personal abuse at him. But it was not until the
last two years of the monarchy that student antagonism broke
out into the open on a large scale, with widespread demonstrations, anti-monarchist slogans and public burnings of royal portraits.[7] At this point the Palace made repeated representations to
the Wafd government calling for the declaration of martial law.

Students and the Government

In the summer of 1946 the prime minister Sidqi Pasha made vigorous attempts to reach a new agreement with Britain to secure the evacuation of British troops from Egypt. One reason for his haste was a desire to finalize the matter before the beginning of the new academic year, a natural response for an Egyptian government in the face of actual or potential student upheavals. During the student uprising of 1935–36 Sir Miles Lampson had endorsed this viewpoint:

> Reports show the urgency of dealing with the student question radically. Until students are put in their proper places no decent government or smooth Anglo-Egyptian relations are possible, whether a Wafd, or anti-Wafd government is in power.[8]

Bashatli Effendi of the Ministry of the Interior took a similar view:

> The danger of the present spirit amongst so many of the irresponsible youths of this country by far outweighs any advantages . . . It would now require a very strong Minister of Education, with the wholehearted backing of the Cabinet, to restore any semblance of discipline in the schools, and it is more than probable that the measures he would be forced to take would have to be repressive and far-reaching.[9]

A comprehensive report[10] prepared for the Ministry of the Interior took a more nuanced and careful view of the problem. It concluded that there were two alternatives in dealing with the student movement, to suppress it or to channel it. The first it regarded as a 'damning back of the flood'; the second as guiding the movement into 'proper channels by organisation, propaganda, and sympathetic handling' while at the same time 'dealing with its unruly manifestations firmly according to the ordinary law'. This latter option was seen to entail a number of measures:

> The creation of a Youth Development Committee under government auspices with the task of turning the energies of the students into beneficial channels such as sport, physical

culture, intellectual interests . . . etc.

An active campaign through the press . . . The isolation of the movement from party politics . . . A reform of the university and educational systems.

Such an approach, though ostensibly more prudent than the repressive alternative, required an effective depoliticization of the university. It had little chance of success in a country whose independence remained severely limited and whose political system revolved around a parliamentary competition between political parties to secure the allegiance of students. The appeals of these factional struggles to the student body remained powerful.

In practice, Egyptian governments applied a combination of these two approaches, among other measures seeking to control the student body through the university administration itself. The Egyptian university—founded by the country's leading intellectuals in 1908 as a private enterprise—was brought under government control in 1925:

The Minister of Education became ex officio Chancellor of the University, and the highest administrative officer in the University, namely the Rector, was a subordinate of the Minister appointed by royal decree on his recommendation. In addition, five members of the University Council were appointed on the recommendation of the Minister. Further, the professors and the teaching staff were civil servants appointed and dismissed by the Minister and subject to disciplinary measures set out in special laws which allowed for demotion and suspension, as well as dismissal. The University was financed from the general budget of the state and was therefore, in this respect also, under strict control.[11]

The demand for university independence, advanced by both students and teachers, was implemented within limits defined by the government. As Dr Taha Hussein observed:

Violation of independence of the university does not necessarily consist of an arbitrary act against this or that dean, or of forcing the university to do something it does not want to do. These things are relatively easy to cope with because we are angrily aware of what is going on and at times actively resist.

The really serious cases are those which appear to have a legal basis. No one can do anything about them, and the consequence is scandalous corruption. I am referring to the government's action in altering examination grades,[12] and University Disciplinary Councils. Although done in a perfectly legal way, it effectively destroyed the university's sacred right to have exclusive control over its internal educational affairs.[13]

In this framework, such incidents as the university being forced in 1932 to grant honorary degrees to politicians, and the expulsion of Taha Hussein himself from his university post for his literary and political views, are far from surprising. In 1937 the rector of the university, Ahmad Lutfi al-Sayyid, resigned over the creation of a campus police force to deal with student strikes.

The timing of examinations proved an effective administrative instrument for restraining students both in the university and in the schools. Commenting on the attitude of schoolboys in the provincial area of Sohag in 1947, the British consular agent wrote, 'Our local schoolboys have realised that their school year has been shortened and that the examinations are fast approaching, so that they tend to pay more attention to their lessons than to politics.'[14] Similarly, towards the end of the national turmoil of 1951–52, the speeches died down and the students returned to their books, after almost a full year of rioting—the examinations were looming.

Governments readily resorted to brief periods of closure of both schools and universities and made a number of legislative attempts to tighten their control over the student body. The government of Muhammad Mahmoud Pasha promulgated, in the absence of parliament, Decree 22 of the Year 1928 for the 'Maintenance of Order in Educational Institutions' which forbade virtually all political activities in the university and schools. The Wafd government of 1937 did not hesitate to invoke this law to suppress student disturbances although the Wafdist parliament of 1930 had declared it void.

Some government departments, however, showed much greater sympathy for the students. During the uprising of 1935–36, for example, Bashatli Effendi noted in his report:

The courts were to a large extent in sympathy with the students . . . The judges were particularly lenient with the offenders. In many cases the accused were acquitted. In the worst cases very short terms of imprisonment, generally with stay of execution, or insignificant fines, were imposed. In one case the judge (Hussein Idris) in his judgement of the 18th November, actually commended the students for displaying their national feelings and excused their attacks on the police on the ground that they were provoked by the aggressive attitude of the police.[15]

In hospitals 'much differentiation was shown by hospital authorities in their treatment of riot casualties—injured students were treated promptly and sympathetically, while the injured police were often neglected'.[16] In many cases even prison authorities treated arrested students much better than the other inmates.[17] Only the soldiers of the riot police (recruited mainly from very poor backgrounds and trained by their officers to detest the students as a privileged minority mainly drawn from the sons of the rich) treated the students with consistent harshness. Before his assassination, the much-hated commandant of Cairo police, Selim Zaki, formed a special division, nicknamed al-Pasha's division, to disperse rioters.[18] Dr al-Fangari recalls being beaten up at a demonstration in 1946 by a soldier who muttered at him, 'Why is it that you can learn while our sons are deprived of education?'[19]

On other occasions, especially when nationalist sentiment ran high, police, and even soldiers, openly showed their sympathy with the students. On 21 February 1946 Egyptian soldiers stood between the demonstrators and the British army and some of their vehicles were daubed with the same slogans as those shouted by the demonstrators. After the bloody confrontation of that day had ended, the student delegation which met the prime minister Sidqi Pasha urged him to allow police and soldiers to join the proposed strike for national mourning on 4 March. When students clashed with the police on 20 January 1952 they were harshly criticized since the police themselves were in direct conflict with the British army in the Canal Zone. A week later, both students and police demonstrated together on the day that Cairo burned.

Students and the Political Parties

On the issue of Egypt's national independence, the different
factions in the student movement reflected primarily the positions of the various political parties. The movement as a whole
was an important area for party competition. Although the uprising of 1935–36 was largely unsuccessful, it nevertheless represented the first serious student attempt to escape this party
tutelage. A report from the Ministry of the Interior noted:

> The most dangerous thing in Egypt, at this juncture, is the
> students' attitude, for at the time when leaders of the national
> front tell students to be quiet and calm, Mohamed Mahmoud
> Pasha prompts a large number of them not to heed this
> advice . . . and to organise themselves in such a manner as to
> leave no Wafd authority over them . . . Although a number of
> students are not with the supporters of M. Mahmoud Pasha,
> these supporters use all means to carry out their scheme . . .
> As Nahas Pasha relies on a number of students who, although
> many, have no influence, it is to be feared that the students
> supporting M. Mahmoud Pasha will succeed.[20]

A police report dated 10 January 1936 confirmed:

> M. Mahmoud Pasha has proposed to Abbas Halim, through
> the mediation of Maitre Hosny el Shintinawi, the legal repre-
> sentative of the Abbas Halim labour union, the creation of a
> group of students to be known as 'The National Students'. The
> object of this body would be to counteract the Wafd's in-
> fluence among students.[21]

These contacts produced a division within the movement that
reflected the struggle for power between the two principal political factions: the Wafd and their rivals, the Constitutional
Liberals. As a report from the Ministry of the Interior explained:

> The students are divided into two parties:
> (a) A Wafdist party under the leadership of Farid Zaalouk
>   which is a tool in the hand of the Wafd and are in direct
>   daily touch with Nahas and receive their instructions from
>   him . . .

(b) The Nationalists, who are under the direct patronage of Abbas Halim.[22]

This position remained essentially unchanged until the early 1950s, except that the anti-Wafdist grouping became increasingly extra-parliamentary in its focus and won over further defectors from the Wafd itself.

Even when the movement came to include a large proportion of extra-parliamentary activists and to adopt a relatively independent framework of action, it did not succeed in avoiding a certain degree of political partisanship. Many of the provincial demonstrations during the 1946 uprising took place under the aegis of the local Wafd Committees rather than under that of the NCWS which had called for the strike. The Wafd leadership, despite its unease at independent action by the students, was confident that it would succeed sooner or later in restoring its hold over them just as it had done after 1935–36.[23]

Students were in most cases the initiators of dissident initiatives by Opposition parties against the incumbent government,[24] especially over the issue of national independence; and they were usually the first to press their opinions in street demonstrations.[25] Not surprisingly, students were seen by the political parties as a valuable political asset and they were courted assiduously:

> Leaders of political parties did not confine their activities to hidden propaganda, but were openly in sympathy with the disturbers of the peace; the victims were treated like national heroes, the wounded in hospital were visited, given presents, and photographed with the leaders.[26]

Administrative aid over admission to schools and universities, fees and examination regulations was given to students on political grounds by all parties in power, including the Wafd, which was particularly eager to retain the allegiance of the majority of students. The harm done by these practices was emphasized by the Egyptian playwright Tawfiq al-Hakim:

> The new state of misconceived democracy had diverted the attention of today's young men from serious work. Political partisanship and the use of students by politicians resulted in

students using politicians in turn to interfere in questions of academic study and examinations.[27]

Student strikes over academic issues were handled by both government and Opposition in the light of their political implications rather than their academic consequences. Dr Heikal, as minister of education, complained that his government's handling of the confrontation between students from al-Azhar and the university over the teaching of Arabic had been determined solely by its effects on the political position of the government.[28]

Student adherents of political parties were attacked by their opponents as party stooges,[29] although on a number of occasions they appear to have acted independently. After the 1935–36 uprising, Bashatli Effendi concluded that:

> The students will no longer consent to be mere instruments in the hands of a political party; they have now a will of their own and this will have been greatly strengthened by the successes—or imaginary successes—which they have had.[30]

This verdict was echoed by Lampson:

> There is evidently some danger of the students imposing their will on all political parties.[31]

A second Embassy official, Walter Smart, also confirmed the dynamism of student action:

> Students, who now regard themselves as responsible for national victory and establishment of united front, are not under full control of leaders and may act independently of them.[32]

When the Wafd took office towards the end of 1936 it found the student body the principal threat to its authority. Lampson noted that:

> The Wafd, having been responsible while out of office for stirring up students and giving them a decisive political position, may now have difficulty in controlling them.[33]

In 1937 the intensity of student opposition forced the Wafd to revive a law which it had repealed only a few years earlier. The dilemma faced by the party was evident to British diplomats:

> The Wafd is now in fact feeling the other edge of the weapon which it itself forged. The students, who for so long have been sedulously incited by the Wafd to oppose authority, appear to be running true to form and to be preparing to oppose the Wafd itself now that it is in power.[34]

Despite these difficulties, however, the student movement remained in the last instance firmly under the control of the political parties and the political skills of their leaders.[35]

The internal divisions within the political parties were often paralleled in the ranks of their student supporters. This tendency explained Nahhas Pasha's reluctance to let Ahmad Maher obtain the Ministry of Education as he had requested (and the control over students which this would have given him) shortly before he led the Saadist secession from the Wafd in 1938. The dispute in the ranks of the Wafd students, the struggle in 1942 between Hasan Yassin and Hafiz Shieha, similarly reflected Sirag al-Din Pasha's efforts to assert his position within the leadership of the Wafd.

Relations between the student leadership and the national leadership within the various parties were not always cordial:

> The dispute between Fouad Sirag al-Din Pasha, the secretary of the Wafd, and Mustafa Musa, the leader of the Wafd students, is a long story. It started with Sirag al-Din Pasha manoeuvring to eliminate the power of the student leader when he began to give direct orders to the heads of the Student Executive Committees. The Pasha followed this up by expelling five students from the committees without consulting the leader of the students. Thirdly, the Pasha directly requested a student to form the committee of the Faculty of Commerce. The fourth crisis took place when the leader of the students published a statement in the Wafd newspapers saying that the Pasha's decision to expel the five students was void. The Pasha made up his mind to get rid of Mustafa Musa who, in his turn, called for a student conference that ended with a demonstration attacking the Pasha and his policies. The Pasha sent a deputy to the student leader's friends to warn him that he would be dismissed from the Wafd. When the

deputy came back to tell the Pasha that the students were furiously attacking him, he said: 'it looks as if it may be necessary to re-open the Taur concentration camp'.[36]

The same tensions, in a somewhat milder form, were also to be found among the extra-parliamentary organizations. The student members of the Communist grouping Iskra pressed their leaders to hasten their union with the EMNL, threatening otherwise to secede from the organization. The only internal dispute suffered by New Dawn was engineered by its own student members. Even in the case of the relatively tightly disciplined Muslim Brotherhood, Hasan al-Banna on one occasion failed to calm his student supporters at a time, just before the murder of the police commandant Selim Zaki, when the organization itself was facing compulsory dissolution. Al-Banna's successor, al-Hodaibi, also encountered opposition from his student supporters over the appropriate means of approaching the issue of national independence; but he dealt firmly with this challenge, insisting that the student resolutions were 'of no value since they had not been issued by the society's headquarters'.[37]

The role of the university as bastion of the new extra-parliamentary organizations was in itself proof enough of the declining influence of the parliamentary parties over the students. As mentioned previously, three-quarters of the five thousand students questioned in 1942 expressed doubts as to the capabilities of the country's leading politicians.[38] A British Embassy report noted similarly that, 'The nation are very angry with the spirit shown by the different political parties . . . Students, in their demonstrations, shout "no partisanship among students".'[39]

Increasing numbers of students discarded their allegiance to political parties and adopted instead the new goals of the extra-parliamentary organizations which they saw as 'bearers of new ideas for solving the country's problems, unlike the power-lusting political parties'.[40] This development was noted also by Ronald Campbell of the British Embassy, after a conversation with Gallad Bey, a source 'close to the Palace':

He agreed with me that there were amongst the younger men those who saw what was necessary in the way of reform in social and political life, but that they were not given an opportunity or encouragement to come up, and could not find the way to do so, moreover, that they had not much heart in any attempt to do so, political parties being such as they were. The danger of this, he agreed, was that sooner or later they might, in discouragement, seek an outlet through undesirable channels.[41]

It was in the midst of this atmosphere of disillusionment with the political parties that the student uprising of 1946 took place and the NCWS was created. In an open letter to the prime minister on 7 February 1946, students justified the establishment of their National Committees by saying that this step would allow them to 'conduct free discussion about the country's rights and aspirations away from political partisanship'.[42]

The slogan of 'national unity' adopted by the students was a vague one. Some students understood it as implying a complete elimination of partisanship, others as requiring unity under the authority of the incumbent government and still others as implying unity under the aegis of the Wafd majority. The raising of the slogan was essentially a protest and a declaration of students' disillusionment with political parties. One of the student statements during the uprising of 1946 called for a National Charter to be signed by leaders of all political parties, regardless of their individual policies, declaring their commitment not to take office unless Britain accepted total evacuation as a basis for negotiations. They also demanded that newspapers should stop their party polemics or be boycotted by students. The students' failure to achieve unity in their own factional squabbles meant that they were no less partisan than the leaders of the political parties. Hence student appeals for national unity were no longer taken seriously by their leaders after 1935–36.

Under the Liberal Regime

Under the liberal regime, with its political parties, national elections and unrelenting rivalry between the Palace and the Wafd, students had many opportunities to become involved in political life; but their role was constrained within strict constitutional limits. In practice these limits subordinated the student movement to the main competing forces within the political system, and students' inflammatory activities were not permitted to endanger the regime itself.

While the nationalist leader Mustafa Kamel had been the first to encourage students to take an active part in Egyptian politics, well before the Revolution of 1919, it was the Wafd which converted the student body into a potent political instrument. On the first day of the 1919 Revolution one of the Wafd leaders, Abd al-Aziz Fahmi, told the demonstrating students, 'You are playing with fire . . . let us work quietly.'[43] A few months later, when the revolutionary movement had gathered strength, another Wafd leader, Abd al-Rahman Fahmi, assured a student audience, 'It is upon you, students, that your nation and the Wafd depend.'[44] Fifteen years later, under the liberal regime, the leader of the Wafd, Nahhas Pasha, refused to allow his two leading rivals within the party, al-Nokrashi Pasha and Ahmad Maher Pasha, to obtain the ministerial portfolios of Defence and Education, seeing these as 'a device whereby one of them would control the army while the other would control our sons the students!'[45]

During the national turmoil of 1946, the Wafd Opposition leader in the Senate, Sabri Abu Alam, stressed the importance of the student role:

> Some would accuse us of attempting to take the country back to the conditions of 1918 regardless of the change that has taken place . . . No, Gentlemen, I would like to take you back to 1935 when the educated young men of the country forced its leaders to respect the nation's will, thus forming the national front and holding the elections of 1936 . . . There is a difference between a revolution and an awakening . . . a turmoil and an expression of sentiments.[46]

When the youthful followers of the Wafd started to publish the magazine *Rabetat al-Shubban al-Wafdiyeen* (League of the Wafd Youth), he welcomed their initiative to 'awaken the deputies and urge the dumb government to speak up'.[47]

While some leading figures of the regime were prepared to tolerate political initiatives by students, even where these were against the law, none was prepared to tolerate their establishing systematic links with peasants and workers or spreading among them the doctrines of radical social change which had found their way into the university through the extra-parliamentary organizations.[48] A student could expect to be treated more leniently by the courts if he was charged with involvement in 'student disturbances' than if he was accused of being an activist in a banned extra-parliamentary organization.

When large numbers of the urban lower classes joined in student demonstrations in Cairo and Alexandria in 1946, the minority governments of the period were alarmed that the students should have allowed 'the subversive elements of the riff-raff to intrude into their innocent demonstrations and submerge them'.[49] Whereas the Sidqi government insisted that students conduct their discussions within the precincts of the university, other opposition parties defended the students' right to demonstrate as the 'enlightened and educated class of the country'.[50] The Wafd endorsed this view when its leader Zaghlul Pasha praised 'our innocent sons—the students' while visiting injured students in hospital.[51] Even the left wing of the Wafd came to the defence of students, affirming that 'the intellectuals represent the vanguard in any popular movement regardless of its class content'.[52]

The attitudes of students towards the working class changed considerably from the 1920s to the 1940s.[53] They rejected the Sidqi government's attack on 'the riff-raff' as unnecessarily divisive at a time of national crisis. This new-found solidarity was expressed in statements by the ECS and in the slogans shouted at the Ministry of Education: 'The Riff-Raff are the Masters' and 'Long Live the Unity of Workers and Students'. It led directly to the formation of the NCWS.

It should not be supposed, however, that this necessarily reflected any very deep identification with the working class or any serious aspiration to play a leading role within it. For most of the students the working class was simply a subordinate ally through which they could hope to achieve greater influence in the country. To advance their nationalist demands, students needed to secure the backing of other political forces.[54] The student-worker alliance, though it gave the student movement a more radical character and led to the adoption of demands for social change in student political programmes, by no means transformed it from an essentially nationalist into a radical social movement.

The sole organizational expression of the alliance, the NCWS, emphasized the many points of agreement between workers and students on the issue of national independence but it made no attempt to define the extent of agreement on the class structure of society or on the position of the working class within it. This neglect was one of the principal criticisms levelled against the NCWS by the Marxist group New Dawn:

The link between the NCWS and the working class is weak. We do not think workers have confidence in it since it did little about workers' wages, unemployment and trade union liberties which are all issues that should form an integral part of the national movement . . . [55] We do not underestimate the abilities of other popular groups, especially our student brothers, in the national struggle but we tell them frankly that their job in this phase of Egyptian history is not to lead the liberation movement but rather to help the working class to express itself.[56]

The worker members of the NCWS were forced to play second fiddle to its student members:

The NCWS did not protest against the arrest of a number of workers shortly before it came into being. The number of students on the committee is equal to that of workers. That is not fair to the working class and the trade union movement. The political proclamation of the committee did not refer to the struggle of the working class. Even the timing of meetings is decided without the collective agreement of workers' representatives (note that workers have to work and produce to support themselves and their families and cannot waste time).[57]

The mere attempt by students and workers to co-ordinate their political activities, however, was alarming enough to elicit a sharply repressive reaction from the Sidqi government, a response essentially shared by other elements of the regime.[58]

The political relations between the student movement and the peasantry were not close, despite the fact that a large proportion of the students came from families which owned moderate quantities of land. The vast majority of the Egyptian peasantry, despite their limited participation in political life, maintained a broad allegiance to the Wafd and were far from receptive to the proposals of the new extra-parliamentary forces. This lack of contact with the rural majority of the population restricted the influence of the student movement in the country at large, and may well have been one of the main reasons for the failure of the NCWS.

In 1936 the British Embassy received a report from, as the oriental secretary put it, 'a countryside notable who was mixed up in the troubles of 1919':

> The fellah is a responsible member of the society who has something which makes him 'get-at-able'. The student is in no way a responsible member of the society. He has none of the ties which exist in the case of the fellah (his wife, his land, his cattle, and his Sheikh) . . . No peasant movement can last very long. They would have, in a few days, to give up and return to their villages. The remaining hooligan type can be shot and imprisoned without anyone minding in the least. In the case of the student, as long as agitation is the order of the day, he can keep it up. He cannot be shot or imprisoned without complications of all kinds. The fellah is always busy. Th student never. No fellah can talk or plan for long, as if he does his 'musga' will flood his field. The student's talk and planning for future troubles can go on without interruption. . . The fellaheen are never concentrated in large numbers. The students are concentrated in the big towns 'like soldiers in a depot' . . . When fiddling out in public transport the fellah immediately gets into trouble. Officials have a tendency to let truculent effendis travel for nothing.[59]

Despite the divisions between students and peasants and the weakness of the links between them, the effects of student political activism nevertheless appear to have trickled down to the countryside. Student demands took in the improvement of the miserable conditions of the vast majority of the peasantry. A foreign commentator recorded that Egyptian students in the early 1950s had told him that they were even prepared to sacrifice their own political freedom for the peasants' sake.[60] Student propaganda reached the countryside, where university students from rural families spent their lengthy summer holidays in their native villages. In provincial towns in the heart of the countryside, student activism spread through the secondary schools and al-Azhar institutes. The spirit of unrest and dissatisfaction[61] helped prepare a welcome among the peasants for the impending political changes.

Not surprisingly, the students appear to have had their closest relations with the urban middle class of which they constituted an integral part. Within this class, the students' closest ties were with the university and school teachers:

> The students were greatly encouraged by their teachers, whose attitude left much to be desired. Not only did they fail to advise them to be quiet and to attend to their studies, but in some cases they actually blamed those who did not join the demonstrators.[62]

Dr Taha Hussein, professor of literature, and Dr al-Sanhouri, professor of law, were famous among many other teachers for closeness of their links with students and for the degree of their influence over them in both scholastic and political matters in the 1930s and 1940s. University rectors such as Abd al-Wahab Azzam and Mansour Fahmi Pasha took part in student activities. In 1951–52 Dr Abd al-Wahab Morroe, the rector of Cairo University, supervised and financed military training for students on the university campus. Other tutors like Dr Said al-Naggar gave students supplementary lectures to compensate for those which they had missed while fighting in the Canal Zone.

The teachers, in turn, were influenced by the general mood of their students. Their own strikes for better salaries and work conditions were timed to coincide with student upheavals. A degree of ambivalence nevertheless remained between the two groups since teachers were also government employees, and were at times required to check the activities of their students.[63] As an ex-minister of education put it:

> Student strikes are acts of disorder which have an effect beyond the confines of the university. It is better that the university authorities should restore order than that the security authorities should restore it with methods that might insult the dignity of the university.[64]

Students also had direct relations with other sectors of the urban middle class, especially shopkeepers and small traders whom they invariably asked to close their shops whenever there was a general strike. Students distributed leaflets among them, and made occasional efforts to convert them. Because the students themselves lived among the urban middle classes, there was daily contact between them. Relations between students and effendis were decisively shaped by the fact that students were potential effendis themselves. Ordinary citizens would greet a student with the title of 'effendi' even before he had actually graduated. When students struck for better conditions for their own future, they were in effect demanding improved conditions for effendis in general.[65] As potential members of the urban middle classes, many students showed a keen interest in the professional trade unions. The students' readiness to join the emerging extra-parliamentary organizations *en masse* made them into the effective striking force of the urban middle class in its confrontations with the authorities and its demand for a larger share of political power.

Over the issue of effective national independence, the student movement was the primary source of pressure on successive governments and political parties. Confident that no solution would be found through diplomatic means, the students' vigorous propaganda and minor acts of violence prepared the way for the subsequent armed struggle in which once again they took an active part.

As Bashatli Effendi asked rhetorically of the outcome of the student uprising in 1935–36:

> Was it not they who forced the leaders of the Wafd to consent to the formation of the United Front? Did they not oblige the British Government to agree to the restoration of the nation's Constitution?[66]

This judgement was essentially shared by the British ambassador:

> This student movement, if not promptly checked, may entirely dominate the Egyptian political stage. Indeed it is already being suggested by many that no government will now dare to adopt a policy entirely unacceptable to the students.[67]

Much the same view, naturally enough, is taken today by leading militants of the period:

> The university *was* the political life of the country.[68]

> There were in Egypt two principal domes—parliament's dome and the university's dome.[69]

In addition, student activists played an important role in exposing the ills of the social and political system and in preparing for its subsequent transformation. Nahhas Pasha advised the student demonstrators of Cairo on 20 January 1952 to moderate their demands: 'We want to save you for the near future to face the critical days . . . We must keep your blood for the battlefield of honour.'[70] But his call went unheeded. The gap between the students and the country's political leaders widened steadily until the entire liberal regime collapsed in July of the same year.

At the time, analysts attributed the prominence of the student movement in the politics of the liberal regime to the leading role of the 'intellectual elite'. As Owen Holloway put it, 'The rapid increase in numbers and consequent unemployment of the students are not the sole cause of this political self-consciousness. The only vocal class in a nation of illiterates must be very vocal.'[71] In addition, however, this prominence was a product of distinctive characteristics of the regime itself and of the balance of social forces in the society at large—the 'nominal independence', which in practice meant the country's entire political subordination; the fostering of organized participation in formal political life and the massive social ills which led many to reject the system in its entirety; the development and rising political influence of the urban middle class; and the comparatively limited political role of the small working class and the even more limited political role of the rural majority of the country's population.

Part Two

1952–73

Students Under the 1952 Regime

Nasserism and Education

The Revolution of 1952 inherited an educational system which had been exposed to severe criticism well before the downfall of the *ancien regime*. Its elitist and fragmented structure was totally incapable of serving the new regime's goals of economic expansion and a widening of its power base in Egypt's social structure. However, the revolutionary regime's pursuit of a more homogeneous and populist educational system did not result in sudden radical change in the system it had inherited. Nor did the more immediate task of consolidating its power allow for anything more than a continuation and elaboration of the reforms that had already been put into practice towards the end of the liberal regime.

In numerical terms, however, the first few years of the Revolution saw some expansion in education: the student/population ratio rose from 71 state school pupils per 1,000 inhabitants in 1952/53 to 102 in 1958/59, and from 1.95 to 3.07 university students per 1,000 inhabitants in the same period.[1] Between 1953 and the end of the first five-year plan (1960–65) educational provision expanded greatly (see Table 6.1).

In 1965, 78 per cent of children went to primary school for six years, 28 per cent of these went on to do three years at a preparatory school, 79 per cent of these went into various kinds of secondary education and 15 per cent were finally admitted to universities and higher institutes.[2] By 1972/73 the corresponding figures were as shown in Table 6.2

Public investment in education in the same period rose from E£2.5 to 33.3 million.[3] Total expenditure on education over the thirteen years from the beginning of the Revolution to the end of the first five-year plan is estimated at three times the entire expenditure on education over the seventy years from the British occupation in 1882 to the outbreak of the Revolution.[4] Expendi-

Table 6.1: Student Enrolment by Educational Level, 1953/54 and 1965/66 (thousands)

	1953/54	1965/65	% increase
Primary	1,393	3,418	145
General preparatory	349	574	65
Vocational preparatory	3	27	800
General secondary	92	209	127
Vocational secondary	19	101	432
Teachers institutes	24	49	104
Universities[a]	54	124	130
Total	1,934	4,502	132 (average)

Note: *a*. Does not include al-Azhar.

Source: Mahmud A. Faksh, 'The Consequences of the Introduction and Spread of Modern Education: Education and National Integration in Egypt', *Middle Eastern Studies*, vol. XVI, no. 2 (May 1980), p. 45, Table 1.

Table 6.2: Student Enrolment by Educational Level, 1972/73 (thousands)

Primary	3,989
General preparatory	1,019
Vocational preparatory	1
General secondary	322
Vocational secondary	297
Teachers institutes	28
Universities	195
Total	5,851

Expenditure on education also rose during the early period of the Revolution (see Table 6.3).

Table 6.3: Expenditure on Education as Illustrated by State Budget, 1952/53–1959/60

Year	(1) State budget (E£)	(2) Ministry of Education budget (E£)	(3) % (2)/(1)	(4) Universities budget[a] (E£)	(5) % (4)/(2)
1952/53	206,000,000	25,317,700	12.3	3,541,400	14.0
1955/56	238,300,000	32,534,500	13.7	6,579,318	20.2
1959/60	318,270,000	41,423,000	13.0	8,769,000	21.2

Note: *a*. The universities' budget increased to E£14,440,306 in 1965/66 and to E£24,209,300 in 1970/71. (Sikas Sanyal *et al.*, *University Education and the Labour Market in the Arab Republic of Egypt* (UNESCO-International Institute of Education Planning, Pergamon Press, Oxford, 1982), p. 228, Table 4.29).

Source: Jean-Jacques Waardenburg, *Les Universités dans le Monde Arabe Actuel* (Mouton & Co., La Haye, 1966), vol. II, p. 120, Table 157.

ture on education reached a peak of 16 per cent of the state budget,[5] an increase of one-third over the last pre-revolutionary figures. This greater commitment of the Nasser regime to educational expansion matched the rate of population growth more closely than it did the rise in national income[6] (which doubled between 1952 and 1962).

The changes introduced into the educational system under Nasser covered a wide spectrum, extending from the abolition of school fees to the introduction of educational planning. They also included measures such as the nationalization of most foreign schools and state supervision of the rest. More important, secondary education was restructured in order to give more attention to technical and vocational education at this level. According to William Polk, technical education was 'virtually a product of the 1952 Revolution'.[7] In fact, the percentage of non-technical education provided at secondary level was rapidly reduced from 85.8 per cent of the total in 1954/55 to 66.6 per cent in 1959/60, with a corresponding increase in the amount of technical education provided from 14.2 per cent to 33.4 per cent.[8]

Equally important was the attempt to provide universal primary education. Whereas in 1951/52 only 42.5 per cent of children of school age received primary education,[9] in 1963/64, 90 per cent of urban children and 65–75 per cent of rural children did so.[10] By 1966/67, 78.2 per cent of all children were receiving a primary education.[11] But universal primary education had to be deferred twice, first to 1970 and then to 1975. Meanwhile, due to the high proportion of children dropping out of classes, the level of participation was as low as 55 per cent, according to some estimates.[12]

Girls' education was given more attention after 1952.[13] The proportion of girls in primary education, however, remained around 35 per cent between the outbreak of the Revolution and the end of the first five-year plan.[14]

State control of education was restricted by the fact that, until the mid-1960s, 6.1 per cent of primary students, 29.1 per cent of preparatory school students and 25.5 per cent[15] of secondary students attended private schools.[16]

The expansion of state education under the Revolution was not without its critics. The most common criticism was that quantitative expansion was not matched by corresponding qualitative progress and in some cases standards deteriorated.[17] In a bid to restore some balance between quantity and quality, the Egyptian government of 1968 put forward a new education law which restricted the movement of students from one grade to another, and from one educational level to another, by requiring them to obtain a certain mark in the examinations. The new law represented a departure from the populist educational slogans of the Revolution itself and led to student protests.[18]

Another area of criticism was the fact that the revolutionary regime had failed to achieve its declared goals of providing universal primary education. It had also failed to increase further the proportion of vocational education at the secondary level and to go beyond the achievements of the early post-revolutionary years. In both cases the level of achievement was decided by social conditions which, in the first case, forced the sons of poor peasants to work in their fathers' fields rather than go to school, and in the second case, meant that the ambition of all middle-class parents was to educate their sons up to the highest level, the university, through the open channel of general secondary education, not the dead end of vocational education.[19] This phenomenon was described by Georgie Hyde as follows: 'Such is the prejudice against manual labour that, given the choice, parents will pay large fees for having their children coached or educated privately rather than see them enter what they consider to be an inferior type of school.'[20] In this context, a young man might well find it difficult to marry a middle-class girl if he were not a university graduate. Thus a high social value was, and to a large extent continues to be, attached to students' performance at the secondary level, upon which their chances of going to university depend. As Yousef Idris put it, 'It is ridiculous that we have got to the stage where the only criterion by which we measure the success and failure of our young men and young women is their performance, namely their marks, in the secondary examinations.'[21]

The development of higher education under Nasser took a distinct form. Between 1952 and 1965 the proportional increase in the number of university students was close to that in primary and in vocational secondary education.[22] Given the increase in the number of students at the higher institutes (which quadrupled over the period),[23] and in the number of students at al-Azhar (which quintupled between its reformation in 1961 and 1973),[24] the expansion of higher education must be regarded as the prime educational achievement of the 1952 Revolution. It represented a development in sharp contrast to the high illiteracy rate prevailing in Egypt[25] and indicated the vigour of the regime's response to the ambitions of the middle class. Between 1954 and 1973 higher education made impressive strides, as shown in Table 6.4.

During this period, a number of reforms were made in the structure of higher education. Whereas before the Revolution, admission to the university was almost automatic after secondary education (regardless of marks obtained in the secondary examinations in the case of admission to the faculties of humanities and social sciences, and with a minimum requirement of 65 per cent for the faculties of science and medicine), under Nasser admission was regulated by introducing, for a period, a qualifying year at the end of the secondary stage. Moreover, selection for university education was based upon a system of 'co-ordination', whereby universities and faculties were classified in different categories and students were allocated to them according to their marks in the secondary examinations.

Other reforms and achievements in the field of higher education included the reduction of fees in 1956 and 1961 and the

Table 6.4: Number and Percentage Increase of University Students by Specialization, 1954/55–1972/73

	1954/55		1959/60		1964/65		1972/73		Disparity over the period	
	No.	%	No.	%	No.	%	No.	%	% increase in No.	% disparity of proportion
Arts	8,894	15.8	15,750	18.8	16,052	13.6	19,703	10.1	121.5	-5.7
Law	14,673	26.1	14,927	17.7	12,048	10.2	21,200	10.9	44.5	-15.2
Commerce	11,567	20.6	19,641	23.3	25,405	21.5	35,491	18.2	206.8	-2.4
Science	1,947	3.5	4,166	4.9	8,443	7.2	8,488	4.4	336.0	0.9
Engineering	6,156	11.0	9,454	11.2	17,563	14.9	20,244	10.4	228.8	-0.6
Agriculture	2,938	5.2	5,464	6.5	12,166	10.3	24,553	12.6	735.7	7.4
Medicine	7,226	12.9	7,260	8.6	11,646	9.9	23,821	12.2	229.7	-0.7
Pharmacology	-	-	1,315	1.6	2,962	2.5	5,631	2.9	328.2	1.3
Dentistry	-	-	779	0.9	1,432	1.2	2,393	1.2	207.2	0.3
Vet.Medicine	484	0.9	1,008	1.2	2,259	1.9	4,188	2.1	765.3	1.2
Dar al-Uloom (Arabic)	1,093	1.9	1,642	1.9	1,548	1.3	3,720	1.9	240.3	0.0
Teacher (M)[a]	436	0.8	436	0.5	3,264	2.8	17,200	8.8	1330.9	6.6
Training (F)[a]	766	1.4	1,159	1.4						
Nursing	-	-	113	0.1	213	0.2	790	0.4	599.1	0.3
Economics & Politics	-	-	-	-	1,096	0.9	1,223	0.6	11.6	-0.4
Girls' Faculty	-	-	1,186	1.4	1,942	1.6	5,087	2.6	328.9	1.2
Archaeology	-	-	-	-	-	-	561	0.3		
Information	-	-	-	-	-	-	502	0.3		
Total[b]	56,180	100	84,300	100	118,039	100	194,795	100	246.7	-

Notes: a. It seems that there is a degree of overlap between university faculties for teacher training and the higher institutes for teacher training in this category. The 3,264 figure for 1964/65 is given as 5,140 in another source.

b. To complete the picture of higher education as a whole we may add to this the total number of students enrolled at the higher institutes which was 11,839 for the year 1959/60; 27,377 for 1964/65 and 48,925 for 1972/73. Figures for al-Azhar University (not included above) are: 4,970 for 1959/60; 10,160 for 1964/65, and 33,640 for 1972/73.

Sources: Compiled from data given in: Mokhtar Hamza, 'Analysis of the Employment Situation amongst the Educated Classes in the UAR', *National Review of Social Sciences*, vol. IX, no. 1 (Jan. 1967), p. 17, Table 1;

Ministry of Education, *Report on Development of Education in 1964/65* (Cairo, 1966), p. 89, Table 1, and p. 91, Table 3; Arab Republic of Egypt, State Information Service, *Egyptian Education*, Table on pp. 36–7; Central Agency for Public Mobilization and Statistics, *Statistical Yearbooks* 1968, 1971 and 1979 (Cairo).

subsequent abolition of fees at all educational levels in 1962; the reform at al-Azhar in 1961 to allow the study of non-theological subjects in new faculties built for that purpose, and the resulting increase in the number of its students (see Table 6.5 below); the introduction of new academic disciplines and other alterations in the syllabus; a greater emphasis on scientific subjects (see Table 6.6 below); the provision of financial assistance to students in the form of awards and loans;[26] and the construction of student hostels with low rents. Other major developments which contributed to the massive increase in the number of students were the introduction in 1953 of the external students system (see Table 6.7 below), the establishment of 43 higher institutes (polytechnics), and the establishment, starting in 1969, of new regional universities and faculties.

Table 6.5: Students at al-Azhar, 1961/62 and 1972/73

Subject	1961/62		1972/73	
	No.	%	No.	%
Theological studies	3,792	61.1	13,608	44.7
Arabic language	1,982	32.4	2,179	7.1
Non-theological studies[a]	334	5.5	14,631	48.2
Total	6,108	100	30,418	100

Note: *a*. Included in 1961/62 one faculty only, commerce, in which the study was semi-theological and in 1972/73 various faculties for modern subjects: medicine, engineering, agriculture, etc.

Source: State Information Service, *Egyptian Education*, Table on p. 52.

Table 6.6: Distribution of University Students between Practical and Theoretical Faculties, 1952/53–1972/73

	1952/53	1962/63	1972/73
Practical faculties (Applied Sciences)			
No. enrolled	15,590	42,130	112,395
%[a]	37.9	43.7	57.7
No. admitted	3,786	8,958	26,066
%[a]	27.9	44.2	54.7
No. graduated	1,961	4,047	15,183[b]
%[a]	44.1	39.3	66.8
Theoretical faculties (Humanities & Social Sciences)			
No. enrolled	25,567	54,295	82,400
%[a]	62.1	56.3	42.3
No. admitted	9,776	11,313	21,601
%[a]	72.1	55.8	45.3
No. graduated	2,482	6,262	7,544[b]
%[a]	55.9	60.7	33.2

Notes: *a*. All percentages are the total for that category.
       b. Figures for the year 1971/72.
Sources: Compiled from data given in: Waardenburg, *Universités*, vol. II, p. 87, Table 118, and p. 92, Table 120; State Information Service, *Egyptian Education*, Tables on pp. 34–9.

Table 6.7: Number of External Students and their percentage of Total Number of Students in the Theoretical Faculties of Egyptian Universities, 1953/54 and 1960/61

	1953/54	1960/61
Number	5,761	19,418
Percentage	16.1	37.8

Source: Louis Awad, *The University and the New Society* (National House for Printing and Publication, Cairo, 1963) (in Arabic), p. 60, Table 16.

The fact that education at all levels had been made free in 1962 and that admission to higher education was now decided on the basis of marks in public examinations were regarded as major achievements by the leaders of the Revolution. This pride is clearly visible in President Sadat's boast to a group of student leaders in 1977:

> You were given, my sons, complete equality of opportunity. It is your performance and marks that admit you to the university. You are accommodated in the faculty of your choice if your marks allow and regardless of who is a son of a minister or a notable. The sons of Nasser and myself did not obtain enough marks for the faculties of their choice. They were put in other faculties where their marks permitted![27]

But this political triumph failed in many ways to transform the educational structure itself. A report on education published by *al-Tali'a* magazine in 1968 insisted that:

> Although the decision to make education free[28] had some far-reaching effects and helped to change the general features of the picture, class barriers remained essentially in relation to admission to preparatory schools and students' distribution between different kinds of education. The prevailing system of examinations ends in effect with a kind of class distinction since the decisive factor in passing such examinations is not real talent and aptitude[29] but rather financial capacity and social environmental milieu.[30]

In this context, the common practice of resorting to private tuition outside school, especially at the secondary level, was particularly prevalent among the sons of well-to-do families.

The middle class[31] remained the main supplier of university students (see Table 6.8). In a sample survey, carried out in 1964, 86.4 per cent of the middle-class parents who responded expected their children to acquire higher education as compared with 43 per cent of lower-class parents, results which were attributed by the researcher to 'the social class imbalance in higher education'.[32] Another sample survey, conducted by Mahmoud Shafshak in the course of his comparative study of al-Azhar University and Cairo University students, revealed that the sons of the middle class occupied about half the places in al-Azhar while they virtually monopolized them in Cairo University.

A considerable proportion of these middle-class families,

Table 6.8: Percentage Distribution of Sampled Students[a] by Father's Occupation, 1962

Father's occupation	Cairo students	Al-Azhar students	% distribution of adult male population in 1960
Professional, technical, administrative, executive & managerial	33.2	17.9	3.7
Clerical	23.0	6.8	3.8
Private enterprise	29.3	19.6	8.1
Manual worker	5.6	2.2	28.3
Farmer	5.8	45.5	54.3
Unclassified	3.1	8.0	1.8

Note: *a.* The sample covered 20 per cent of senior students in both universities in 1962; 475 for Cairo and 175 for al-Azhar.

Source: Mahmoud Shafshak, 'The Role of the University in Egyptian Elite Recruitment: A Comparative Study of Al-Azhar and Cairo Universities', *National Review of Social Sciences*, vol. V, no. 3 (1968), p. 442, Table 1.

however, were not well-to-do. The results of a two-stage sample survey published in 1969 and 1971 indicate that around one third of the students in the major universities of Cairo, Alexandria and Assiut had to endure difficult living conditions in order to pursue their education.[33] In the case of al-Azhar, the proportion was around one half. The position of students at the higher institutes was similar to that of students at the three universities.[34] The position of students at the American University in Cairo, on the other hand, was comparatively comfortable, only about one tenth of them suffering in this way.

The numerical expansion of higher education through the system of external students in the theoretical faculties, the establishment of scores of higher institutes, and later, the spread of regional faculties and universities, implied that massive numbers of students were being educated with very few resources and facilities. This entailed, on the one hand, a deterioration in the quality of higher education and, on the other, a surplus of university graduates.

The case of the external students[35] is a peculiar one in this context. The percentage of external students who were able to pass the examinations was as low as 12, 8 and 15 per cent of their total number in the three academic years 1959/60, 1960/61 and 1961/62 respectively.[36] Meanwhile, this system proved contradictory to the regime's policy of promoting technical education since it encouraged a number of vocational secondary school-leavers to give up a vocational career and attempt instead to obtain a theoretical university degree.

The opening of some of the higher institutes indicated clear defects in educational planning. Although supposed to be 'polytechnics', providing the cadres for the economic development of the country, they soon assumed an essentially academic character and the distinction between them and the universities disappeared. Their students acquiesced in this transformation since many of them had actually hoped to go to a university in the first place.

On the other hand, the lack of co-ordination between the expansion of higher education and the extension of the labour market resulted in a surplus of university graduates, particularly from the theoretical faculties. In line with its social policy, the government elected to shoulder the burden itself and filled its offices with unnecessary staff. Mokhtar Hamza's survey of graduate employment affirmed that a relatively high proportion of graduates of the theoretical faculties worked in jobs where their academic studies made no direct contribution and which could have been performed adequately by others with no higher education.[37] The position of these graduates was unenviable:

The university graduates constitute a growing force of un-usables whose social and economic expectations have been raised to unrealistic levels by their education . . . The result of mass higher education has been to redistribute poverty in the name of social equality, in a manner that threatens simply to replace an illiterate class of unemployed proletarians with a literate and more sharply alienated one . . .

The disappointments are sharp as thousands of not-so-bright young men in their soiled collars and cheap suits eke out a shabby and insecure but desperately respectable existence on ten pounds a month as minor clerks, book-keepers, school teachers, and journalists. They are assured from time to time in the press and in the president's speeches that as educated men they are the 'vanguard' of the nation's progress, but they are impotent to fashion even their own progress.[38]

Hence, despite the regime's emphasis on scientific rather than theoretical studies, both in general secondary and in higher education,[39] its admissions policy for the theoretical faculties was the main cause of real and masked graduate unemployment. It was in these faculties that the deterioration of academic standards manifested itself most clearly and educational commentators were its sternest critics. Even Louis Awad, who complained about 'the persecution of theoretical sciences for the sake of applied sciences in the name of development',[40] felt compelled to criticize this policy for its intellectual content:

> The order of priorities between academic disciplines based on the transient needs of development would only result in dispersing scarce talents into branches of study (i.e. the scientific ones) which do not require special talent. It would also result in loading the theoretical faculties with the retarded students, contrary to the natural order which assumes that scarce talents are usually the theoretical ones.[41]

The overcrowding of Egyptian universities was bound to affect the quality of the education they provided, in tuition, examinations and research. In this regard, it is well known that the teacher/student ratio in Egyptian universities has constantly been very high. While it was 1:20 in 1950[42] it had increased further by 1958/59, as shown in Table 6.9.

Table 6.9: Teacher/Student Ratio in Some Egyptian Universities, 1958/59

University	No. of students	No. of teachers	Teacher/student ratio
Cairo	33,773	1,566 total	1:21.5
		968 qualified	1.35
Alexandria	18,037	928 total	1:19.5
		587 qualified	1:32
Ain Shams	23,258	984 total	1:23.7
		587 qualified	1:40

Source: Awad, *University and New Society*, p. 90, Table 12.

Moreover, the ratio varied considerably from one faculty to another. In 1962/63 it was 1:15 in medicine, 1:22 in science, 1:32 in agriculture, 1:43 in engineering, 1:45 in economics and dentistry, 1:54 in arts, 1:92 in commerce and 1:95 in law.[43] With the exception of the Faculty of Law, the teacher/student ratio had improved by 1972/73 to be: 1:10 in dentistry, 1:12 in medicine, 1:13 in engineering, 1:15 in agriculture and economics, 1:36 in arts and 1:80 in commerce.[44] This high ratio was bound to have a bad effect on the quality of tuition given and on the students' ability to adapt to the structure of the academic institution and identify with its academic and social activities. A study comparing the students of Ain Shams University (where the teacher/student ratio in 1966 was 1:50) with those of the Jordanian University (where it was 1:15)[45] showed that the latter displayed much greater adaptability.[46]

University students accordingly transferred the technique of rote learning, which prevailed in secondary schools, to their work in the universities. 'Memorization for the examination' became the accepted approach. As Joseph Szyliowicz put it:

> In Egypt the emphasis remains upon formal lecture, and students are accorded little opportunity for discussion, questioning, or meeting with the professor. Moreover, the student is graded only upon his success in the annual examinations . . . Students resort to cramming and memorising the factual information contained in the lecture notes or the textbook.[47]

Hence, there was an obsession with textbooks, in many cases no more than an adaptation of Western works. The situation was made worse by the fact that university libraries were poorly equipped. There were between two hundred thousand and three hundred thousand books in each of the libraries of the three major universities in 1958/59. Moreover, university libraries were poorly used.

The quality of research, which was made subject to government orientation, deteriorated in Egyptian universities:

> If we know that the average lecture time for the student is 24 hours per week and for most teachers it is 20 hours per week (more than that of the secondary school teacher) we must immediately realise that there is no time or place for academic research, reading, and discussion within the campuses of our

universities. If we add to this the burden of the exhausting examinations, it will be easy to perceive the deteriorating state of scientific research in our universities. A university without scientific research, without reading, without thinking, without discussion, is no more than a workshop to train labourers at the hands of foremen![48]

This statement must be read in the broader context of intellectual debate about the function of the university in the Arab world as a whole, and in Egypt in particular. What Awad called a 'workshop' has been labelled by other commentators a 'laboratory for spawning government employees'[49] and a 'factory where degrees and aspirations for social mobility gave education a utilitarian character as a means for practical ends'.[50] According to Jean-Jacques Waardenburg, 'If the bourgeois Western ideal of the University does not coincide with the Marxist or the technocratic ideal, the Arabs too can have their ideal of what a university is. But what is there, is no more a university.'[51] With its high student density and its exhausted lecturers, the university, as Waardenburg sees it, is no more than a secondary school. It is certainly not where intellectuals are born and bred.[52]

This outcome is attributed by Awad to the method of selecting students for university education:

The Co-ordination Bureau distributes students between university faculties in an arbitrary way, based on their marks and the artificial grading of these faculties into different classes as if they were classes of hell and paradise. The result is that the thousands who want to study medicine, engineering, or science have to make do with the study of arts, law, or commerce . . . many talents are displaced because of the mental compulsion which forces a person who has an interest in engineering or chemistry or agriculture to study history, banking, or law, thus producing for us not a mediocre engineer, chemist, or agronomist but a low-standard history teacher, banker or lawyer.[53]

The force of this line of argument was clearly demonstrated in 1971. A new post-graduate diploma was proposed for the Institute of Information at Cairo University and applicants were summoned for a general knowledge test. The result, as described by the examiner Dr Gamal al-Otaifi, was appalling:

It became clear that most applicants had no clear idea about the history of Egypt, to the extent that some graduates of the history department failed to know elementary facts about modern history . . . This serious lack of knowledge did not only apply to events of the past which these young men had not witnessed or studied but was apparent also in their answers to questions about contemporary affairs like issues of socialist construction in Egypt, which they had studied for years in the syllabus of every faculty of the university . . . As for their knowledge of world affairs, it proved to be non-existent or seriously confused . . . There was a graduate of politics who did not know who Gomulka or Ceaucescu was and a graduate of law who did not know Montesquieu's theory . . . One of the applicants for the television and broad-casting diploma thought the BBC was the International Court of Justice![54]

Dr al-Otaifi concludes:

This phenomenon reveals two things. First, the way that the civics curricula has been taught in previous years has proved ineffective. Second, the failure of some graduates to answer questions well within the realm of their specialization under-mines the credibility of university degrees as a proof of quali-fication. What does all this mean? Does it prove that our young men do not read?[55] or care for what is happening around them, and that they join the university only to obtain a degree as a passport to a job? . . . Who is responsible for this? Is it our young men themselves? Or what? It is a question that should be posed in public for wide discussion and for a brave and frank answer.[56]

An answer was given the following day by Awad:

The young men of the present generation have an immunity against history, all history: ancient, medieval, and modern! Why? Because history books in our schools are no more books of history. They are rather books of pure politics . . . The young Egyptians have lost their sense of history and, con-sequently, their sense of politics. Dr al-Otaifi should not be surprised that some of his examinees are totally ignorant of the history of land reform, the history of socialist measures, or even the history of the Revolution of 23 July 1952 itself.[57]

The Nasser regime paid particular attention to the curricula at schools and universities and reformulated textbooks of geography, history and civics (together entitled the social curriculum). The National Charter of 1961, which itself became a school textbook,[58] declared:

> The object of education is no longer to turn out employees who work at the government offices. Thus, the educational curricula in all subjects must be reconsidered according to the principles of the Revolution. The curricula should aim at enabling the individual human being to reshape his life.[59]

To define the new outlook on education, the National Charter referred to the distortion of the curricula in the past:

> Successive generations of Egyptian youth were taught that their country was neither fit for nor capable of industrialization. In their textbooks, they read their national history in distorted versions. Their national heroes were described as lost in a mist of doubt and uncertainty while those who betrayed the national cause were glorified and venerated.[60]

The subjects of the 'social curriculum' were firmly politicized and written in a highly demagogic language that mingled national pride with political loyalty to the regime. The treatment of history in the textbooks was as selective as in the pre-revolutionary texts mentioned in the National Charter. Omission of historic events and personalities became so frequent[61] that Awad considered the history textbooks to be little better than fairy tales:

> Such rulers as Abbas, Tawfiq and Fouad are ignored, and except for the 1952 Revolution the student would never learn of the existence of King Farouq . . . The French student does not learn the opinion of the minister of education on Louis Philippe or Napoleon III but the poor Egyptian student does not learn anything that is not accompanied by either scorn or praise, as if he were reading a paper or listening to the radio![62]

Awad called instead for:

an objective view of what the fundamentals of a modern state are, beyond the social and educational myths which prevailed for about twenty years in the name of development necessities, ideological unity, and national integrity . . . [63] Our education is imbued with the ideological and national myths which were inserted into the syllabus in the name of civic education . . . We should treat social sciences the way advanced countries treated them, stressing the history and geography of our country without being obsessed with ancestor cults or personality cults, or claiming that we are superior to others.[64]

Other commentators criticized the changes in the 'social curriculum' in the schools as changes in presentation rather than in content. *Al-Tali'a's* educational report of 1968 referred to the social curriculum of the revolutionary era as:

basically the same curriculum as the 1940s . . . any mention of socialism or imperialism in it is usually superficial and unelaborated . . . it does not provide the student with a genuine awareness of the country's and the world's problems . . . [65] if education emphasized national issues in general, it did not, however, keep pace with the social revolution.[66]

Moreover, educational practices within the schools and the universities served to support:

the pattern of passive non-participatory political life among educated Egyptians. Educational practices emphasised the authority of the teacher, rote learning, formal curricula, strict uniformity, discipline, and routine . . . In the primary and preparatory schools, great efforts were made to develop a strong loyalty to the regime.[67]

At the level of higher education, the revolutionary regime took various measures to control the universities politically, educationally and administratively. Political control will be examined later (see pp. 119–22). Administratively, responsibility for the universities and other institutions of higher education was transferred in 1961 from the Ministry of Education to the new Ministry of Higher Education. Although the universities remained technically independent institutions, a further attempt to integrate them into the government system was made through the creation of a Supreme Council of Universities under the chairmanship of the minister of higher education.[68]

The reformulation of the syllabuses in the universities included a compulsory curriculum, known as the 'national curriculum', to be studied by all students. It consisted of three parts—Arab Society, Revolution and Socialism. Although less demagogic than the 'social curriculum' of the secondary schools, these courses were not essentially different in content. The Arab Society course, though aimed at providing a better understanding of the country's social and economic problems, failed to provide any objective analysis.[69] Nor did the curricula of the broader study of social sciences, which dealt with these same problems, offer a significantly better understanding. The revolutionary regime, as Awad noted, 'has produced very little speculative, analytical, and critical theory in the fields of political science, economics, sociology, and moral philosophy'.[70] The curricula of the Faculty of Economics and Politics, founded by the Nasser regime, provided a good example of this.

Nasser himself complained to university teachers about this problem:

At the Law Faculty you teach political economy—Adam Smith's theory of supply and demand—and you say that such theories are ideal. People would then look at us in surprise and say: What we have learnt at the Law Faculty differs from what is being applied here! I say: No, the process is not one of supply and demand. We are forging a new system . . . Some authors have written books on economics that were simply copied from other countries. Who has written a book on the economy we are now dealing with? . . . When I realize that these economics books are merely a repetition of what we were taught at the Law Faculty in 1936, then I am filled with endless disappointment.[71]

The regime tried to deal with the dualism in the educational system, as evident in its attempt to modernize al-Azhar and assimilate it to the pattern of other universities. Al-Azhar students were very much at odds with those of other universities, particularly Cairo: Azharites were traditional and fundamentalist, rather than modern, secular and liberal.[72] The government achieved a measure of success, but failed to unify the educational system effectively. To this day al-Azhar remains an autonomous institution with a predominantly pan-Islamic orientation.

Despite changes in the curricula of all sections of the educational system, students' values remained very much at odds with the aspirations of the regime. Some 50 per cent of the male students in the three major universities of Cairo, Alexandria and Assiut were opposed to the idea of equality between the sexes, a proportion identical to that among al-Azhar students, and even one quarter of the female students were opposed to the idea. The students of the American University were the only ones with a clear majority in favour of it (only 6 per cent of its male students and 12 per cent of its female students rejected the idea).[73]

A second example is the students' attitude towards manual labour. Amid the clangour of socialist slogans in the early 1960s, there remained among the students:

> a definite attitude against manual work—none of those with a higher education and only 4.1 per cent of those with a secondary education were doing manual work of any kind, and none of the persons with a higher education who worked during their vacation or did part-time jobs during study took manual work.[74]

This attitude may have changed slightly by the late 1960s and early 1970s with the exodus of Egyptian university students to explore Europe and take employment in its restaurants as manual workers, and under the pressure of the contracting white-collar labour market. But by that time the shouting of such slogans had died down.

Political Containment

The Revolution of 1952 inherited a political system in which the universities played an important role both in the national movement and in the struggle for power. To consolidate its power at the outset, the military regime had to win over a politically active student body which, in common with other political groups, had become accustomed to the liberal framework of political activity and found it difficult to come to terms with the rule of the armed forces. Students and workers were seen as a potential source of political disturbance. As President Sadat put it, 'He who wants to inflame the political situation in Egypt will find the incendiary device in the students or the workers.'[75] It is not surprising that the first major confrontations faced by the military regime were with workers of the industrial city of Kafr al-Dawwar in 1953 and with the universities in 1954.

The confrontation with the universities, both teachers and students, resulted directly from the conflict between the liberal intelligentsia and the autocratic tendencies of the military rulers. The new regime offered to do away with the parliamentary system in return for providing a number of social achievements which that system had notably failed to produce. While the promise of social change appealed to large sectors of the intelligentsia, the accompanying political restrictions provoked their vivid animosity. As Awad put it, 'Many people thought they could have a republic and agrarian reform and at the same time keep the classical forms of liberal democracy.'[76]

The university was one of the three platforms (the other two being the lawyers' and journalists' syndicates) from which the intelligentsia could voice its opposition to the new military regime. During the political crisis of March 1954, the teaching staff of Alexandria University—ironically the first body in the country to have declared its support for the Revolution on its very first day—pioneered the opposition, calling for an end to martial law and for the dissolution of the Revolutionary Command Council (RCC). In his capacity as general military commander, Nasser ordered the arrest of a number of university teachers, ignoring the advice of his intellectual fellow-minister, Dr Abbas Ammar, who warned Nasser against provoking the university. At a meeting with a group of university teachers, Nasser denounced the university as an opponent of the Revolution, to which the teachers replied that:

the university had prompted the Revolution before he carried it out[77] and its teachers were the only group in the country to have refused to meet the deposed King . . . the university supported the ends of the Revolution and not its means since the university believed strongly in freedom, democracy and individual dignity.[78]

When the RCC asserted its authority by liquidating its internal and external opponents, Nasser took the unprecedented step of sacking university teachers *en masse*.[79]

The position of the students resembled that of their teachers. Most students maintained their political affiliations and the Free Officers were at a loss as to how to integrate them into a regime whose ideological framework at this initial stage barely existed. As Khalid M. Khalid put it in 1954:

> The Muslim Brotherhood and the Communists are the two forces which contain most of our active youth. To deny this is naive and conceited . . . The young men could be removed from them and transferred elsewhere at some future date . . .or another pole of attraction might in due course make its appearance to which the students would rally. Either eventually might or might not arise. But at present this was how things stood.[80]

Immediately after its outbreak, however, the Revolution enjoyed enormous support in the ranks of students. A student Front was formed from various political groupings and pledged its allegiance to the Revolution.[81] Even the Muslim Brotherhood, although it did not join the Front, aligned itself with the Revolution at this stage. When the issue of 'democracy' came to the fore, however, threatening to split the RCC, student support for the military leadership (except for the renegade officers, led by General Naguib, who advocated civilian rule) began to diminish. The student Front took an anti-government stance and called for struggle against military dictatorship. An officer of the pro-democratic Cavalry Division asked Nasser, 'Suppose students took to the streets in support of General Naguib . . .can we really fire at them?'[82]

Although university students were, as Professor Zakariya put it, 'clearly in favour of democratic rule, so that not a single student demonstration supported the other side',[83] their attitude cannot be interpreted as one of unequivocal support for a return to liberalism. The attitude of the students of the Muslim Brotherhood in particular reflected the power struggle between the military regime and the Brethren, who were not necessarily devout believers in a liberal regime.

The Muslim Brotherhood had many supporters among university students,[84] who expressed their support for the organization's pro-Naguib stance. Students of the Brotherhood went further in their protests than the leadership of the organization itself, which adopted a policy of *attentisme* at intervals in the course of the power struggle. On 14 January 1954 the Brotherhood—which had earlier been given favourable treatment by the new regime, being exempted from the dissolution of political parties on account of its being a 'religious' society—came under direct fire from the RCC and was declared a political party, to be treated like the others and dissolved accordingly. The excuse for taking such a step was an episode which had taken place in the university two days earlier.

In the course of commemorating Omar Shaheen and Ahmad al-Minayyisi, two of their celebrated martyrs in the guerrilla warfare of the Canal Zone, the Brethren clashed with secondary school students representing the youth section of the government-sponsored political organization, the Liberation Rally, on the campus of Cairo University. The students had been brought to the university in government lorries with loudspeakers. The Brethren put on to the rostrum the famous Iranian terrorist Nawab Safawi, who delivered a speech to the shouted accompaniment of their traditional slogan, 'God is Great . . . Thanks to God.' The youth of the Liberation Rally answered back with the slogan, 'God is Great . . . Dignity to Egypt.' A fierce battle followed and the Brethren gave the youth 'a hell of a beating' as one of their leaders admitted![85] During March the Brotherhood became closely aligned with the general movement for a return to democratic rule. The students of Cairo University announced the formation of another student Front to express their opposition to military rule, this time including the Brotherhood.

Student strikes in this period resulted in fierce battles with the police, one student even firing at the police. The university was closed and, when reopened, was readmitted piecemeal with a gradual resumption of studies in one grade after another, in order to avoid more trouble. Government pressure upon the student body was intense:

The revolutionary government of the 1950s was a new situation for us . . . It considered itself to be right and everybody else to be wrong . . . Whoever was not its friend was taken for an enemy . . . The University Guard within the campus beat and spied on students . . . The lorries of the Security and the Military Police formed cordons to check the identities, kidnap and load up the daily quota of university students to be beaten for no reason and remain in custody for days, months in some cases, without even being questioned . . . In the Faculty of Engineering, I have seen the harvest of two years of early Revolution—two martyrs at Qasr al-Nil Bridge and 20 injured in Qasr al-Aini Hospital, plus a series of assaults, beatings and arrests of whoever dared to visit an injured colleague or attended a victim's funeral. The punishment was so severe for kind acts which we had always cherished as tokens of respect. . . Thus, the prospects looked bleak and a whole generation was forced to retreat and relinquish its role, leaving governing to the governors![86]

The confrontation of 1954 marked the beginning of a long period of hibernation for the student movement in Egypt. It became relatively 'tame' and the characteristic activities of the pre-Revolution student movement became simply historical memories. Those students who supported the new regime's reformist social policy channelled their support through its official political organizations; those who could not accommodate themselves to the new orientation resorted, in the face of an authoritarian power, to the politics of withdrawal. An alternative that became of especial importance was football. Professor Zakariya noted, 'From my personal experience I can assure you that 90 per cent of student discussions at the university are on the subject of football . . . The young men on whom the future of the country depends are obsessed with an opium called football.'[87]

In 1970, and after the resumption of student activism in 1968, the percentage of students in Sultan's sample who agreed with the statement 'I resent students' apathy towards political discussion' differed markedly from one university to another:

Cairo	Alexan-dria	Assiut	Al-Azhar	American University	Higher institutes
M. F.	M. F.	M. F.	M. F.	M. F.	M. F.
61 56	57 57	35 25	47 60	25 37	42 44

The percentage of students who expressed their resentment at political debate in agreeing with the statement 'I resent too much debate on political principles and tendencies among students' was a more consistent percentage for all universities other than the American University:

Cairo	Alexandria	Assiut	Al-Azhar	American University	Higher institutes
M. F.	M. F.	M. F.	M. F.	M. F.	M. F.
38 29	36 31	33 23	31 28	0 10	33 31

The percentage of sampled students who agreed with the statement 'I resent seeing some students preoccupying themselves with political organizations' was higher and similarly consistent:

Cairo	Alexandria	Assiut	Al-Azhar	American University	Higher institutes
M. F.	M. F.	M. F.	M. F.	M. F.	M. F.
40 36	43 42	41 38	40 42	19 15	44 42

It is also notable that almost one half of the sampled students in these universities, again excepting the American University, held a narrow-minded attitude, influenced by official propaganda, towards the flow of human thought worldwide. The percentage of them who agreed with the statement 'I resent some students' adoption of foreign ideologies' was:[88]

Cairo	Alexandria	Assiut	Al-Azhar	American University	Higher institutes
M. F.	M. F.	M. F.	M. F.	M. F.	M. F.
51 48	49 48	43 35	43 40	6 32	13 17

This demobilization and demoralization of what had been an autonomous political movement was engineered through a combination of coercion and socialization. Indirect political control of the student population through the university administration was made tighter and strengthened by direct political control. A special Ministry of Higher Education was established and in the early 1960s this was supplemented by the Higher Council of

Universities. Earlier still, more direct measures were taken: a military figure was appointed general secretary of the university administration, and elected faculty deans were replaced by appointed ones.[89] This helped to preserve in the university a kind of 'theological hierarchy where senior professors with vested interests monopolized the seats in the administrative councils of faculties and universities, with the younger generation of teachers having merely token representation'.[90] Students were not, and are still not, represented in these councils although they have always demanded such representation.

The regime appointed university staff to ministerial and departmental committees and gave them some consultative power in the administration of various government and industrial departments. At the same time, their academic independence diminished under political pressures and governmental intervention. The minister of higher education drew an elusive distinction between the principle of freedom for university staff and their independence. Academic freedom suffered so severely under Nasser that one university teacher maintained that it had been snuffed out altogether—'The current of freedom was halted, and the university gave up its leading cultural position.'[91]

More serious was what Zakariya terms 'the moral deterioration' of the university:

> The greatest calamity that affected the university since the early years of the Nasserite experience was government intervention in university affairs, in such a manner that the university staff lost their balance and slid into inevitable moral decline . . . The university lost its esteem in the eyes of the government when its staff started to quarrel with each other and flatter any one who was a favourite of the government, even if he was less learned than their students.[92]

Under these circumstances university teachers with no reputation or special talent and no obvious capacity for public service could find themselves promoted to high positions, even to ministerial portfolios.

Another method of controlling teachers and students alike was to put them under the surveillance of the security agents. The presence of these agents was resented by most teachers and students, although they were recruited from the ranks of students, teachers and administrators.[93] Some senior university academics and administrators considered security work an integral part of their duties. Zakariya claims to have seen university rectors taking telephone orders from junior security officers.[94] During the student uprising of 1972–73 a number of deans, vice-deans and professors—one of whom, Dr Kamel Laila, subsequently became minister of higher education and speaker of the Egyptian parliament—were notorious for tearing down student wall-magazines.[95] During the student uprisings of 1968 and 1972–73 teachers and senior university administrators competed with one another to delate the student movement to the authorities.

The teachers' capacity to influence their students[96] was affected by the strains to which they themselves were exposed. Dr S. Asfour, one of those sacked in 1954, maintained that:

> the university teacher could not advance or implement his message properly, especially in developing the self-confidence of his pupils, unless he had the courage to express his scientific and critical views without fear of reprisal. The one thing that weakened the relationship between students and their teachers was that the latter were unable to answer student questions on public affairs.[97]

This view is endorsed by Zakariya: 'One reason for the violence that characterizes student revolt is the huge moral and mental gap between them and their teachers.'[98] In their first political statement since 1954, a group of university teachers admitted their lack of influence on their students when they declared during the student uprising of 1973 that the university staff were unable to play a mediatory role between students and government because they themselves were deprived of the right to organize their own professional union.[99]

The other side of the government's policy of coercion was the direct discipline of the students themselves. The first such measure was the introduction of a mid-winter examination to occupy students' time. In addition to the temporary stationing of troops at the university gates in 1954, there was the permanent presence of the University Guard, consisting of uniformed policemen in each faculty, under the control of the Interior Ministry instead of the university rector as had been the case before the Revolution.[100] In spite of the student movement's continuous demands for the abolition of the Guard, it was finally disbanded only in 1972, to be replaced by the less provocative civilian Security Bureaux which nevertheless remained a target for student resentment.

Moreover, the University Ordinance prohibited any form of political activity among students.[101] For example, paragraph 4 of article 87 prohibited the formation of or participation in student societies without due permission (not readily available) from the university authorities. A similar prohibition was imposed in paragraph 5 on the distribution of leaflets, the collection of signatures and the issuing of wall-magazines. Paragraph 6 prohibited demonstrations in the universities. The disregard of these rules was an offence punishable by administrative penalties, ranging from a warning to expulsion from the university. The student movement constantly objected to this part of the ordinance and demanded that it be altered to allow students freer political activity.[102]

Beside these coercive measures the revolutionary regime attempted to channel student political activism into a number of political organizations of its own, starting with the Youth Bureau of the Liberation Rally in 1953 and ending with the Socialist Youth Organization (SYO) in 1965 and the underground Socialist Vanguard in 1968.[103] Other non-political organizations were created under the supervision of the government bodies established to take care of the sports and welfare activities of young people and students. The most important among these were the Higher Council for Youth Welfare and the Ministry of Youth, set up in 1954 and 1966 respectively. These organizations arranged for a stadium to be built in every province, a youth centre (club) in every city and over 800 rural clubs. They organized such events as the University Youth Week, the School Youth Week and a multitude of summer camps and community service projects, all with extensive student participation. A Youth Welfare Office was established in every university faculty or higher institute under the supervision of the Ministry of Higher Education and in close co-operation with the Ministry of Youth and the Higher Council for Youth Welfare.

The government-sponsored political organizations to which students were invited to belong, and which were sometimes in competition with each other, were mostly short-lived experiments which had to be frequently altered in line with changes in the mother organization, the Liberation Rally, which subsequently became the National Union and finally the Arab Socialist Union (ASU). The most homogeneous and durable experiment was the SYO, established in 1965 in the shadow of the power struggle between Nasser and the army command and in the aftermath of the discovery of the Muslim Brotherhood's clandestine organization. Nasser showed a particular interest in the creation of the SYO and wished it to establish itself first in the industrial, rural and residential areas before being introduced into the universities, where, as one of his aides put it, 'political activity [i.e. recruiting support for the regime] was a difficult task'.[104]

Students and young graduates soon became the majority (65 per cent) of the SYO, however, leaving only 35 per cent of its membership to young workers and peasants. This was scarcely surprising since membership was open only to those who were literate. Justifying this trend, a leading figure of the SYO said:

> The SYO concentrated upon the recruitment of university students because, as is well known, they form a versatile and active leadership wherever they are. The SYO wanted to arm them with socialist thought to undertake their social duties. On the other hand, the emphasis on students was a response to the very evident attempt by reactionary forces to recruit them.[105]

Despite the SYO's attempts to recruit within the universities, it achieved only limited success over the three years during which it was present on the university scene, before being finally withdrawn after the student uprising of February 1968. The last secretary of the SYO admitted this when he said:

> In the university the link between the SYO's leaders and its members was missing. Its political activity, like that of the ASU itself, was weak. This is attributable to our neglect of the organization at the university and to the general conditions of political activism there . . . It is not the SYO only which failed at the university.[106]

The decision to withdraw the SYO from the university, taken by the top leadership of the ASU headed by Nasser and not by the leadership of the SYO, was criticized as an admission of defeat. In the *al-Tali'a* symposium on the SYO, Dr Ibrahim Saad al-Din, himself an ex-director of the Higher Institute for Socialist Studies which produced many of the SYO's cadres, put forward the following argument:

> There seems to be a fear of the youth movement within the university, and because of this, the SYO is excluded from acting there. I put the question this way: the reason why the SYO must be in the university is because if it cannot take a lead in the university and the higher institutes it will mean that this role is left for others . . . To organize the student members of the SYO outside their natural setting would be an odd thing. The university and its activities have a decisive influence on events in our society and we should face up to that.[107]

Despite continuous debate on the question, however, especially after the student uprising of 1972–73, the SYO was never re-introduced into the universities. There were many reasons for its apparent failure in this setting. First, it encountered a large body of students who were apathetic[108] because of the revolutionary regime's policy of banning political opposition. Second, the ideological sympathies of the politicized minority lay elsewhere, either with the anti-regime Muslim Brotherhood or with the Marxists, with their mixed feelings towards the regime. Third, many students were not attracted to the kind of mindless exhibi-tionism for which the SYO was renowned: pro-regime proces-sions, parades, and so on.[109] They also resented the fact that some of its activists took on the role of security informants by writing secret reports on the political situation in the university and the political stance of opposition elements within it.[110]

The most important factor in undermining the base of the SYO in the universities and in forcing it finally to withdraw was the existence of an alternative organizational platform in the Student Union. Although the existence of the SYO, as well as the pro-regime organizations and groupings which preceded and suc-ceeded it, caused a division within the Union between those who succumbed to and those who resisted such pressure to conform, the Union itself remained essentially an oppositional force. The antagonism between Union and SYO activists was most conspicuous at the time of the Union elections. In these elections the SYO usually ran its own slate of candidates in competition with other slates. Such electoral contests were not purely political, since they also included a strong element of personal rivalry. Union veterans and beneficiaries fought hard to retain the prestige of their Union seats and, in some cases, to preserve their opportunities for corrupt manipulation of Union resources.

In the early stages of the SYO's introduction into the university, official policy preferred it to the Union, with a consequent weakening of the latter. (Union activities at a national level were frozen between 1966 and 1968.) But conflict between the two made the SYO's task of recruiting students to support the regime a difficult one. In order to ease tension at the universities immediately after the student uprising of February 1968, the SYO was withdrawn from the campuses. The resulting victory for the Union's point of view was underlined by its president Abd al-Hamid Hassan (later minister of youth in President Sadat's cabinet) in a speech to the National Congress of the ASU:

> I beseech the Congress to respond to the view of the youth at the universities and higher institutes that the Student Union is the right political framework to enhance their political action and unite their thought, and avoid a return to the duality and conflict between the Union and other organizations within the universities and the institutes.[111]

But a much earlier attempt to depoliticize the Union had already destroyed its chance of proving an effective political organization. This attempt had involved both direct intervention in its work by the government and amendments to its constitution which restricted it to the essentially cosmetic activity of applauding official policies. Government intervention had started in 1953, when elections for the Union were suspended, representatives being appointed instead by the university authorities. When elections were resumed in 1959, intervention took the form of disallowing candidates from taking part in them, or of interference in the day-to-day running of the Union under the close supervision of the university authorities.

The Union's constitution, laid down by a Presidential Decree, requires special analysis. It was reformulated several times to guarantee the Union's loyalty to the regime and restrict its organizational autonomy. In its 1958–59 version, the constitution provided for a Union concerned solely with social and welfare matters, political and religious activities being forbidden. Its objectives were listed in six clauses, one of which affirmed commitment to 'the Arab national revival' and 'the principles of democratic co-operative socialism', the other five reflecting its social and welfare concerns. Both students and teachers were eligible for membership, with the latter given the final say. Its Higher Council in the last year of its currency, 1962/63, comprised twelve teachers, nine graduates and eighteen students.

The alteration[112] of the constitution in 1963 brought it closer to being a true 'student' union. Membership was confined to students, but a number of teachers continued to play a supervisory role as 'consultants of the Union's committees'. In 1966 they became 'guides of the committees and councils at all levels', with administrative powers of veto. This last provision was a major focus of student complaint and was commonly known as 'the system of tutelage'. After the first phase of the student uprising in 1968, it was finally removed from the constitution. This triumph, however, was short-lived. After the second phase of the uprising, at the end of 1968, it was reinstated as the much-hated article 56–8:

> The councils and the committees of the Student Union at all levels are to have guides from the teaching staff. Meetings held without the presence and the presidency of the guides are void. Cheques must be signed by the guide in addition to the president of the Union and its financial and administrative supervisor. Appointment of the guides for the council and the committees at the faculty or the institute level is at the discretion of the faculty dean with the approval of the vice-rector of the university. The latter is to be the guide of the Union council at the university level and he is empowered to appoint guides for the committees at this level. The appointment of the guide of the Union council at the national level[113] is at the discretion of the organization committee of the Arab Socialist Union.[114]

The constitution in its 1968–69 version[115] provided for a variety of activities. The objectives of the Union were listed in the seventeen clauses of article 4, of which four clauses reflected the political character of the Union while the remaining thirteen reflected its social, welfare, and trade-unionist character. The four 'political clauses' were:

(1) to formulate student opinion upon national and world affairs;

(2) to design and organize national projects and programmes through which students could serve the country's goals and contribute positively to the process of social and cultural construction;

(3) to promote Arab national consciousness among students, to inculcate socialist concepts and to provide students with knowledge of the Arab world's struggle for freedom, socialism and unity;[116]

(4) to let students practise the free expression of their opinions and develop their personalities.

Article 5 clearly indicated the Union's subordination to the regime:

The GUSUAR aims at realizing the following: (1) strengthening the ties between the Student Union and the political organization (ASU) in the national interest; (2) strengthening the ties between the Student Union and executive bodies working on youth affairs; (3) resisting the conspiracies of reaction, imperialism and world Zionism which aim to isolate our nation, hindering its progress and destroying its vital interests.

This is further enforced in the stated objectives of the Union's Political Action Committee at the national level in article 26 which essentially repeats article 4.

The apparent contradiction in the constitution is its almost exclusive emphasis on the political character of the Union's organization at the national level and its organizational provision locally for a correspondingly exclusive concentration on social and trade union activities.

At the national level the Union Council was divided into five committees, of which three were explicitly political (Political Action, Arab Relations and Foreign Relations), one was non-political (Internal Relations) and one was mixed (Information and Publications). The Political Action Committee was in fact the only one to be presided over by the president of the Union himself while other committees were left to the vice-presidents (article 27). Locally, however, there were six committees, of which only one was political (Political and Cultural Activities) while the other five were devoted to non-political activities (Art, Social, Sports, Rover Scouts, and Travel and Camping).[117] Even in the case of the professedly 'Political' Committee, politics was diluted with broader 'cultural' activities which in practice were clearly predominant.

At the national level, the objectives of the Political Committee were identical to those of the Union itself. But the objectives of the local Political Committees were formulated simply as the provision of information:

> Article 30: The Committee of Political and Cultural Activities aims to realize the following objectives: (a) organizing lectures, debates and conferences as well as issuing publications which will *inform* students of what is happening inside and outside the country; (b) *informing* students of the characteristics of Arab society and the requirements of its development, and enhancing the role of university students in achieving the goals of the Arab world (author's italics).

In other words, the political functions of the Union were exercised by its upper echelon and not extended throughout its membership. This structure made it easier for the government in power to control the Union's political activity, as is indicated by the structure of the Union's finances:

> Article 43: Each student at the universities and the higher institutes is required to pay an annual Union subscription fee of E£1.50 to be distributed as follows: E1.00 to the faculty or institute's Union, E£0.40 to the university or the higher institutes' Union and E£0.10 to the GUSUAR.
>
> Article 44: The financial resources of the GUSUAR constitute its portion of the subscription fee together with the aid given to it by the state . . .

Thus, local branches of the Union financed their preponderantly social activities exclusively from members' subscription fees. Of these fees they kept 66.6 per cent, leaving 26.7 per cent to the middle echelons, which had similar committees and activities, and forwarding only 6.7 per cent to the national level, which therefore had to depend on supplementary funds from the government, effectively guaranteeing government control over its political activities. The financial regulation of the Union's budget was identical to that of any department of the civil service, and its funds were subject to direct state control as public funds.[118]

It is clear from this that Union membership was (and still is) automatic[119] for every student admitted to higher education, subscription fees being collected along with tuition fees by the faculty treasurer. Some have interpreted this as indicating that 'the Student Union is the democratic representative of all students in the university faculties and higher institutes since every one of them is a member of it'.[120] In reality, however, the Union's large membership was far from rendering it genuinely democratic in operation. Union elections were contested by candidates against a background of an apathetic membership and frequently with a very low turnout. This state of affairs was implicitly recognized in article 53 of the constitution:

> The validity of the elections for the Union at faculties and institutes is conditional upon a 50 per cent turnout of the electorate. If this proportion is not reached the elections are to be postponed for a maximum of three days, and are then to become valid with at least a 25 per cent turnout of the electorate.

In many cases, only the minimum turnout was attained.[121] The findings of Sultan's survey of 1970 give a striking indication of the kind of relationship that existed between the Union leadership and its membership (see Table 6.10).

It is clear therefore that the Student Union was far more a welfare or recreational club than a representative political organization. As a Cairo student committee complained:

> The liquidation of the political movement was reflected in the student movement through the replacement of the elected Union by an appointed one between 1953 and 1959. When elections were held once again in order to constitute the Union, they were combined with every device which could mutilate it and paralyse its effectiveness, the student body having already deserted it in the years when it was a purely appointed body, since they felt that it was not their real representative. A variety of forms of tutelage and corruption were practised—intervention in the elections, security bodies

Table 6.10: Percentage of Sampled Students[a] Affirming Certain Statements about the Student Union, 1968 and 1970

	Cairo Univ.		Alexandria Univ.		Assiut Univ.		Al-Azhar Univ.		American Univ.	
	M.	F.	M.	F.	M.	F.	M.	F.	M.	F.
The Council of the Union does not represent the large mass of students.	63	53	64	59	63	47	47	47	38	17
It does not try to explore students' views on many issues.	67	61	68	63	71	59	52	64	44	28
Some unsuitable elements assume the leadership of the Union.	62	50	64	54	66	47	44	40	31	20
Some students assume the leadership through undemocratic means.	51	39	53	46	14	32	42	30	19	12
Some student leaders benefit from their positions.	61	51	63	56	66	47	45	36	25	15

Note: a. The sample covered 5,977 students (4,081 male and 1,896 female) from the third-year students of the five universities.

Source: Emad-eldin Sultan, 'Problems of University Students', *National Review of Social Sciences*, vol. VIII, no. 1 (Jan. 1971), p. 18, Table 7.

outside the university proscribing certain candidates, ordinances making it difficult for the student movement to act spontaneously, tutelage by the 'guides', and splitting the Union up into separate segments (committees). All this resulted ultimately in its transformation into a charitable society practising welfare and recreation activities.[122]

Despite financial regulations which on paper appeared extremely strict, the corrupt behaviour of some of the Union leaders went unchecked by the government authorities who were supposed to supervise them. One Union leader went as far as to accuse the government of encouraging such excesses in order to weaken its prestige.[123]

But events in the national arena such as the defeat of 1967 and its aftermath gave the Union the chance to assume an actively political role during the first phase of the uprising of 1968. This chance, however, did not last long in the face of the second phase of the uprising, which was taken by the government as an excuse to retreat from its earlier concessions over the Union's constitution.

In addition, from 1968 onwards the regime recruited many of the emerging student leaders into its underground Socialist Vanguard, giving them a misleading taste of power and a promise of change from within the system. The Vanguard contained some very able student leaders, side by side with outright opportunists. It helped to politicize the Unions of those faculties and universities which its members controlled, as in the case of Ain Shams University. But its militant support for the regime prevented other emerging political factions, especially the Marxists, from expressing their own views. As a result, discreet antagonism between the two sides gave way to open clashes. In these, the Vanguard members were taunted with being 'security agents' by their opponents, although this was perhaps an exaggeration.[124]

After the military defeat of 1967 and the student uprisings of 1968 it was the Socialist Vanguard which was principally responsible for preventing the immediate re-emergence of an autonomous student movement. When in the course of a power struggle in 1971 the Vanguard was disbanded, it was possible for other political factions to come to the fore and lead a new wave of political activism with the uprising of 1972–73. Despite the belated attempts of a number of its members,[125] this was not a role which the Student Union itself had the capacity to carry out.

Government control of the student body was not, of course, based on coercion and manipulation alone. It depended also on the wider social and political achievements of the regime. Like many other Egyptians, students welcomed the social and economic achievements of the Revolution and responded to the euphoria and sense of national pride[126] inspired by Nasser's leadership. They also responded to the government's offer of wider educational opportunities and guaranteed employment upon graduation. At times, their support was absolute enough to prompt Malcolm Kerr's conclusion that 'the younger intelligentsia as a whole were the most reliable enthusiasts of the regime . . . and it was they who constituted the proletariat that Nasser's dictatorship represented'.[127] Only after the massive national defeat of 1967, and the slowing down of the regime's social programme due to the burden of military expenditure, did an eventual split between the regime and its student body become a real possibility. The split itself was initiated by a generation of students who 'had the achievements in their memory and lived the defeat in reality'.[128]

7
Confrontation

After the curtailment of independent political activity in 1954 there was little opportunity for self-expression for educated Egyptians. The heavy-handed rule of the officers had alienated the country's intelligentsia. One scholar has gone so far as to label the Revolution of 1952 itself as 'anti-intellectual'.[1] Within the framework of the economic development brought about by the regime, however, there was room for considerable co-operation between the officers and the technocrats and many intellectuals supported enthusiastically the new reforming social policies. The lack of political freedom, however, remained a serious ground for reservation in their attitudes towards the regime.

The officers' conception of the political role of the educated Egyptian was not that he should participate in government but rather that he should confine himself to responding to it in a more or less favourable way. There was only one policy, and everyone was expected to adhere to it. As far as individual opinion was concerned, however, the situation was by no means comparable with the period of Savak terror in Iran. As Leonard Binder put it, 'Opinion may be expressed with relative freedom, but in the end the wise citizen bows to the acknowledged sources of authority . . . Argument can proceed only to a certain limit and then must cease.'[2]

Collectively, intellectuals were not only deprived of participation in power but were also denied a forum in which they could speak frankly. Even the official political organizations did not provide a platform for any reasonable degree of collective self-expression.[3] The scholar Amos Perlmutter goes as far as to say, 'The problem in Egypt is not a crisis of political participation. The problem is the suspension of politics as an autonomous goal.'[4] This is a blatantly tendentious formulation, however. It is possible to 'suspend' political movement but even under the most repressive of regimes one cannot speak of 'suspending' politics. For most educated Egyptians the problem was precisely one of political participation: namely the opportunity for self-expression.

The traditional forums of self-expression for university graduates, the professional trade unions, were put under strict control. Their councils were dissolved in 1954, and in 1958 legislation was enacted restricting membership of their councils to members of the ruling party. Furthermore, army officers with professional training moved into influential positions within them and virtually all of their leaders were directly or indirectly installed by the government itself. The political influence of the professional unions in general was weakened despite an increase in their number with the creation of new unions for previously unorganized professional groups. (Some professional groups such as university teachers remained without unions.)

The regime's ban on independent political activity by intellectuals, and the limited degree of self-expression that they were allowed within official organizations, weakened the influence that the intelligentsia had attained during the liberal era. It ceased to be a cohesive and self-conscious elite and its grievances were not, until 1967, manifested in acts of open protest. Many intellectuals sank into a state of apathy. Only the small minority among the non-technical *literati* who possessed ideas of their own and a desire to engage in honest criticism had the opportunity to express dissatisfaction; and naturally, they used the limited scope available to them in the official press to criticize only the detail of governmental policies and the remaining members of their own class. As Kerr noted:

> The intellectuals are publicly encouraged to blame themselves . . . Journalists and university teachers may debate at great length in the press about the failing of their own class, provided that the conclusion drawn is not that the army has monopolised power and deprived intellectuals of the right to free self-expression, but that the intellectuals had ignominiously abdicated responsibility . . . Breast-beating has thus become a fixed posture of the intellectual in the public press as he self-consciously discusses the 'crisis' of the university, the 'crisis' of the free professions . . . etc, and searches for

reasons why it is not his class that has lately stood in the forefront of change.[5]

According to Muhammad Hasanain Heikal, the regime's *de facto* intellectual spokesman, the regime 'could not absorb the rightist traditional intellectuals because of their class position,[6] neither could it absorb the leftist intellectuals because of their political position'.[7] Heikal himself attempted to absorb on the paper *al-Ahram* leading writers of different persuasions. But this, of course, did not significantly alter the terms of the relationship between the regime and the intelligentsia; it merely enabled Heikal to conduct a small liberal experiment on the surface of political life in Egypt.[8]

The national defeat in 1967 brought the problem of self-expression to a head. For the country's students, the defeat, as Szyliowicz noted:

> shattered the remaining sense of dynamism and momentum among the youth and created a climate wherein their frustrations concerning the university environment, the kinds of positions to which they could aspire, and the repressive political context became as explosive as in the past.[9]

The uprising of February 1968 marked the students' initial reaction to the defeat and the beginning of their confrontation with the regime. It reflected the failure of the official youth organizations, indeed of the whole range of official political organizations, to contain their movement. Its intensity was attributable to the scale of the military defeat itself as much as to the constraints on self-expression among students and intellectuals long before the defeat.

In *al-Tali'a's* report on the political organization of the youth (February 1966), Zakariya raised the issue of self-expression:

> The right attitude to be taken by the state is to encourage the young men by all means to think in a positive way, giving them the feeling that all problems are open to discussion and analysis, and that they themselves are capable of playing some part in solving them . . . The ability of the young men to develop an independent critical mind may in the first instance appear contradictory to society's endeavour to unify its plans and attain its collectively agreed objectives. But I see

no contradiction in this . . . The young men's response to social objectives would be greater and more enthusiastic if these were subject to their analysis and conscious discussion than if they had to accept them blindly.[10]

Zakariya's call went unheeded, and a national defeat on the scale of 1967 was needed to convince the country's rulers of the truth of his argument. As one of the SYO leaders put it:

> We should realize that the youth at this stage are not prepared to accept predetermined propositions in any field . . . After the defeat, a political reappraisal had to take place in every field and we could not expect a continuation of the previous forms of commitment, as for example in the case of the SYO. Commitment can no longer be a form of mental compulsion nor should it be an obstruction to the freedom of opinion of the youth.[11]

The state of apathy into which most students had sunk before 1967 changed with the defeat, and increasing numbers of them showed more interest in national affairs. The basic political freedoms which Khalid Muhammad Khalid had claimed for the nation in the early 1960s became the central issue in the public debate which followed the defeat. In his speech to the National Congress of the ASU, the student leader Abd al-Hamid Hassan took 'freedom' as his principal theme:

> The value of freedom in a given country is to be measured by guaranteeing every mouth to tell the truth and every pen to write what is real. Chanting for freedom is no substitute for practising it . . . There should be no censorship in the press in other than military matters. Censorship should not be subjective arbitration by a handful of individuals.[12]

To reinforce his point, Hassan put forward a common argument of the period, 'If we had been allowed to talk without fear and speak our minds there would have been no defeat.'[13] In fact, many people in Egypt were obsessed with this idea. Although freer expression could have facilitated an earlier disclosure of the abuse of power by the army command—which was proved to be negligent during the war—it is unlikely that this would necessarily have averted defeat. The prevalence of this idea was essentially a reflection of the sense of national humiliation and the strenuous desire of the Egyptians to reform the political system in order to offset the effect of the defeat.

The theme of political freedom was carried from street corners into the regime's institutions themselves. At a meeting of the ASU branch in the Ministry of Culture, for example, members complained that 'they were not allowed to share responsibility in political affairs and that fear and apathy had permeated every corner of the society'.[14] The recommendations of a conference of the ASU branches in Cairo University in July 1968 focused on the basic freedoms and listed them as follows: 'Freedoms of the individual to criticize and express himself, of assembly and open political discussion, of peaceful protest and of the press and other media.'[15] They also called for: (a) the formation of a Constitutional Tribunal; (b) the drawing-up of a permanent constitution; (c) the recognition of the people's right to withdraw their confidence in representatives at all levels; and (d) the recognition of the people's right to be correctly informed of developments in the political situation.[16]

The call for freedom came from a wide range of groupings and institutions, from the young *literati* who gathered at a conference in 1968 'facing the omnipotent minister of the interior with what he never imagined he would hear',[17] to the judiciary, who met in their club in March 1968 and issued a declaration calling for the establishment of basic freedoms, the independence of the judiciary from the executive, the exclusion of judges from political organizations (i.e. the ASU) and the removal of non-specialized (i.e. military) personnel from the work of the judiciary.

Even in Nasser's own cabinet the subject of 'freedoms' was actively discussed. In a cabinet meeting, Dr Helmi Mourad, the liberal education minister of the period, hinted that Nasser's strict concept of 'social freedom' was invalid in the conditions of Egypt after the defeat:

In the discussions on freedom which are now taking place in this country, there can be no doubt that social freedom is essential for political freedom. But political freedom is also essential because it defines an important issue, that is, participation in the expression of opinion and the government of the country.[18]

Although Nasser remained adamant about his theoretical belief in 'social freedom',[19] in 1968 he responded to public demand and issued his famous Programme of 30 March, offering a relative liberalization of the political system and promising to embody liberal principles in his proposals for a permanent constitution, proposals which had still not been drawn up by the time of his death.

In an attempt to prove that the Programme was working, *al-Ahram*, probably with Nasser's direct or indirect consent, opened a debate on an issue of particular relevance. Under the headline 'A Serious Incident', on 13 October 1968 the paper wrote:

> Today, *al-Ahram* draws public attention to an incident which we think has an effect on the spirit of the Programme of 30 March . . . In brief, three weeks ago the state security prosecutor together with the Public Intelligence Agency arrested a director of a prominent scientific research centre, one which plays an important role in the field of social and economic studies . . . He was interrogated on the basis of information provided by General Gamal Askar, the president of the Central Agency for Public Mobilization and Statistics [CAPMS], who claimed that one of the research projects of the centre contained information the release of which the CAPMS does not approve.

Al-Ahram also mentioned that the person in question had been arrested at dawn in his house by the 'dawn visitors' (security men in colloquial Egyptian). The dawn visitors, said the paper:

> are a phenomenon which we do not want in this country . . . it is against its patriotic and revolutionary nature. [Furthermore,] a line should be drawn in the activities of the CAPMS, in order to avoid the excesses from which we have suffered in the past [adding that the whole of this discussion] would have been inconceivable before the Programme of 30 March; it would then have been a great risk!

The following day, and for a whole week, *al-Ahram* sustained a public debate with General Askar, who defended the overwhelming powers of his agency, and, for the first time ever, with the secretary of state for intelligence, affirmed that the Programme 'clearly decided that the centres of power should be dismantled, and we abide fully by that decision'.[20] In a series of articles, liberal and Marxist university teachers rallied to the support of *al-Ahram*.

In an article entitled 'Obstacles in the Path of Scientific Research', Dr al-Otaifi wrote:

> I know of an incident when the CAPMS informed the police against a university professor who was conducting research in a village without its permission . . . If we ask university teachers to study the enemy we should provide them with the necessary means to collect enough information on it, information that is available in scores of books and periodicals published abroad, which should not be subject to the narrow view of censorship.[21]

Professor Sarhan of the Institute of Statistical Research and Studies complained:

> University teachers who conduct research either individually or by committees feel bitter about the need for lengthy formalities and correspondence with the CAPMS, as though the latter were interrogating them on the content of their research in order to give them permission to conduct it.[22]

Dr Amr Mohieddin of the Economics Department at Cairo University noted:

> The freedom of scientific research is not an abstract concept or a slogan to raise in the air, it is a pressing necessity dictated by the pressing need for the country's development.[23]

A post-graduate student abroad sent *al-Ahram* an eloquent letter in answer to the CAPMS's refusal to let him carry out a sample survey of the country's administrative cadres, stressing the underlying issue of political loyalty:

> My questionnaire is prepared under the supervision of Professor Iskander, who helped to train socialist cadres at the Higher Institute for Socialist Studies and who received a state award for his academic contribution. He is undoubtedly as concerned with the country's interests and security as the general . . . In our whole history, no university teacher or

research student has ever been implicated in espionage, treason or the abuse of power.[24]

Dr Ismail S. Abdalla confirmed this:

The concept of secrecy leads us in the end to deny access to information to our fellow countrymen, whose aim is to serve the country, without in fact being able to prevent the enemy from obtaining it.[25]

Dr al-Otaifi summed up the debate:

Any discussion that does not lead to clear-cut conclusions and proposals is purposeless and no more than expenditure of words, which may release our frustrated energies without laying down guidelines for political participation . . . Some people have written to *al-Ahram* saying: 'Good of you to raise the issue of scientific freedom and freedom in general . . . but what about all those cases of people arrested or convicted for political activity which have remained unresolved for many years?' Such questions can only be answered in enacting legislation which guarantees basic freedoms.[26]

Al-Otaifi's fear that the debate might be fruitless was also expressed in Abd al-Hamid Hassan's speech to the Congress of the ASU: 'The young men of this nation would like to feel that the role assigned to them is meant to utilize their capabilities, not to defuse their outrage.'[27] The scepticism of both men proved well founded. After a few months of liberal deeds and declarations the trend was reversed and Egyptian politics reverted to its authoritarian mould.

In explaining this regression, some commentators suggested that Nasser had been obliged to introduce a short spell of liberalization as a means of absorbing the shock of the 1967 defeat and avoiding its potentially serious repercussions. One commentator contended that vocal public criticism in this period 'made no impact and led nowhere since it was merely a shock-absorption exercise on the part of the government to give Nasser time to put his house in order and devise his new plan of operation'.[28] Even Nasser's supporters were forced to admit that there was some truth in this argument. One of his closest aides admitted:

> I heard Nasser say in those days that the home front would not remain stable for long, and that people would not bear the shock for more than six to nine months . . . Therefore, he was trying earnestly to introduce a comprehensive change in the style of his rule before the débâcle he anxiously expected. In fact, Nasser's fears were realized: seven months after the defeat major demonstrations broke out.[29]

Nasser's handling of the situation, however, was not merely a short-term expedient. The exigencies of the continuing military confrontation with Israel compelled him to try to soften public criticism of the abysmal performance of the Egyptian army in the war.[30] Public criticism of the police state, however, put him in a dilemma. He was obliged, on the one hand, to respond to that criticism without reducing the efficiency of the security institutions on which he relied so heavily[31] in the absence of effective political institutions. On the other hand, the drive for liberalization met with fierce resistance from the hard-line members of his government. While the first wave of student turbulence in 1968 helped the more liberal elements to put forward their reforms, the second wave of unrest in the same year reinforced the position of those disposed to take a harder line.

More importantly, the immediate pressure on Nasser for liberal change was in fact an appeal for improvement within the system itself, and not a fundamental challenge to it. The public demand was for greater efficiency and less repression. The millions of demonstrators calling for change were not led by an alternative force with a different political programme. As Dekmejian noted: 'One aspect of the political process which remained relatively unchallenged was the sacrosanct realm of ideology.'[32] Some commentators advised the regime to treat the slogans of public criticism as a mere call for reform and not as a threat:

> The students' demand to be able to withdraw their confidence in their representatives distinguishes for the first time between the Revolution and those in power. It makes possible a change in the personnel who hold power without the collapse of the Revolution itself, and it makes the endeavour to change the ruling power a legitimate act within the framework of the Revolution and not an instance of high treason that should entail the death penalty . . . [33] Students' demands

do not contain anything that is in contradiction with Nasser's declared revolutionary objectives.[34]

It was this absence of an ideological alternative that led an author such as Dekmejian to contend:

That a generally authoritarian regime would permit significant liberalisation and dissent during a time of national emergency was a demonstration of systematic strength. One would find this type of behaviour hard to conceive of even in the Western democracies under conditions of war and occupation similar to Egypt's.[35]

The 1967 defeat, however, sowed the seeds for the development in the longer term of ideological possibilities in Egypt as in the wider Arab political arena. According to Ali Hilal Dessouki, the Arab intellectuals who explained *al-Nakba* (the defeat) by historical and long-term factors, who saw its wider significance, and who made a sincere attempt at self-analysis and self-criticism, could be classified into three groups:

(1) representatives of the secular liberal response who stressed the importance of education, science, technology, planning and secularization;
(2) representatives of the Islamic fundamentalist response who advocated the return to Islam as the only solution;
(3) representatives of the revolutionary socialist response who advocated complete modernization of society along revolutionary lines.[36]

The polarization of these responses and the emergence of fully fledged political movements along their respective lines was a gradual process that ruffled the surface of Egyptian political life until the mid-1970s, following Nasser's death in 1970 and Sadat's accession to power. This delayed impact marked the resilience of Nasser's regime and led commentators—even after the death of Nasser himself—greatly to overestimate its stability: 'The participation crisis in Egypt is at present invisible or suppressed. That there is no open pressure for increased participation and that only the most harmless of private murmuring goes on is certainly the case.'[37]

In 1972–73, however, a further wave of student revolt broke

out, bringing the issue of self-expression before the Egyptian public once again. And this time its meaning was broadened to include the ultimate freedom of ideological choice. It is not surprising that a student declaration of this period was bold enough to proclaim that 'students measure the sincerity of their leaders by their patriotic attitude, not by their ideological commitment'.[38]

8
The Uprising of 1968

Phase One: February

The student uprising of February 1968 was the most vocal expression of public unrest following the defeat of 1967. The students, who had remained politically silent between 1954 and 1967, spearheaded public criticism. The re-emergence of student activism was an integral component of the general pressures on the regime to break the mould of Egyptian politics by allowing a greater degree of self-expression to various sectors of the population. The position of the students in the national arena was particularly strengthened by the fact that the regime's attempts to restructure the army relied upon using university graduates to form the backbone of a better-educated army.

The uprising was initiated on 21 February by workers in Helwan, an industrial suburb of Cairo. It broke out immediately after the announcement of the military court's verdict on the charges of negligence brought against the leaders of the Egyptian air force, who were widely held responsible for a major part of the military defeat. The workers in the munitions factories and fellow-workers in other industries considered the sentences to be too lenient. They reacted by taking to the streets, where scores of them were injured in clashes with the police outside Helwan police station. What had started as a protest by the workers escalated into a wider mass uprising in which students took an active part.

The twenty-first of February happened to be Students' Day, celebrated every year in memory of the famous Bloody Thursday of 1946. The day's festivities turned into a series of forums for political discussion where university and government officials attempted to answer questions from the students on the political situation in the aftermath of the trial. In the following days students passed beyond the university gates and made their presence felt on the streets of Cairo and Alexandria for the first time since 1954. They remained there, together with their fellow-demonstrators from the industrial areas and other areas of the two cities, until 27 February. The uprising in Cairo alone resulted in 2 workers being killed, 77 civilians and 146 policemen being injured, and 635 people being arrested, in addition to damage to vehicles and buildings in the capital.[1]

Thousands of students from the major universities in Cairo and Alexandria participated in the uprising. A distinctive part was played by the students of the Engineering Faculty (Polytechnic) of Cairo University. They were at the heart of two incidents of particular importance. The first occurred on 24 February, when a group of engineering students formed the core of a delegation, drawn from the students demonstrating outside parliament, who were allowed inside to present their demands to the Speaker, Anwar al-Sadat, later the President of the Republic. Having registered their names, the delegation members expressed their fears that they might be arrested. The Speaker gave them his 'word of honour' that none of them would be molested and, moreover, gave them his phone number in case anything of the kind happened. Later the same night, however, the students' fears proved to be all too well founded when they were arrested at home.[2]

The following day, enraged at the arrest of their colleagues, students held a mass meeting and decided to organize a sit-in inside the Polytechnic.[3] Although the government had decided to close the universities on 25 February, the sit-in, the second major incident in the uprising, took place on that day and lasted for three days, while the uprising in the rest of the country was dying down. The first day of the sit-in was marked by a battle with the riot police besieging the Polytechnic, in which stones were thrown at the police. The police subsequently withdrew to a nearby park while other forms of pressure were brought to bear on the students. Both teachers and parents of students were brought in to persuade the students to give up their protest. In the end these tactics proved successful, and the five hundred students at the beginning of the sit-in were reduced to some one hundred and eighty by its end.

The compromise formula which ended the sit-in, offered to students through the mediation of Professor Ibrahim Gaafar, was for students to present their demands at a meeting with the Speaker of parliament. They were transferred from the Polytechnic to parliament in a fleet of cars provided by government and the proposed meeting took place in the evening of 28 February as the finalé of the sit-in and, indeed, of the entire February 1968 uprising.

The meeting itself took the form of a fierce debate between ministers, state officials and MPs (with the Speaker in attendance) on one side, and the students on the other. One of the students boasted subsequently, 'I can recall no other incident where a group of ministers were ridiculed as they were at this meeting!'[4] The debate centred on the demands formulated in the course of the sit-in. When the students insisted that their declaration be published in the press, the Speaker declined to do so and refused the declaration itself *in toto*:

> I reject this declaration in form and content . . . I read it last night . . . Isn't it that of 'freedom to be taken not to be given!?' . . . I say no to this . . . This declaration has been based on bad temper and not on our democratic discussion of today.[5]

The content of the students' demands is crucial to an understanding of the uprising of February 1968. The government tried to suggest that these demands were related essentially to the case of the officers who had been tried for neglecting their duties. After lengthy discussions with student representatives, the Speaker described their demands as centred on three issues—the sentences passed on the officers, the workers' demonstration in Helwan and student grievances at the behaviour of the University Guard. Reporting the demonstrations in Cairo, *al-Ahram* mentioned one which had occurred outside its own premises. A delegation of four students had entered the building and expressed the demands of the demonstrators: 'The university youth record their objection to the verdict in the air force case. While they reiterate their support and loyalty to President Nasser they beseech him in the name of university youth to revise it.'[6] Heikal's lengthy article on the events was entitled, 'On the Verdict . . . the Demonstrations . . . and the Retrial'.[7]

In fact, however, the demands of the uprising were far from restricted to the question of 'the verdict'. In their slogans, declarations and discussions with government officials, the students' demands covered a much wider spectrum of issues. The declaration by students participating in the Polytechnic sit-in, for example, listed the following demands:

(1) the release of arrested colleagues;

(2) freedom of expression and of the press;

(3) a truly representative parliament in a real and sound representative system;

(4) the withdrawal of Intelligence personnel from the universities;

(5) the promulgation and enforcement of laws establishing political freedoms;

(6) a serious investigation of the workers' incident in Helwan;

(7) a declaration of the extent of the air force officers' responsibility;

(8) an investigation into police intrusion in the universities and police assaults upon students.[8]

Three of these demands bore on the question of democracy in the country as a whole, three referred to the absence of democracy in the university in particular, and only two concerned the question of the air force case and the events to which it had led.

The slogans daubed on the walls of the Polytechnic during the sit-in included: 'Stop the rule of Intelligence', 'Down with the police state', 'Down with Heikal's lying press', 'No life with terror . . . No knowledge without freedom' and 'Don't discuss the air force question, discuss freedom.'

Another example of the main thrust of the students' demands was provided by the recommendations of the student meeting held at the Faculty of Pharmacology at Alexandria University. The meeting resolved that the government should:

(1) point out who was really responsible for the air force disaster;

(2) build an effective political organization and reconstitute the existing youth organizations;

(3) punish those responsible for the Helwan incident;

(4) allow freedom of the press and free criticism;

(5) dismiss al-Lethi Abdel-Nasser [Nasser's brother in charge of the ASU in Alexandria];

(6) abolish paid full-time work in political organizations;

(7) convey the university's recommendations directly to the presidency;

(8) stop the Intelligence service interfering with people's freedom, and stop them spying on individuals.[9]

Here, then, there were four recommendations for democracy in the country at large, one for democracy at the university itself, one local political issue of some significance because it may have been aimed indirectly at Nasser himself, and finally two recommendations arising directly out of the recent events.

Some of the slogans frequently shouted by demonstrators were also directed specifically against the regime itself: 'Down with the Intelligence state!', 'Down with the military state!', 'Heikal, you are a liar . . . stop lying, you cheat!', 'Nasser there are limits to patience . . . The tenth of June will never happen again' and 'On the ninth of June we supported you . . . Today we oppose you!'

Furthermore, the discussions between student representatives and state officials, like those with the Speaker of parliament, ranged more widely than mere protests at the military court's verdict. Most significant among these was the discussion between Nasser himself and a group of Student Union leaders[10] after the uprising. In a meeting scheduled to last for half an hour but extended to some three and a half hours, student representatives discussed with Nasser seventeen questions which they had prepared more than a week before the meeting. All of them concerned the national political situation[11] and none mentioned any student grievances. It was only at the end of the meeting that Nasser himself prompted them to describe the problems of students in particular. They responded briefly, concentrating their complaints on the question of teachers' tutelage of the Student Union.

The student uprising of February 1968 was no mere protest at the military court's verdict upon a group of allegedly negligent officers. It was, as Zakariya put it:

a summing up of the outrage that spread all over the country after the 1967 defeat . . . the general spirit behind the uprising, however, was more than mere outrage—it was in fact an expression of discontent with a whole style of rule of which the military defeat was but one feature.[12]

The government reacted to the uprising by trying to contain it in its early stages in Helwan. While workers were planning a demonstration outside parliament and the Presidential Palace, the ASU leaders persuaded them to confine it to the ASU headquarters of Helwan zone, at a short distance from the police station where the confrontation between workers and the police eventually took place. This is what Nasser meant when he referred to 'the contradiction of the uprising—that the ASU was leading the demonstrations and the police were confronting it'.[13] This is also what led some people, including a number of MPs, to believe that the demonstrations were organized by the ASU and the SYO.

The fact is that the workers' uprising was spontaneous. As Khalid Mohieddin argued in parliament, 'That the ASU led the demonstrations does not mean they were not spontaneous . . .it was the general political atmosphere which made them inevitable.'[14] Moreover, the ASU leaders' control of the demonstrations did not last beyond, at very most, the first few hours. After this point the demonstrations became wholly out of control. This is admitted implicitly in the minister of the interior's statement before parliament:

> On the evening of 20 February the agreement between the ASU, the SYO and the Interior Ministry was that demonstrations should not be organized and protests should be restricted to indoor meetings at which opinions could be expressed. But the demonstrators set off and their leaders failed to get in touch with the Interior Ministry to receive instructions.[15]

The government's initial attempts to contain the uprising also included the pre-emptive arrest of a number of alleged provocateurs. Nasser himself, however, ordered his minister of the interior to let the demonstrations proceed if these arrests failed to bring them to a halt.[16] The scale of the uprising was in fact too massive to be contained either by pre-emptive arrests or by the riot police. Still relatively weak at that time, the riot police were to be transformed after the uprising into a powerful and heavily armed battalion known as the Central Security Forces.

The containment of student participation in the uprising started within the university itself. *Al-Ahram* reported that on 24 February, the first day of student street demonstrations, Dr Helmi Mourad, the rector of Ain Shams University, succeeded in persuading his own student body to confine their action to within the university boundaries. In his statement to parliament, the minister of the interior described a meeting between students and the minister of higher education at which it was agreed that student demands were to be considered by appropriate official bodies like the ASU, the Student Union and the university administration, while their views on the air force case might be conveyed to the presidency without their needing to resort to demonstrations.

When the attempt to contain them within the university had failed, students were advised through the media to leave the streets, on the grounds that 'other elements' had penetrated their ranks during the demonstrations.[17] More important, students were told that any breach of the official ban on demonstrations would be 'an insult to the national struggle, at a time when the Arab nation was having to face a wide-ranging conspiracy by imperialist forces and Israel.'[18] This theme featured in official accounts of the uprising, along with a simultaneous declaration of confidence in the country's students, a gesture aimed at dividing the majority of students from their active leaders, thus leaving the leaders to bear alone the accusation of undermining the national struggle and serving the enemy.[19]

At the conclusion of his statement to parliament, the minister of the interior summed up the situation: 'Students are in fact our sons and brothers. The security of the home front is vital to the security of the military front. It is the duty of every individual in this nation to combat malicious elements.'[20]

His cabinet colleague the minister of higher education also maintained that:

The whole country has every confidence in university students. It is entirely appropriate that they should express their opinions through free and constructive discussion . . . Our position now is dependent on the strength and security of the home front at a time when our forces are facing the enemy . . . Unobstructed production provides the basis both for the home front and the armed forces. The disruption of production helps no one, and the disruption of studies is in fact a disruption of production.[21]

The same argument was even advanced by Heikal. Although at an earlier point he claimed that:

holding demonstrations is a healthy phenomenon despite their excesses; it is a form of concern for the country's destiny which should be appreciated, even if people try to exploit them, [he still warned that] demonstrations may give a wrong impression of the stability of the home front, which is the only clear and solid basis for the country's steadfastness in the face of the enemy.[22]

At the other end of the spectrum of opinion within the Nasser regime, a radical MP like Khalid Mohieddin also argued that 'although universities admittedly have certain defects, they can wait . . . the enemy on our doorstep cannot wait'.[23]

The accusation that the uprising would or might affect the country's domestic political stability was linked with the allegation that it had direct connections with the reactionary forces left over from the old regime. Students' criticism of the ineffectiveness of parliament was taken by some of its members as a slur on its social composition: the 50 per cent of its seats given to workers' and peasants' representatives. It is possible that some individual students had in fact, as one MP alleged,[24] expressed such hostility. But it was in no sense a demand of the mainstream of the movement. The government, however, frequently claimed the existence of such a connection with elements of the old regime. At his meeting with the students of the Polytechnic, for example, Sadat himself reiterated it:

> With your demonstrations you gave courage to elements which had been eradicated or had retreated. A car was spotted today touring the schools in the Heliopolis area and inciting students to strike. The passengers in the car were sons of the old feudalists.[25]

In his speech immediately after the uprising, cleverly delivered in the industrial suburb in which it had begun, Nasser pressed this argument on the public, making it an integral part of his analysis of the significance of the uprising which, he admitted, he had been following personally 'minute by minute'.[26]

Combining themes from the official statements of the minister of the interior and the semi-official articles of Heikal, Nasser offered a more elaborate account of his own. While admitting that the students had 'the right and duty to care about the affairs of their country,' he emphasized that activists who had taken the movement on to the streets were a mere 'fifteen hundred to two thousand out of the one hundred and forty thousand to one hundred and fifty thousand university students in the country'.[27] His conception of the motives behind the uprising was comparatively complex:

> (1) The post-defeat unrest—'Our young men feel restless, they feel torn apart, they feel the impact of Israel's aggression . . . The verdict in the air force case has had an emotional impact on them.'
>
> (2) The 'misunderstanding' between students and the authorities in the course of the uprising.
>
> (3) The existence of 'anti-revolutionary, anti-popular and pro-imperialist elements' who were trying to exploit the situation to encourage the killing of a number of demonstrators and the disruption of domestic political stability.
>
> (4) The failure of the press fully to report what had occurred for reasons of national security.[28]

Enemies of his socialist revolution, Nasser warned, had found their way into the ranks of the country's students:

> We all know that in the past workers and students were misled by reactionaries. The process which started spontaneously here in Helwan, then in the university, ceased to be spontaneous after a while . . . I am telling our brothers at the university that before following any slogan they should first see who is raising it. Everyone has his class position. There are people whose property was confiscated, whose land was seized and whose factories were nationalized. The sons of these people are living amongst us . . . That is how the forces of reaction operated: through exploiting student demonstrations, in which they raised the slogans of freedom and democracy.[29]

While it is logical to assume that those who benefited from the *ancien regime* would try to profit from any such uprising, Nasser's claim was not convincing: it was clear to many that the uprising had been principally a response to the 1967 defeat, and to those evils of the regime which people had discreetly complained about before the defeat, and more openly attacked after it. In some cases the accusation was treated with contempt: 'It is ridiculous and insulting to the Egyptian student of today to connect him with, for example, the deposed Wafd . . . Many students do not even know who Nahhas Pasha or Sirag al-Din

Pasha were!'[30] But it was, of course, possible that the slogan of democracy had been raised by opponents of the regime as well as by those of its supporters who merely hoped to democratize it.

The ideological orientations of the core of student activists who led the uprising of February 1968 did not bear out Nasser's claim. The best description of these was given by an Islamic fundamentalist student:

> While the right and left were heavily represented in the discussions, the Islamic tendency was absent . . . The leftist tendency was influential but the majority consisted simply of students who advocated freedom and reform without a defined ideological approach . . . The interrogation of the arrested students was aimed at finding out which tendency was directing the movement . . . It was clear that the ruling power feared the leftist drive . . . that is best exemplified by questioning the arrested students on their views about the Sino-Soviet dispute . . . Although I felt uneasy about the fact that the movement was not led by the Islamic tendency, I must truthfully admit that the 1968 movement was the only one that encompassed students of all tendencies and that it remained pure until its very end, because it was not affected by conflicting ideological tendencies.[31]

The political impact of the uprising was considerable, both in the country at large and within the universities. Nationally, it forced Nasser to order the retrial of the officers charged with negligence and to form a new cabinet with a civilian majority,[32] mostly of university professors, for the first time in his rule. More significantly, it made him seek a renewed legitimacy for his regime through the promulgation of the Programme of 30 March, with its promised liberal reforms of the political system.

Within the universities, the uprising paved the way for the lifting of a number of restrictions which had severely hampered the activities of the student movement. Although the University Guard remained on the campuses, it no longer meddled in the political activities of students, nor did it have the authority to censor student articles in the wall-magazines. This made the wall-magazines, as one student put it, 'the freest press in Egypt'.[33] A central student newspaper was also authorized for publication by the Student Union (the GUSUAR). A new constitution for the Student Union was issued by Presidential Decree to give students what they had wanted for so long: a union without tutelage by the teachers. Students also received a number of other welfare benefits—a reduction of the cost of living in student hostels from E£7.50 to E£5.00 and an increase in the funds assigned to the Student Bank from E£1 million to E£3 million.

Meanwhile the Nasser regime had gained greater understanding of the potential threat to its stability from the revival of the student movement in the aftermath of military disaster. Special efforts were therefore made to recruit student activists to the emergent underground organization of the ASU, the Socialist Vanguard. In this organization, the independence and initiative which the students had begun to develop during the uprising were restrained by the discipline of the attempt to reform the system from within.

The most important legacy of the uprising, however, was the spirit of self-confidence which spread through the student body in its aftermath. By spawning the activists who were to lead them, the uprising had also laid the foundation for a later series of student actions, and begun the process of ideological polarization in their own ranks which led to the re-emergence of organized political factions in the student movement, each of which viewed the events of February 1968 with particular strength of feeling.

Phase Two: November

For a few months after February 1968 a measure of self-confidence was restored to the Egyptian students' ranks by their publicly acknowledged role in paving the way for political reform in the aftermath of defeat. But the relative calm of the student body was abruptly terminated by the outbreak of a second wave of student turbulence in November 1968.

The occasion was the promulgation of a new Education Act which restricted the existing practice of allowing secondary school students to stand for examinations an indefinite number of times, and to secure an overall pass despite failures in two of the subjects (most often, mathematics and foreign languages). The act raised the minimum level for a pass in a number of secondary subjects, put an end to automatic progress from one grade to another in primary school and fixed a minimum mark for admission to preparatory school. Under the act, it became necessary for students to attain a certain minimum standard in all of their subjects in order to achieve an overall pass in their examinations. There is no doubt that the general impact of the act upon educational standards was beneficial. But for those attempting to earn educational qualifications, its effect naturally appeared severely restrictive.

The November 1968 student uprising began in the Delta city of al-Mansoura. Students of the city's secondary schools took to the streets on 20 November in protest against the act, following its publication in the press the previous day.[34] Official sources attributed these demonstrations to the pupils of one particular private secondary school in al-Mansoura who were renowned for their above-average age and their repeated failure in secondary examinations. But the fact that they were rapidly joined by students from other secondary schools in the city makes it difficult to attribute the demonstrations merely to the pupils of a single school. The students had been expecting to have the opportunity to proceed to higher education as a result of the expansion promised by Nasser's populist educational policies. It was the new act's emphasis on quality at the expense of quantity which brought the students onto the streets.

The first day of demonstrations in al-Mansoura ended with a student gathering in a government secondary school, at which the governor assured students that the act would not be enforced retrospectively and that certain allowances would be made for students already in school at the time of its promulgation. The substance of the governor's assurance to students had been conveyed to him by phone by the minister of education after discussing the act with officials of his ministry at a meeting held in Upper Egypt.

On the following day, 21 November 1968, the students continued to demonstrate. This time the demonstrations began among the two thousand students of al-Azhar's Divinity Institute whose pupils, though not subject to the act, feared that they might be affected by it. The demonstrators headed towards the Security Administration of the province, where they came face to face with the police force stationed inside. Shots were fired, killing three students and one peasant; thirty-two[35] demonstrators, nine senior police officers and fourteen policemen[36] were injured.[37]

The government took measures to curb the spread of the disturbances, and the official press sought vociferously to discourage further student protests. *Al-Ahram* reiterated the advantages of the new Education Act and claimed that the demonstrations had been 'infiltrated by non-student elements' which had attempted to attack the Security Administration in al-Mansoura.[38] Once more it stressed 'the country's exceptional circumstances which oblige all efforts to be directed at the foreign enemy'.[39]

One reporter from *al-Ahram*, Makram Muhammad Ahmad, attempted a more informative and analytical account without repudiating the official version.[40] He raised the issue of the responsibility of the province's director of security: 'Why did the director of security not tell the whole truth in his statement? Why not report the events as they actually happened? Why did he not say that the four demonstrators had fallen dead right on the doorstep of the Administration? Is there something to hide?' He continued, however, to lay all the blame on the students: 'Why was there so much violence against reforms which put an end to the nonsense that affected the educational system for many years?' He quoted the minister of education's address to students: 'You were crying out last February for a strong nation and a strong citizen. Now that you are affected by reform you rail against it . . . What a strange position!', and severely criticized them:

The student force in Egypt, which had the opportunity last March to be a force of reform in society, should not be obsessed with the idea that what it believes is always right. Its attitude towards the events of al-Mansoura reveals that the student movement in Egypt needs to correct its own mistakes continuously . . . It should be agreed that the climate in which the events of al-Mansoura took place differs totally from the climate in which the uprising of last February took place. There was then a clear public appreciation of how student demonstrations contributed to reform . . . What happened in al-Mansoura was not the right thing at the right time[41] . . . The students of al-Mansoura should be severely censured for not having exhausted other means of conveying their views. The problem is that we do not use the available channels effectively in order to express our views on various problems . . . They could have held a meeting at the school, they could have involved the parents' associations in the issue, they could have presented the problem to the ASU to handle politically and lastly they could have prompted the Student Union to take its share in the matter. None of these did they do. Demonstrating is easier![42]

Makram Muhammad Ahmad provided the most eloquent and the least demagogic semi-official account of the events at al-Mansoura. But he failed to suggest an effective alternative to the action adopted by the students. They did not ignore the pre-scribed channels through gratuitous eagerness to play the hooligan. They had long lacked confidence in any of the insti-tutions in question and the brief period of reform was wholly insufficient to dissipate the deep-seated mistrust. In his own article, Makram quoted some of them as saying, 'There should be a strike . . . Who would guarantee that the promises made by the province's governor will be fulfilled?'

The news of the bloody events in al-Mansoura swiftly spread to the University of Alexandria which housed a number of students from the Delta province of al-Dakahliya, of which al-Mansoura is the capital. Anticipating trouble in the university, and particularly in the Engineering Faculty (Polytechnic) where there was a core of political activists, the governor of Alexandria held a meeting on the morning of Friday 22 November with the director of Security, the rector of the university, five members of the teaching staff of each of its faculties, all headmasters of the city's secondary schools, a number of headmasters of the large preparatory schools and the heads of the city's districts.[43] They discussed the possibility of disturbances and agreed that lectures at the university should start five minutes earlier than usual and that the director of Security should prevent any street demonstrations by students. No student representative was invited to the meeting.

In the evening of the same day two engineering students returned from al-Mansoura to confirm the news of the bloody confrontation. An urgent Student Union meeting[44] was held after midnight and a decision was taken to organize a peaceful protest march the following morning. From early morning students started to gather at the Polytechnic. The two students from al-Mansoura informed a student meeting of the situation there and mentioned that the police had surrounded the city's mosques during Friday prayers. Slogans were shouted against the minister of the interior,[45] Shaarawi Goma, and after two hours of hot debate the meeting ended (in chaos, according to *al-Ahram*) and students took to the streets.

The demonstration was led by the president of the Student Union of the Polytechnic, Atef al-Shater, who carried its banner. The inevitable clash with the riot police took place in front of the Agriculture Faculty; thirty-five policemen and thirty students were injured.[46] In the course of the demonstration al-Shater and three colleagues were arrested while negotiating with the police and taken to the Alexandria Security Administration. The demonstrators were dispersed and students reassembled in the Polytechnic.

The governor of Alexandria chose courageously to confront students in person inside the Polytechnic to persuade them not to increase the tension. Upon arrival he was seized by students and kept in the guards' room which was under student control. The students cut off outside telephone links. The governor was not finally allowed to leave until he had ordered the release of the four students. When they arrived at the Polytechnic a student meeting was held and the governor was allowed to address it. He had little success in face of the pandemonium which greeted his remarks; but he agreed to meet a delegation of students in his office the same evening.

Before he left the Polytechnic the governor met al-Shater and two of his colleagues. They gave him a handwritten copy of student demands which included a call for the resignation of the minister of the interior, and demands that the officials responsible for the events in al-Mansoura be put on trial, that the students arrested during these events be released, that press censorship be lifted, that the rule of law be established and that the universities be improved.

The proposed meeting with the governor took place and was attended by some twenty students representing the Student Union and the several hundred students who had already started a sit-in in the Polytechnic. The meeting ended in deadlock.

The students taking part in the sit-in strengthened their position by seizing the faculty's roneo printer and began to publish a series of statements, all of which were widely distributed in the city. They declared the Polytechnic the permanent headquarters of the sit-in, and formed a 'committee of observation and exploration' and a 'committee to follow up demands'. The latter was made the responsibility of Dr Esmat Zein-eddin, the 43-year-old associate professor of nuclear physics at the Polytechnic who supported the students and took an active part in their uprising. A four-student committee was formed to broadcast statements through a loudspeaker attached to the faculty fence.

The following day the cabinet, in place of its planned discussion of the housing issue, discussed the students' actions and decided to close the universities. Meanwhile, thousands of students had joined the sit-in. Students from the surrounding schools also began to demonstrate but were dispersed by the police surrounding the Polytechnic.

On Monday 25 November there was a strike in Alexandria and the city witnessed demonstrations on an unprecedented scale, ending in a bloody confrontation with the police.[47] As the casualty figures show, not only students were involved: 16 people were killed (3 students, 12 other inhabitants and a twelve-year-old schoolboy, trampled underfoot by the demonstrators), 167 inhabitants reported to hospital with injuries and 247 police (19 officers and 228 policemen) were injured.[48] There were 462 people arrested, of whom 78 were released because under sixteen years of age and 19 were released for lack of evidence, while the remaining 365 were detained.[49] According to the minister of the interior, who had received a report, with photographs, from the governor, property damaged during the demonstrations included 50 public buses, 270 tram windows, 116 traffic lights, 29 traffic kiosks, 11 shop windows—including one co-op whose entire contents were looted by the demonstrators—the windows of several private and official cars, a number of street lights and the furniture of the Governorate Staff Club which was set on fire.[50]

Those students still inside the Polytechnic, whose request for a visit by a senior official had been refused, ended their sit-in that evening, according to al-Ahram because of 'their sense of guilt and regret over the latest destruction in the city', as described to them by five of their colleagues who had made a tour of inspection at the request of the governor and the teaching staff. Beside this sense of guilt, they allegedly felt 'that they had been deserted by the man-in-the-street who was bewildered at their unwarranted attitude'.[51] The heavy involvement of the non-student inhabitants of the city in the demonstrations does little to confirm the accuracy of this sense of desertion.

The real reasons for the end of the sit-in were practical. They included the lack of food needed at the end of a Ramadan fast day, electricity cuts caused by heavy rains, the pressure brought to bear by students' parents, the fact that the president of the Union withdrew from the sit-in and refused to provide the participants with more food and the governor's warning to students that the Polytechnic would be evacuated by force and his effective preparations for doing so.

At Cairo University, which lacked strong links with the province where the first protests had taken place, a meeting in the Engineering Faculty on 23 November issued a statement and decided to reconvene the following day. In the Faculty of Medicine there was a call for a sit-in. The next day, following the cabinet decision, Cairo University was closed and the students were dispersed before they could gather. The events in Cairo did not reach the scale of those in Alexandria, not because Cairo University lacked a similar core of political activists (it may well have had more activists than Alexandria) but because the news spread slowly and left insufficient time to organize an uprising.

The government's handling of the November uprising is unique and deserves some attention. There was little serious attempt at analysis in the press, especially in contrast to the question of academic freedom which had been discussed at great length in *al-Ahram* the previous month. Only two contributions attempted to do so: Heikal's two-part article entitled 'The Question of Youth'[52] and 'Youth Between Fire and Ice',[53] and Dr al-Otaifi's article entitled 'Questions in Search of an Answer'.[54]

Heikal prefaced the first part of his article with an admission that discussing the question of youth was like 'tampering with dynamite'. He then drew a distinction between the youth movement in general and 'the incomprehensible blunder committed by a few students at al-Mansoura and the convulsive unrest experienced by Alexandria'. He contended that 'the only way to maintain a dialogue with the younger generation is to avoid addressing it in a patronizing manner'. The main thrust of his argument was that 'the Egyptian youth movement, though subject to local conditions and pressures, is nonetheless a part of and an extension of the world youth movement'. He offered little more than variations on this theme and failed to give concrete evidence to support his argument except in so far as the student revolt in Egypt coincided with student turbulence worldwide.

In the second part of his article, Heikal noted that some young men had criticized the views expressed in the first part. He responded merely by emphasizing that the local movement arose out of the international movement:

> If our youth live their time in their world they should be
> affected by what affects others, and that is natural. If they are
> not affected, they are then isolated from their time and their
> world, and that is not natural.

Only when discussing the local issue did he become more specific:

> We may agree that the vast majority of students did not take
> part in the demonstrations. We would be wrong, however, if
> we assume that they stayed away because they are content
> with things around them . . . They are at present faced with a
> number of contradictions:
> a contradiction between their ideals and the failure of reality
> to match them;
> a contradiction between over-enthusiasm during the war of
> 1967 and the extent of the subsequent defeat;
> a contradiction between the pre-war mobilization and the
> post-war dispersal of their energy;
> a contradiction between the supposed continuity of the war
> and the discontinuity of fighting; and
> a contradiction between the aggression of the enemy and
> Egypt's lack of aggression in defence of its national rights.

Although Heikal focused his attention on the external threat facing the country, he implicitly acknowledged the responsibility of the country's political system for part of the dissatisfaction. It took him four years to become more explicit:

> A lot of what the Programme of 30 March contained was
> confronted in practice with a seemingly logical obstacle which
> was in fact half-true and half-false, i.e. the contradiction
> between the necessity of change and the necessity of con-
> tinuity. While Nasser was trying to implement changes, the
> power centres were hindering him.[55]

By contrast, Dr al-Otaifi's article offered a more coherent analysis:

> It is not sufficient in the face of the recent regrettable events to

refer to the importance of quiet and disciplined debate or the necessity of having a steadfast home front. Nor is it sufficient to explain away the events by concluding that some irresponsible malicious elements infiltrated the ranks of students, and be satisfied with such an explanation . . . It is not sufficient either to publish the findings of the prosecution and base our analysis and conclusion on them alone. The prosecution findings can identify those responsible for the events but cannot by their very nature analyse the phenomenon or consider its social and political implications. Neither prosecution nor security measures are the effective answer to such events.

Instead, Dr al-Otaifi posed a number of questions:

What is the role played in the universities by the ASU committees of which students are a part? . . . What is the nature of the discussions in these committees? Were the opinions and trends they revealed conveyed to the upper echelons of the ASU?

What is the role of the Student Union? . . . How can it be made genuinely representative of the broad student base? How can its democratically elected Councils be made the channel through which students freely express themselves?

Is the method of teaching the national curricula effective in generating real awareness amongst students? Or is it a bitter pill swallowed by students in order to pass the examinations?

Are there close links between students and their teachers? Do teachers know the views of their students and discuss things freely with them?

Would it be proper to allow students to be represented with the teachers on the Faculty Councils in order to understand the problems and share the responsibilities?

Dr al-Otaifi went further and posed a challenge which nobody took up:

Should there be a sociological inquiry into the categories of students who took part in the recent events? I am afraid such an inquiry might conclude that some of the students whose class and social interests are identifiable with the socialist transformation are exposed to other influences against which they have no line of defence. To provide them with this line of defence it is not sufficient to say to them, 'You are the sons of the Revolution', or to remind them of what it did for them. Instead, we should know what they are thinking and respond to it . . . For four years I have been listening to the opinions of these young men through my lectures for the Department of Journalism in the Faculty of Arts at Cairo University. From my discussions with them I realized that they have certain questions to which they were not given any answers, either by the ASU committees, the Student Union or their teachers. Although what happened is unjustifiable we should identify the disease before prescribing the remedy.

The regime's legal handling of the November uprising entailed the arrest, at the end of the sit-in at the Polytechnic, of scores of students, a number of teachers from the Polytechnic and other persons believed to have given assistance to those directly involved. After five weeks of interrogation and some three thousand pages of information, the charges against the defendants were announced by the public prosecutor and published in the press on 30 December 1968. The list contained the names of forty-six defendants—forty students (of whom thirty were from Alexandria Polytechnic), three members of the teaching staff of the Polytechnic (an associate professor and two teaching assistants) and three graduates (of whom two were ex-presidents of the Student Union of the Polytechnic). Of the forty student defendants, twelve were Student Union leaders (four of whom were presidents of the Union in four faculties of Alexandria University—Engineering, Medicine, Pharmacology and Commerce). They were charged with five criminal acts: agitation with intent to topple the regime, use of violence against public employees, sabotage of public and private property, looting of assets and goods, and demonstrating without permission. In addition, twenty other students and two more teaching assistants were handed over to the university authorities to be disciplined.

In the cabinet and in the Executive Committee of the ASU the question of punishing student activists was discussed. Despite a call by some members for them to be severely punished, Nasser was careful not to show any sign of retreat from his policy of liberalizing the political system. He argued against the previous practice of internment:

I am against this idea because of the practical problems it would entail. It would lead to the internment of many people. For example, in the Polytechnic of Cairo University there are seven rebellious students. If we were to intern them that would not necessarily keep the peace in the faculty because they have their close circle of supporters and friends. We would therefore have to intern a hundred students at least.[56]

Nasser preferred to refer the matter to the judiciary. But in the end no trial was held, and after about three months of imprisonment the students were released and their ringleaders were sent to serve in the army. Although Nasser did not initially favour the idea of treating the army as a penal institution, this seemed to be a practicable compromise. The arrested university teachers were released in May 1969 after pressure by the teaching staff, while the other graduates remained in prison until 1970.

Nasser's fiercest attack on the student movement was waged instead on the political front. The official press was engaged in a two-week long campaign[57] to undermine whatever measure of support the student movement enjoyed in the country at large. The uprising was presented as subversion by an irresponsible minority of *agents provocateurs* inspired by the counter-revolution and, to an even greater extent, by foreign influences aimed at undermining the stability of the home front in wartime. Under the headline, 'The Hidden Hands behind the Incident of Alexandria', *al-Ahram* of 29 November made special reference to the distribution of student leaflets to the consulates of various foreign countries in Alexandria: 'The distribution of leaflets to foreign embassies is a phenomenon which ended in Egypt a long time ago.' *Al-Ahram* also referred to the important role played in the street violence by an unnamed person.

The culmination of the campaign was the convening on 2 and 3 December of an emergency session of the National Congress of the ASU.[58] Nasser inaugurated the session with a long speech in which he referred to the importance of having a stable home front in the face of the psychological warfare waged by the enemy and the sabotage of the counter-revolution. He recalled the reforms he had instituted since March 1968, including the positive response to all student demands for a freer Student Union. While emphasizing that 'there should be no contradiction between the Revolution and its young men, especially those in the universities', he blamed a minority of them for a blunder which 'would continue to be a shame and a disgrace to everyone who took part in it'.

Nasser seemed concerned about the effect of student disturbances on the image of his regime abroad. He maintained that the country's enemies 'had anticipated the student disturbances as long as several months previously, as manifested in their press'. He quoted comments about the instability of his regime from the London *Observer* of 1 December 1968. 'It is dangerous', he said, 'to allow any sign of weakness in the home front . . . that might give the impression of weakness'.

In a remark intended for his student audience nationwide, Nasser gave an example of how student demonstrations were treated in another part of the world. He read a long column from the *Daily Telegraph* of 29 October 1968 reporting clashes between students and the police in London and concluded that:

> There is no country in the world where demonstrations are allowed to proceed unrestricted. To organize one you must have permission. In England, if you deviate from the agreed course of the demonstration you will be arrested. If you hold a stick you are carrying an offensive weapon. I am reciting this in full in order to clarify that, contrary to some people's belief, disorder is not freedom and it is not the right of everyone to demonstrate and assault the police.

Other government officials supported Nasser's argument in what seemed to be a carefully stage-managed event. The minister of the interior, Shaarawi Goma, who was a target for students, condemned the breach of security and, not surprisingly, defended the police. He emphasized that the police had not entered the Polytechnic to bring a forcible end to the sit-in, but 'in order to prevent further casualties and to counter any possible future accusation that the police had trespassed on the sacred precincts of the university'. The minister of higher education, Dr al-Burullusi, added his voice to the general condemnation and pledged that 'responsible men in the university have undertaken to be firm and resolute and will never allow a disobedient minority to take advantage of the honour of belonging to the university'.[59] Ironically, the person who was the least condemnatory was the minister of education, Dr Helmi Mourad, who had originally inflamed the situation by his educational reforms. Focusing on the reforms, he exclaimed, 'While students in France demand the enhancing of the curricula with subjects related to technology and modern mathematics, in our country we hear voices calling for an increase in the number of examination failures!'

A distinctive report was presented to the Congress by the minister of justice. Although couched in legalistic terms, in substance it was political. The minister gave a detailed account of student disturbances but offered an abrupt report of the police behaviour. He came to the Congress without having held a full investigation of the incidents in which demonstrators had been killed. With regard to the incident in al-Mansoura he failed to give the results of the forensic examination. He did, however, attempt to substantiate the allegation that there were foreign influences behind the uprising by revealing that an Egyptian soldier, Muhammad Mahmoud al-Haddad—recruited to spy for Israel when a prisoner of war—had played an important part in inciting the demonstrators to commit acts of arson and violence during the bloody confrontation of 25 November in Alexandria. The evidence given against al-Haddad was clearly controversial but this revelation provided the papers with sufficient ammunition for their front pages during the following days. Nasser himself took up the thread and declared an amnesty so that all those who had betrayed their country could give themselves up and be pardoned.

Other speakers in the Congress included a number of ASU officials. They added their voices to the condemnation, and in addition either defended or criticized the actions of their own organization's handling of the events. The secretary of the ASU in Alexandria read a statement prepared by the ASU Congress there:

> The people of Alexandria declare that those responsible for inciting the demonstrators are agents of the counter-revolution within the country, and of imperialism and Zionism from outside.
>
> The people of Alexandria condemn the movement of students and others for betraying the sacred cause of the country.
>
> The people of Alexandria call for strict administrative measures to purge from the ranks of students the absurd and irresponsible elements, and to review the position and the

political colour of some members of the teaching staff and to remove those who are opposed to the socialist revolution.

A number of university teachers and administrators who spoke in the Congress generally expressed a hard-line view.[60] However, two university professors—Dr Ahmad al-Sayyid Darwish, the dean of Alexandria's Faculty of Medicine, and Dr Ismail Ghanem, the vice-rector of Ain Shams University—put forward a different point of view, though initially mouthing condemnation. Dr Darwish, in response to his colleagues' repeated condemnation of the deviant 'minority' of students, called for 'a consideration of the position of both the minority and the majority to find out why the latter consented to the leadership of the former'. He defended the students of the Polytechnic: 'I lived with them in Alexandria for three days not noticing any tendency to subversion. No window, lecture theatre or laboratory was ever damaged.' Dr Ghanem attributed the events to 'the general problems the country was facing, and the novelty of student political activism after years of it being banned'. He also referred to the failure of the SYO and the fact that some Union leaders were in effect representatives of the government not of the Union membership, and criticized the teaching of the national curricula as being 'propaganda'.

The two student voices in the Congress were those of Muhammad Farid Hasanain and Abd al-Hamid Hassan. Hasanain delivered an incoherent speech which did not diverge from the main tone of the Congress and failed to offer any distinctive student view. His only concrete proposal was 'to lengthen the academic year to a whole calendar year since a nation at war should waste no time on vacations'. Hassan's speech was more convincing. He cautiously put forward a different view. After condemning the violence as a 'mean conspiracy neatly drawn up to isolate students from the rest of the nation' he turned to address his audience in the following terms:

As a student I do not like to put myself on one side of a dispute and you on the other side. I do not like to see any of you putting yourselves in that position either. There is one cause and you together with your sons the students form one side in it . . . If a historic trial of students is required now, it is more urgent to try ourselves as fathers and leaders of the ASU . . . Where was the ASU in the universities? What has it offered?

Every time a disaster occurs, we hear of it holding conferences and meetings. How long must organized action take place only as a reaction to events? Was the ASU rebuilt only so that one could say the Programme of 30 March had been carried out? Or was it a genuinely necessary step?

The position of the Student Union during the events was referred to by a number of speakers in the Congress. The secretary of the ASU in Alexandria accused the Union of having 'participated in stirring up the disturbances instead of quietening them'. Certainly, many union leaders took an active part in the events. Union leaders represented 30 per cent of those students charged in connection with the disturbances. However, other Union leaders had tried to quell the troubles.[61] Even al-Shater himself seems to have been reluctant to take action at the Alexandria Polytechnic. In a newspaper interview about the November uprising he said, 'The angry students gathered in the morning and called for a protest against what had happened in al-Mansoura. I calmed them down, but under pressure we decided to organize a silent protest march.'[62] Towards the end of the sit-in he was reported to have responded to pressure from the government by withdrawing from the sit-in, and stopping the Union providing meals for the students taking part in it.[63]

In fact, the Union was caught between the drive of its members and pressure from the authorities. The performance of its activists vacillated during the events, and many of them acted on their personal initiative rather than as representatives of an organization. Typical of its performance under the contradictory pull of two poles was a six-point statement by Cairo University Union which Hassan read out in Congress. The statement:

(1) condemned acts of subversion;
(2) declared non-student any student who was in any way associated with its instigators;
(3) declared its faith in the impartiality of the prosecution and called for the results of the investigations to be published;
(4) authorized certain lawyers to represent the arrested students;
(5) proposed a code of conduct for student activities;
(6) presented the transport authorities with a bus to be bought by the Union from its own budget, symbolizing its regret for the damaging of buses during the demonstrations.

The Union, however, became the first victim of the November uprising. A number of speakers in the Congress proposed putting the Union under strict supervision. 'Tutelage is natural, not obnoxious', said Dr Mustafa Abu Zeid Fahmi, then professor of law, and later the socialist public prosecutor. He went further by suggesting that Union activities be restricted to 'welfare matters and sports affairs'. Subsequent articles in the press called for similar restrictions. As Heikal put it, 'The big mistake of the ASU is that it originally tried to transform the youth into a "political instrument" not into a "political force" . . . After February 1968 its approach became the opposite . . . the regime looked like trying to placate the youth not to guide them.'[64] Another journalist maintained, 'The university authorities must have the first and foremost word in all that relates to student affairs . . .students are not greater than the university where they study.'[65] The minister of higher education announced that 'the question of lifting tutelage was premature since students cannot handle their affairs by themselves'.[66] Guidance of the Union committees by teachers was then reinstated in the Union's Constitution as a new article enforced by a Presidential Decree.

The November 1968 uprising represented a step backwards from the point of view of students' freedom of action.[67] At the level of national politics, it did nothing to strengthen the hand of the liberalizers. One of these liberalizers, Dr Mourad, the minister of education, called upon his colleagues in the Congress 'not to be perturbed by what had happened and to continue the serious endeavour to implement the Programme of 30 March'. This call did not meet with much response and it was the hardliners who won the day.

The November 1968 uprising broke out over an educational issue in which the government was indeed more progressive than the students of al-Mansoura. The confrontation with the police in al-Mansoura, where people were killed and the government subsequently failed to make any serious attempt to investigate the incident, enlarged the scope of the uprising. Referring to the strike in Alexandria, the minister of education said; 'It was a protest against the al-Mansoura incident, to which students added other political issues which were unrelated to the original cause.' Students were so angry that they not only protested against the incident itself but also aired their grievances against the political framework which allowed it to take place. As

Mahmoud Hussein put it, 'Once the movement was launched and the confrontation with the forces of repression took place, the contradictions between people's global aspirations and government policy were crystallized; the educational issue subsided and political concerns came to the fore.'[68]

The events of Alexandria were the culmination of this process: it resulted in a political uprising which broadly reiterated the slogans of the preceding uprising in February 1968 without developing a more comprehensive political programme for the student movement. Despite the losses that resulted from it, the November 1968 uprising paved the way for greater polarization of political forces within the movement. The strengthening of the regime's grip on the universities, far from producing the desired result, encouraged the students to wriggle out of the regime's ideological containment and prepared the soil for the emergence of a more militant student movement in the years that followed.

9
The Uprising of 1972–73 [1]

January 1972: Rebellion

President Sadat acceded to the presidency after Nasser's death in September 1970. He disposed of his rivals in power in May 1971 and made 'political freedom' the main theme of his promised 'rectification' of the political system. He also pledged himself to make 1971 a decisive year for resolving the problem of Egypt's occupied territories, an undertaking which created an atmosphere of anticipation in the population at large.

In the universities, the growing current of political activism was beginning to develop into a fully-fledged movement. Students published a multitude of wall-magazines, organized numerous student societies and held frequent conferences. The impact of the wall-magazines was particularly marked.[2] Although they covered a wide variety of political, economic and social issues, their principal focus was on the demand to free the occupied territories and democratize the political system. Students of a variety of political tendencies took part in publishing these magazines, with those from the left making the greatest contribution.[3] The tone of the magazines varied from the serious to the cynical. With the remainder of the press subject to official censorship,[4] they were the only way in which students could express themselves freely. They were in fact, as one student claimed, 'the freest press in Egypt'.[5] Although they contained a great deal of information and analysis, their main impact upon students was to spur them to further political efforts. There can be no doubt that they helped greatly to allay the fears, hesitations and passivity of the student body.

The formation of a variety of societies helped to provide students with a platform for collective activities and discussions. While some were primarily social and cultural gatherings, usually called 'Families' and supervised by a member of the teaching staff, others were overtly political.[6] The most prominent political group was the Society of the Supporters of the Palestinian Revolution (SSPR), established in Cairo's Faculty of Engineering by a group of activists, some of whom had previously visited Palestinian camps and guerrilla groups in Jordan. Although each of these societies contained not more than a few score of students they helped to develop co-operation and to strengthen the morale of the student body and in due course spawned the leaders of the student movement.

A third medium for student activism was provided by the public meetings. These were either spontaneous gatherings or else assemblies held at the invitation of one or other of the student societies or unions. Some of them had a limited audience; others were massive. They usually ended with the issuing of a statement or declaration for publication and distribution. They presented an appearance to the government which was acutely alarming. According to Dr Kamal Abul-Magd:

> Rebellious or revolutionary activism on the part of students started to take a unique form called the 'student conference'. This is a special form of action and not just a gathering of students . . . To arouse people's feelings in the conference a single issue is harped on continuously in a highly charged atmosphere. A histrionic and one-sided presentation of the issue is maintained until one view prevails. This view hardens into mental conviction, which, backed by emotional enthusiasm, is not open to discussion, bargaining, or even the airing of a different view.[7]

Notwithstanding the hostility of Dr Abul-Magd's description, it is a fair reflection of some of the meetings that took place in this period. Others, however, were conducted more democratically and a variety of sometimes complex views were expressed in them. In addition, there were smaller-scale student meetings to which speakers were invited and at which discussions were conducted in the manner of a seminar.

One of the early indications of the students' growing propensity for collective action was a sit-in of students at Cairo's Veterinary Medicine Faculty at the beginning of the 1971/72 academic year over the issue of their post-graduation salaries. An earlier indication of students' growing interest in political affairs was the attempt by a number of leftist candidates to politicize the usually non-political contest for Union seats in the preceding academic year,[8] an attempt repeated at the beginning of the 1971/72 academic year.[9] During the earlier campaign these candidates had demanded the abolition of the University Guard. This was a demand to which Sadat chose to accede, with the result that in the year following the Guard's removal, there was a major student uprising.

This uprising, in January 1972, was sparked off by the president's speech of 13 January in which he excused his failure to keep his promise to make 1971 a decisive year by referring to the outbreak of the Indo-Pakistani war. He claimed that there was no room in the world for two simultaneous major wars, and that Egypt's Soviet ally was too preoccupied to provide adequate aid, especially as a Soviet-backed Egyptian assault on Israeli-occupied territory might well provoke retaliation by the US. This predicament he described as 'the fog' which hampered his actions.[10]

Student reaction to the speech was unenthusiastic. According to the *Guardian*'s correspondent:

> Some of his children certainly did not believe it. The 'fog' speech may have lulled, confused, or even convinced the naive. But for the country's ardent youth, the students and the political activists, it was a red rag to a bull.[11]

The same judgement was voiced by *The Times* correspondent:

> Right from the beginning there were many who felt that setting deadlines, which there could be no certainty of keeping, was a grave error. And even the most ardent supporter of President Sadat will admit that his excuse . . . [for] cancellation of a planned December attack into Sinai was a tactical blunder . . . It carried an anxious and impatient audience beyond toleration point.[12]

'The message of students was that they thought the fog lay in policies'[13] and if 'anyone was creating all the fog it was Sadat himself'.[14]

The uprising began at Cairo Polytechnic, where the active core of the SSPR was located and where publication of wall-magazines was particularly extensive. Only a few days before the president's speech, on the anniversary of the Palestinian revolution, an exhibition had been organized at the Polytechnic and a meeting held in its support. The following day, in response to the publication of the president's speech in the press, spontaneous group discussions were held at the Polytechnic and on the second day a call for a public meeting was accompanied by a spate of wall-magazines and placards commenting on the speech and criticizing the government. Large numbers of students attended the meeting, with SSPR activists playing the leading role. During the night, it turned into a sit-in. Dr Kamal Abul-Magd, the ASU secretary of youth and later the minister of youth,[15] himself attended one of the conference sessions but failed, despite his acknowledged eloquence, to placate the student critics. He evaded some of the more pointed questions by claiming that the only person who knew the answer was the president himself. But the student audience responded by taunting him with being a mere emissary and not a political figure in his own right and he was reduced to leaving the meeting amid a barrage of catcalls.

Developments at the Polytechnic encouraged discussion at other faculties of Cairo University and meetings were held, concluding with the printing and distribution of public resolutions. The production of wall-magazines[16] and placards[17] also increased sharply. The resolutions from meetings in the different faculties again demonstrated the unreadiness of the student body to accept Sadat's justification for his inaction. None of this ended in a sit-in, however, and those who wished to participate in more action accordingly moved to the Polytechnic. At the conference of the Economics Faculty there was a call for a larger inter-university meeting to be held on 20 January. A moderate student suggested that the president himself should be invited to this meeting, since he was 'the only man who can answer the students' questions'. It was at the Economics Faculty that the slogan subsequently adopted as the motto of the movement was first raised.[18]

While these developments were in progress within the university, President Sadat announced changes in his government. These included the appointment of Sayyid Mara'i as secretary-general of the ASU. He had been minister of agriculture under Nasser and was an eloquent veteran politician from a landowning family (and dubbed accordingly by the students 'Feudalist'). Dr Aziz Sidqi, minister of industry under Nasser and a close ally of Sadat in his struggle of the previous year, was made prime minister. He was to head what was called 'the comprehensive confrontation cabinet', comprising mainly technocrats. The cabinet met immediately and approved twelve austerity measures to prepare the country's economy for the battle ahead. The minister of defence announced that the army was now open to student recruits, and that the military training given to students in institutions of higher education was to be intensified. In the meantime, student delegations flocked to the ASU headquarters to convey the declarations of their meetings to its new secretary-general, receiving in return his assurances that the ASU and the government would do their best to consider student demands. [19]

Neither the cabinet's austerity measures nor the assurances by the ASU's new secretary-general deterred the students. The night before the proposed meeting, the Polytechnic sit-in adopted a suggestion that a Higher National Committee of Cairo University Students (HNCCUS) should be formed, with representatives from different faculties of the university. Later the same night a declaration was drafted which summarized student demands and called upon the president to respond to the students' appeal and to attend the meeting. Should the president fail to comply, the students were to organize an inter-university sit-in until he responded.

The declaration was printed early in the morning at the university press and distributed immediately afterwards, when thousands of students flocked to the venue of the proposed conference, the university's main hall. The formation of the HNCCUS was endorsed at the beginning of the meeting and the Economics Faculty representative was nominated as its president. The HNCCUS was enlarged by representation from other faculties, each of which began to form its own National Committee. The conference also set up a small committee to draw up a 'student proclamation' combining the issues and demands raised by the various meetings.

A student delegation was formed to take the proclamation to the president's house with an invitation to come to the university to address the students. They were given no definite reply by his secretariat, and the proposed sit-in began the same day. While several thousand students had attended the meeting during the day, about one thousand took part in the sit-in during the night. The following day another delegation was sent to the president but returned empty-handed. The sit-in went on for four days of lengthy discussions, internal wrangling and the publication of wall-magazines and declarations.[20] A similar sit-in was held at the University of Ain Shams.

The attitude of the official press served to confirm its position as a permanent student bugbear. Before 20 January, although cautious in its reporting of the students' meetings, it had mentioned briefly some of their demands. After this date it concentrated on assisting the government in its efforts to disperse the movement, giving, for example, front-page headlines to the president's having agreed to meet the students of Alexandria and Cairo at the invitation of their unions. *Al-Ahram* also published a front-page picture of the PLO leader Yasser Arafat chatting with a group of students at ASU headquarters.[21] The student proclamation, despite the moderation of its phrasing, was not even mentioned, nor was there any coverage of the events at the two universities of Cairo and Ain Shams or of the embryonic uprising developing at Alexandria University and a number of the higher institutes. The chief editors of major papers wrote articles whose tone varied between cautious criticism of the movement and fierce assaults upon it.[22]

The only exception to this was an article by *al-Ahram*'s Muhammad Sayyid Ahmed, entitled, 'The Question Students are Posing is the Preoccupation of all Patriots'.[23] He saw the students' concern as a right, indeed a duty, and argued that they were fully entitled to be informed of the intricacies of the situation. Another article which did not deal directly with the student movement but upheld one of its main arguments was published in *al-Ahram* on 21 January by Dr Louis Awad under the title, 'A Report on the Egyptian Question'. It contended that although the Egyptian bourgeoisie had the potential to face its Israeli counterpart, it was unwilling to make the same sacrifices.

Having failed to persuade the president to face them, the students agreed to a compromise solution proposed by the minister of the interior (later prime minister) Mamdouh Salem, and conveyed to students by the rector of Cairo Unviersity, Dr Hasan Ismail. The compromise formula included an invitation to a large student delegation to attend parliament to present their demands and end the sit-in. The HNCCUS accepted this proposal and persuaded the meeting itself to adopt it. Three MPs came to the university and were informed of the students' decision. They returned to parliament to prepare to receive the students. The Ministry of the Interior provided a number of coaches to carry the student delegation, which represented all faculties and numbered some two hundred.

The meeting in parliament was chaired by the deputy Speaker, since the Speaker was abroad. The president of the HNCCUS outlined the position of the students and in the ensuing hot debate students were by turns flattered and attacked by MPs. The MP Mahmoud Abu Wafia, a relative of Sadat, dismissed the students' request that their proclamation be published in the press on grounds of 'secrecy' in wartime. The president of the HNCCUS answered:

> There are no real secrets in this world even in military affairs. Publicizing the student movement will not mar the country's image. On the contrary, it might shake the enemy to learn that there is in Egypt a nation willing to fight.[24]

One MP, Dr al-Otaifi, addressed students with particular eloquence:

> Parliament is not a paralysed institution. But we appreciate your lack of confidence in it. Your presence here and your movement at the university, where you have formed the HNCCUS, are proof of the working of democracy. We in parliament do not represent the government. We have our contacts with the country's young men. I personally lecture to them in the university. We have been following your movement, and we know that trying to contain it would give only temporary relief and would not cure the problem in the end. . . Your student proclamation can be published but with some amendments.[25]

An agreement was reached for a number of amendments to be made to the proclamation and it to be published in the press the following day, in return for an end to the sit-in. The delegation returned to the university, leaving two students behind to arrange the amendments in conjunction with Dr al-Otaifi. After hours of bargaining an amended proclamation was agreed for publication. Minutes before the two students left, Dr al-Otaifi hurried up to them and informed them that nothing would be published and that President Sadat himself would hold a meeting with representatives of various 'social forces', including students, to discuss the situation in two days or so.[26] He also informed them that a second Student Union delegation had arrived in parliament and was presenting a quite different view.[27]

The two students returned to their colleagues, to be greeted by screams of hysterical abuse directed against the 'council of hypocrites' (parliament). There was a call to organize a march into the centre of Cairo the following morning.[28] After the atmosphere had calmed down somewhat the HNCCUS held a closed meeting to decide what to do next. In the course of its discussions the members were informed that Dr Kamal Abul-Magd was at the gates of the university and wished to talk to someone in authority. In what seemed a last-minute bid to avert disaster, the minister advised the committee's representative to bring the sit-in to a speedy end. When he was asked whether he could guarantee the safety of those who had taken part in the strikes, he said he would need to ask the minister of the interior about this.

Shortly afterwards, at dawn on 24 January, the minister of the interior gave his answer: he ordered his special forces, the Central Security Forces, to storm the university and arrest the students.[29] The leaders of the sit-in at Cairo University surrendered peacefully, while in Ain Shams University there were initial clashes. In this way the decision which the authoritarian minister of the interior had refused to make in 1968, and which he prided himself on having avoided, was taken by his supposedly liberal successor in 1972.

Although the university authorities decided to close the universities for the mid-term vacation, students flocked into the two universities that same morning to discover that their colleagues had been arrested. Some twenty thousand infuriated students headed towards central Cairo, where the security forces failed to disperse them. This was the first occasion on which President Sadat had had to face street riots, and it set a precedent which he never forgave or forgot.[30]

The demonstrations continued throughout the day, and in the evening a further sit-in took place around the column in the centre of Cairo's Liberation Square.[31] A second Provisional National Committee was formed to organize this. The unusual scene attracted Cairo inhabitants who tried to help the students in whatever way they could, from providing them with food to supplying them with covers and blankets on this cold January night. Later that night the chanting students were warned to disperse by the commander of the Central Security Forces.

Having refused to do so, they were dispersed by force at dawn, only to reassemble in smaller groups which toured the central shopping area in Cairo shouting 'Egypt arise'. The demonstrations continued until midday, with the president holding his meeting only a stone's throw away. Little damage was done by the demonstrations. As *The Times* correspondent wrote from Cairo, 'A number of shop and office windows, including those of the Pan American Airways office, were broken but there were no signs of deliberate attempts to damage property.'[32] On the same day the papers published the Ministry of the Interior's proclamation banning demonstrations, phrased in surprisingly mild, even placatory, terms:

> The security authorities with the guidance of the political leaders had been careful not to interfere, in appreciation of the patriotic motives of students, and because what they call for is accepted by the nation and its leaders.[33]

At the meeting of 25 January Sadat delivered an extremely nervous speech in which he declared that the decision to fight to liberate the occupied lands was final and irrevocable, but that he could not describe the military and political implications of this decision in public. The president justified this discretion by invoking a distinguished precedent:

> Churchill wrote in his memoirs that the cabinet fully authorized him, together with a five-man ministerial committee, to direct the battle reporting only what he chose, when he chose. The same thing happened when Churchill and the war cabinet were given a similar authority . . . The British people stood firm because they reposed their confidence in their country and in its leadership . . . Now look what is happening here. With the battle raging, they want me to give details and tell them what is happening! Did they face Churchill and say 'Come here and account for your actions?'[34]

Despite the diffference in context, the president's analogy had some broad validity. Its crucial weakness, however, was that the students had never demanded detailed information about 'the battle' since their concerns were essentially political. The declaration of the Arts Faculty meeting, for example, had stated categorically that 'students naturally have no wish to know the timing of the battle hour by hour, minute by minute, since the logic of the battle does not permit this'.[35] On the other hand, Sadat, unlike Churchill, was not fighting an actual war. Students, like many others in Egypt, felt uneasy at the demand to remain calm for the sake of a 'battle' which had failed to materialize ever since Nasser raised the famous slogan, 'No voice should be louder than the voice of the battle.'

To justify use of force against students, the president had recourse to further precedents:

> What was the outcome of the student uprising in France in 1968?—the collapse of the French economy . . . In France—and you all know and speak about the freedom of expression in France— what did De Gaulle do when he became certain that the student movement would ruin the French economy and that it was organized by the Zionists and the Americans? He stormed the university. In Egypt there was not a single injury and the police intervened only after seven days.

The president's analysis of the uprising itself, drawn from a security report, was utterly condemnatory. He attacked students for insulting the minister of youth, who was 'a professor worthy of their respect'. He condemned the wall-magazines portraying him personally with a disrespect which went 'beyond all limits'. He accused the student delegation which went to his house of having 'written and signed a piece of paper that could be interpreted as an attempt to breach the country's internal defences and prompt sedition'. He described the National Committee 'as the Committee of National Treason' and presented its activities at the university as an 'occupation' over which 'there could be no bargaining'. The uprising as a whole he portrayed as the work of a 'deviant minority', of some thirty students, carrying out 'a carefully planned operation from outside the university'. To define the political composition of this 'minority', the president employed the well-known terminology of the security services: 'students of special leanings', 'elements of certain colours' and 'remnants of the deposed centres of power'.

To placate the 'majority', Sadat affirmed that 'the student body as a whole was basically healthy'. He promised that they would be given 'more democracy if they rid themselves of their extreme elements'. He also promised 'not to restore the University Guard despite what had happened'. He advised the country's students to concentrate their efforts on their studies, bearing in mind that 'study time should be for studying'. Finally, he reminded them that there were three acknowledged authorities in the country—legislative, executive and judicial. 'Students have no authority', he said.

Sadat received the unqualified support of a number of those present at his speech.[36] The vice-rector of Cairo University[37] gave an absurdly exaggerated account of the resources on which the students had been able to draw:

> The meeting at the university was in fact like an organized government . . . . Certainly the wall-magazines came from a single source. Forty magazines in one day—that cannot be the work of any student or university body . . . The amount of paper needed for their leaflets was not available at the university. What they obtained exceeded what the university had in stock. Where did they get all that from?

Some of the president's audience, however, were more sceptical. They included Professor Ibrahim Gaafar of Cairo Polytechnic, who had followed the movement closely and had more than once proposed compromises to students to avoid confrontation with the government. He said to the president:

> Our sons have certain questions. We as professors do not have the information to answer them. They should have freedom to speak and to criticize in order that they may participate in the country's reconstruction . . . The accusation now is directed at thirty students. I hope we do not put them on trial in the present circumstances.

The President's immediate answer was, 'It is not a question of timing. The ranks of students must be rid of this epidemic.'

Sadat's task was not an easy one. Beyond the ranks of his immediate audience, the student uprising enjoyed a measure of support in the country at large. The student movement had galvanized the Egyptian intelligentsia, and the professional unions came to the support of the uprising on the very day that students demonstrated in Cairo. Four of the most influential of these unions—the teachers, the lawyers, the engineers and the journalists—issued declarations which were published in the press[38] praising students' patriotism and upholding their call for serious preparations for war. While some of these declarations (such as those of the teachers and journalists) attempted a compromise between the positions of the students and the government, others (like that of the lawyers) unequivocally supported the students' demands. All of them, moreover, seized the opportunity to call for the lifting of press censorship. A further declaration by five of the country's top writers[39] was issued, though not published. It urged that, 'If some mistakes or excesses in expression have marred student calls and demands, they should be attributed to the enthusiasm and lack of experience of the young men, not their lack of patriotism.'[40] A meeting was also held between senior officials of the ASU and representatives of the professional unions who reiterated their defence of the student movement, insisting that, 'It is unacceptable to say that there is deviation in the ranks of students . . . The only conceivable deviation is when a student is convicted of being a spy.'[41] In another ASU meeting with a delegation of university teachers there was a call for the release of the arrested students.

In the face of these pressures, and after a sober consideration of the situation, Sadat adopted a less intransigent attitude. There were sharply differing attitudes within the government over the issue of student activism. According to Dr Abul-Magd:

> The members of government, as a whole, did not all have the same attitudes. Some attributed the entire episode to activities of the disbanded Socialist Vanguard. Others insisted that it had all been a carefully organized Communist movement from outside the university. President Sadat held a balanced view which took into consideration both these opinions while at the same time recognizing the objective reasons for unrest.[42]

Dr Abul-Magd himself claimed that he and other colleagues had tried to 'handle the phenomenon politically'.

Much the same attitude was reflected in Heikal's article, 'The Cause of this Generation', in *al-Ahram* of 28 January. After drawing his usual distinction between 'the problem of youth, and the case of thirty or forty students who may have committed their excesses', Heikal admitted that the country's young generation had a deserving cause:

> Despite any mistakes, impatience, or even harm to the

> solidity of the home front . . . When we face youth move-
> ments in our land we must abandon our obsessive fear of
> scandal. We often view social phenomena with a tribal logic,
> forgetting altogether that we are already in the industrial
> age . . . The pressure of public opinion could be of great
> value in showing everyone that there is an impulse and a vocal
> public opinion behind the government.

President Sadat finally decided that the issue must be handled
politically. Like Nasser in 1968, he called a special session of the
National Congress of the ASU, which he inaugurated with a
conciliatory speech:

> The discontent expressed by the Egyptian youth movement
> has echoed the general atmosphere of impatience in the
> country at large. It was only natural that this impatience
> should surface first among the youth . . . I have no wish to
> contain, isolate or crush the youth movement.

Nevertheless he also announced two major decisions: that the
SYO was to be rebuilt and that the arrested students were to be
released and transferred to the university authorities to be dealt
with by the 'Disciplinary Councils'.

On the second day of the session, however, Sadat echoed
Nasser once more by implying that students had been prompted
by an active espionage network of Israeli agents and by the
distribution of leaflets advancing claims just like those of the
students.[43] The reports by Sadat's ministers to the Congress
supported his position. The foreign minister defended UN
Security Council Resolution 242 and the relationship with the
USSR, both of which had aroused misgivings among the
students. The defence minister invited students to go to the front
and see the serious preparations in progress there, and
welcomed visits from students of the Polytechnics to the technical institutions of the army. Unlike his two colleagues, whose
reports had been delivered in closed sessions, the justice minister's statement was broadcast and televised on Sadat's instructions.

Unlike the report by the justice minister in 1968, this statement
was purely political and couched in the terminology of Intelligence reports, referring to the 'minority', the 'extremist
elements' and those of 'special leanings'. It presented the move-

ment as directed from outside the university, with its leaflets printed externally and 'huge' financial subsidies also provided from outside. The minister accused the 'minority' of 'using violence against the true patriots', and charged one of the student leaders with evading his military service and another with having made suspicious trips abroad. He alleged that troops had been sent to the university following reports that students had armed themselves with sticks and implements for a possible confrontation with the security forces. He stressed the damage caused to seven shops in central Cairo by demonstrators and emphasized that 67 policemen had been injured, while ignoring any casualties among the students.

The 224 students (112 from the university sit-in, 61 from the Liberation Square sit-in and 51 from demonstrations) mentioned in the report as having been interrogated were supposed to appear before the Disciplinary Councils of the universities. Thirty of these students were ordered not to enter the university until the Councils had looked into their cases. In the face of student pressure, however, and in view of the relatively moderate attitude of the rectors of Cairo and Ain Shams Universities towards the movement, the university authorities turned a blind eye to the students slipping into their lectures, and in the end no Councils were actually held.

After the release of the detainees in the second half of the academic year, student activism continued but on a lower note. Students' Day on 21 February was greeted with fresh meetings and declarations renewing their earlier demands. They reaffirmed their confidence in the 'leadership of the uprising', condemned the security forces for having trespassed onto the sacred precinct of the university, and refuted some of the allegations levelled in the justice minister's report.[44] They also rejected Sadat's call to concentrate on their studies since any 'contribution to the national cause cannot be related only to high achievement in academic work; it must also relate to people's right to discuss and debate in the execution of their duty to work and rebuild the country'.[45] Their firm opposition to plans to reintroduce the SYO into the university ultimately forced the government to give up its attempt.[46]

The demands of the January 1972 uprising were sweeping, despite an early attempt by a handful of students to confine them to the question of students' military training.[47] Criticism of the government focused on three distinct issues. The first was the

Israeli occupation of Egyptian and other Arab land. Students had little faith in UN Resolution 242 or in the efficacy of attempts to liberate the occupied land by diplomatic means, through international pressure, to which Israel had all too often proved immune on earlier occasions. They believed rather that the land should be recovered by force, in an all-out 'people's war'.

The main brunt of their criticism fell on the regime's chronic indecision in its handling of the issue. As *The Times* correspondent[48] put it:

> Not that the decision must necessarily be war. But they have made clear that they do want a decision and they want it straight . . . Certainly the complaints go deeper than the bland call to take up arms and head for the front.[49]

Even an Israeli analyst reached the same conclusion:

> The students made the issue of confrontation with Israel their main goal not to bring about an immediate war with Israel but to demonstrate that the regime is politically bankrupt.[50]

The very first paragraph of the students' proclamation made clear the depth of their hostility towards the slogans of the regime:

> The students of Cairo University who are now gathering inside its precincts condemn the policy of hiding the truth from the people and insulting their intelligence by the plethora of vacuous calling for 'Continuity', 'Steadfastness', 'Deterrence', 'Attrition', 'Decisiveness', 'Confrontation', 'Triumph', and so on.[51]

Secondly, students turned their attention to the political system as a whole and focused their demands on the question of democracy. Building on the arguments put forward in the student proclamation, another student statement maintained:

> Our conscious people were enraged by the policies themselves not by ambiguous or misleading phrases in an official statement. They knew (and showed in their recent uprising) that the way to play a real role in political life is by partici-

pating in making decisions, not simply by watching them being made.[52]

In this period, however, there was no direct advocacy of a multi-party system, the main emphasis falling rather on the freedom of the press.[53]

The third principal issue was the country's socio-economic structure. In a somewhat unsophisticated way, students saw this issue as linked with the national cause, insisting that in a 'war economy' each social class should make a 'proportional sacrifice' based on its ability to contribute. The most radical proposal in the proclamation was the demand that the highest income should not exceed a multiple of ten times the lowest income. Linkage of the Egyptian economy with imperialist interests through free trade zones was also rejected. In addition, student declarations expressed criticism of the extravagance of the upper echelons of the bureaucracy—extravagance which the new cabinet had itself attempted to restrain by its austerity measures—and rejected the appointment of Sayyid Mara'i as secretary-general of the ASU, on the basis of his 'feudal' background. They also demanded the release of the Helwan workers and the rehabilitation of the trade union committees which had been vilified as a result of their strike in 1971.

The demands of the January 1972 uprising were lengthier than those of either of the uprisings of 1968. On this occasion they denoted an uncompromisingly militant stand. This militancy was the fruit both of years of disappointment and of the efforts of the political activists who had emerged during these years. The government's response to these demands naturally concentrated on the militancy of the activists rather than on the objective situation which had been the underlying cause. Senior members of the government, including Sadat himself, were to simplify the issue of student demands. While the president of the HNCCUS told parliament that there was 'a strategic difference between the government's view and the student view over the national question',[54] Sadat's response was more irritable:

> Their meeting rejected the diplomatic solution (I also rejected it), called for the preparedness on the home front (the papers also said so), asked about the attitude of the Soviets (I have said let us have high-level negotiations with them), required

there to be a war economy (this has been published and it is our policy). There is nothing new in this; it has all been published in the papers long ago.[55]

Dr Abul-Magd was more candid:

The government did not know for once what student demands were. It is a problem we should now emphasize. The government always thought that students had no specific demands. What were presented as 'documents' were prepared in a fiery atmosphere, hastily formulated, and were not given careful consideration by anyone. The only goal they wished to achieve was the creation of more trouble and tension. That is why, frankly, no one in government took these demands seriously.[56]

It is perfectly true that 'running through these demands was a good portion of less-than-realistic assessment'[57] and that 'it took students some time to clarify their programme'.[58] But there was one clear and definite demand: the quest for a solution to the national problem and the democratization of the political system. The government's response showed the extent of its ignorance of and insensitivity to the feelings of a particularly volatile and politically concerned section of the public.

Despite this gap, however, the two sides avoided a complete break. Students were addressing their political programme to the government as much as to other sections of the nation and more than once expressed their confidence in the patriotism of the ruling power.[59] In doing so they showed their lack 'of a clear vision of the economic and social nature, i.e. class nature, of political power and thus confined the student movement to the role of merely "commenting" on the behaviour of this power'.[60]

The leaders of the January 1972 uprising formed the most politically conscious group of activists since the dispersal of the student movement in 1954. Its allegiance was generally to the left, though not exclusively 'Communist' as both the government and the right wing of the student movement claimed. The underground Communist movement in Egypt at the time was still embryonic and in search of a power base within the student movement. As one Communist organization reported:

Our organization put all its energies into this movement. It helped to develop it but was also developed by it. The workers' movement did not receive the same attention at the time. Therefore, some thought we had a petty bourgeois or a student bias.[61]

While the Communist movement provided the uprising with a number of activists who had some ideological influence on the larger core of student activists, the uprising itself formed a turning-point in the development of the Communist movement through the recruits which it brought to Communist organizations.

The influence exerted by Marxist students and the presence of a number of them in the HNCCS antagonized the right wing of the movement, both liberal and fundamentalist, and even to some extent the Nasserite left. The right, sometimes sheltering behind the façade of the Student Union and at other times acting independently, attempted to split the movement at an early stage. During the sit-in in Nasser Hall they assembled a number of students, mainly from the Engineering and Medicine Faculties, and demonstrated vocally against the Communists. They also prepared a more moderate proclamation. Their attempts were unsuccessful because many students saw them simply as government agents.[62] A brave step taken by the left was to press the government on the extent of Soviet support to Egypt,[63] a gesture which misled some into inferring that the leadership of the uprising was Maoist or New Leftist (in a European sense).[64]

The January uprising was organized through independent National Committees, described by Sadat himself as 'Soviets'.[65] These Committees offended the government not only by their evasion of the legal framework of the Student Union, but also by their symbolic echoes of the National Committees of the 1940s while Egypt was still under British occupation.[66] The government's conclusion was that the HNCCUS was the product of a conspiracy organized from beyond the boundaries of the university. The first statement by the HNCCUS claimed explicitly to be a product, and not an instigator, of the uprising itself.[67] This claim was justified. The spontaneous rioting in the streets of Cairo described by the *Guardian*'s David Hirst was matched inside the university:

Today's riots are undoubtedly the fruit of a spontaneous upsurge from below. It all grew separately in various colleges and faculties, but is now beginning to coalesce in a single stream with a single acknowledged leadership.[68]

The HNCCUS was formed, as one of its members put it, 'in an attempt to uphold people's right to organize themselves independently, outside the framework of the paralysed official institutions'.[69] It became the mouthpiece of the uprising and had the support of a number of Student Union leaders despite the general antagonism of the Union towards it. Having seen the extent of its support among students, and in a bid to bring the sit-in to an end, the rector of Cairo University issued a brief statement on 23 January recognizing the HNCCUS as the students' legitimate representative.

The initial formation of the HNCCUS reflected the Student Union's denial of a platform for self-expression to the student body. As Dr Abul-Magd admitted:

There was a growing awareness of Union corruption. This corruption took the form of impotence, misconduct and dependence on certain bodies in the government, to the degree, on many occasions, of executing orders from these bodies. Students felt too that it was not a genuinely representative body because of the low turnout in its elections and there were constant rumours about the mishandling of funds and individual speculation through Union office.[70]

The supplanting of the Union in the leadership of the student movement followed very different trajectories from one university or faculty to another. In Cairo University, as Dr Abul-Magd noted, the real leaders of the student body were:

Totally opposed to the Union . . . Our contact with them was occasional . . . They remained sceptical and unco-operative . . . In Ain Shams University the situation was different. There the Union was in control and most of its leaders were ex-members of the Socialist Vanguard . . . many of them had long-standing links with us through camps and meetings which were organized under pro-Nasser slogans. They believed that there was common ground between us and we had similar attitudes, at least towards some questions . . . Therefore communication continued with them except in periods when they themselves lost control of events.[71]

The Union leaders 'were divided between loyalty to the regime and forced sympathy with those they were supposed to represent'.[72] They tried to pacify the movement before it gathered momentum,[73] but in its course they inundated President Sadat with telegrams affirming their loyalty.[74] In his speech of 25 January the president chose to read out a number of these telegrams, including one from the Union of Cairo Polytechnic. He called it 'a telegram of special significance, because the movement had begun at the Polytechnic'.[75]

Under student pressure following the arrest of some of their colleagues, the Union of Cairo University issued a statement calling for their release and declaring its support for the movement, while at the same time 'recording the democratic steps taken by President Sadat'.[76] The national leadership of the Union faced a similar predicament. As one of its leaders reported:

> In the evening I went to the headquarters of the Union and found the full Council in session discussing what to do. The Ministry of the Interior requested them by phone to go to Liberation Square, talk to demonstrating students and form ringleaders into a committee which would discuss the situation with the government after the demonstrations had been ended. When we arrived at the square we found the confrontations had already started and the security forces were using tear-gas to disperse the demonstrators. We could not do anything and our attitude therefore changed. We issued a joint statement from the Union deploring the intervention of the police and supporting the mass of students.[77]

At the meeting of 25 January Sadat urged the Union to reassert its authority:

> Some sincere Union leaders actually tried to challenge the leadership of the sit-in. I want political activity to be through the elected Union . . . They say you do not represent students but I say you do because you are the elected ones . . . Thirty students were able to turn the tables on you, the legitimate representatives of the student movement.[78]

The Union representatives in the president's audience expressed their eagerness to follow his injunctions. The president of the Union of Ain Shams University boasted that he had already done

so: 'We were able in Ain Shams entirely to control the movement, on its first appearance in the Faculty of Medicine. We were
able to crush the so-called National Committee even in the
Medicine Faculty itself.' Others, however, told him that the
Union had been discredited in student eyes because it was under
government tutelage, but the president showed no intention of
abandoning this tutelage.

In the aftermath of the January uprising the Union continued
to find it hard to assert its authority. Further confrontations took
place at the meeting of Cairo Union, held in al-Mansoura, and at
the Political Camp organized by Ain Shams Union. When the
government responded to student pressure and authorized the
Union to hold its national conference, for the first time in three
years, the conference's deliberations merely underlined the
Union's reluctance to engage in political activity.[79] This gave the
government some short-term satisfaction, but it did nothing to
strengthen the Union's claim to be a genuinely representative
body.

Some early assessments of the student uprising of January
1972 were fairly ludicrous.[80] Others, like that of Professor
Zakariya, were rather more balanced:

> I witnessed the student movement of 1972–73, when student
> awareness reached its peak. In fact, this awareness had come
> as a surprise to many university teachers, myself included.
> The prevailing opinion among us was that these young men,
> brought up in the shadow of educational curricula which
> presented a one-sided picture of history and redolent of the
> cult of personality, would fail to grasp issues which the older
> generation, by virtue of its very different education and the
> discretion and comparison which this permitted, could per-
> ceive clearly. But these students showed sometimes a better
> understanding of the country's problems and their solutions
> than the older generation. This surprising revelation is what I
> remember most about these events, which brought back hope
> to us at a time when we thought that the younger generation
> had become subdued and forced into conformity . . . We all
> felt that whatever we did would remain a small effort com-
> pared to that of these young men, who stood alone in express-
> ing the suffering of a whole nation.[81]

In this way the student movement, which in 1968 had been

essentially a mere reaction to the national defeat, became in 1972 more of a political movement acting on behalf of other social classes and 'inspiring in turn movements of their own.'[82] It acquired a more coherent platform from which to speak its mind and to formulate its political programme. It also forced upon the attention of the regime the political danger of procrastination and vacillation over the burning issue of the occupied territories, restricting its subsequent freedom of manoeuvre in the quest for a diplomatic solution and opening the way for a full-scale military attempt at their recovery. In the meantime it served an early warning upon Sadat's regime that 'democratic' slogans alone would not be sufficient to secure its political future.

The Academic Year 1972–73

The summer of 1972 witnessed the preliminaries to a second wave of turmoil in Egyptian universities. Three forces were being shaped in this period. The first was the leftist core which had led the uprising of the preceding academic year. This consisted of two distinct groups—a harder core of activists who began to develop organizational links with the emerging Marxist organizations in the country, and a more heterogeneous group of independent activists with general leftist and Marxist leanings. The second force was the Nasserite students, especially those at Ain Shams University, who were closing their ranks to play a more active role in the movement by advancing a more radical programme aimed at undermining the position of their Marxist rivals. Third, the right wing of the movement was closing its ranks to counteract the left, on a platform of Islamic fundamentalism.

Student activities that summer clearly indicated the divisions in the student body: a left-dominated seminar was held at Cairo University; a Union conference was held at Ain Shams University and was dominated by the Nasserites; and another gathering at Ain Shams was organized to commemorate Nasser.[83] The national leadership of the Student Union held a government-sponsored political summer camp at Alexandria, aimed at 'filling the political vacuum in the student body through meetings with government officials'.[84] In reality this was an attempt to recruit supporters for the government within the student movement.

In the meantime there were rumours—which could be substantiated only when the academic year had actually got under way—that special squads of students were being prepared to halt the resurgence of student political activism by the use of force, and that many of these squads were under the direct supervision of Muhammad Uthman Ismail, organization secretary of the ASU.[85] Dr Abul-Magd,[86] while not himself accused of adopting such tactics, later admitted that his colleagues had done so: 'Some circles in the government, in the broad sense of the word, resorted to the formation of student groups to attack the activities of student leaders, thus creating the phenomenon of internal violence within the universities.'[87]

The right wing of the movement began to polarize around the nucleus of the Youth of Islam, established in Cairo Polytechnic at the beginning of the academic year 1972–73, as, according to one of its founders, 'a new society to assert the Islamic political presence' and as 'an alternative to the Communist leadership'.[88] It was immediately approached by government officials, offering money and inciting its members to use violence against their leftist rivals,[89] an offer which the society turned down.[90]

Against this background the academic year 1972–73 started with a crescendo of wall-magazines. The subject matter of these magazines, which President Sadat described as 'obscene', was that of the preceding year, but now more defiant towards the government.[91] They were described by the state security prosecutor:

> From a perusal of these wall-magazines it is apparent that they contain an attack on the present regime and its policies, on the practice of socialism in Egypt, on the legitimate constitutional institutions of the state and its various bodies, such as the ASU, the People's Council [parliament], the armed forces, the media and the security forces. They also contain an attack on the foreign policy of the state since it represented what they call a policy of kneeling before the US and of trembling before imperialism. They also attacked the policy of Arab states, alleging that the Egyptian government is allying with the Shaikhs and Sultans against national liberation . . . These wall-magazines also contain a discussion of what they call the question of freedom and democracy, alleging that democracy is absent and that liberties are shackled and there is no free press in the country. Meanwhile, they alleged that the university administration applies repressive measures against the

student movement, and that the legitimate Student Union is an agent of security bodies.[92]

Student meetings—where, according to a prosecution witness, 'questions related to the country's political and social situation, the problem of the Middle East, the liberation of the occupied territories, and democracy were discussed'[93]—started this same year. The first was a right-sponsored gathering in Cairo Polytechnic questioning Sadat's decision to expel from his cabinet and from the army General Sadek, the defence minister, who was renowned for his anti-Soviet stance. The government's attitude towards that meeting was ambivalent. On the one hand it welcomed the resurgence of the right to counter the influence of the left, while on the other hand it felt uneasy about the right's allegation that the minister had been ousted at the behest of the USSR. The left did not give much credence to the allegation and tried to play down the issue: 'We are totally opposed to the manipulation of the student movement by one side against another in the struggle for power.'[94]

The following weeks witnessed an intensive production of wall-magazines dealing with the broader issues of the country's political situation. The government's response was twofold: first, it pressed the university authorities to take harsh measures against the activists, and, second, it unleashed its student squads to use violence against its opponents. This included sabotaging student meetings and conferences, tearing down wall-magazines and beating up activists. The activists did not retaliate lest they damage their political cause.[95] While these methods led many students actively to reject them, they also forced the students to discuss the issue of internal democracy within the universities at the expense of their discussion of national issues. In the meantime, it became somewhat easier for the government to intervene under the pretext of putting an end to violence in the universities.

Events took a serious turn when in early December the vice-dean of Cairo Medicine Faculty, Professor Hassan Hamdi, tore down a number of wall-magazines and required their editors to appear before a Disciplinary Council. On 17 December four students were due to appear before the Council which their lawyers[96] were entitled to attend. The Council, however, was not convened because its members did not turn up in order to avoid a confrontation with students who were occupying the area around the university administrative offices.

The student gathering took the form of an open-air conference which was reconvened almost daily for the remainder of the month. Calling itself the National Democratic Grouping, it organized marches within the university and issued statements and declarations reiterating students' political demands and adding a call for democracy within the university. This included an invitation to students to form an independent Union if the elections for the official Union, which were long overdue, were not announced by the end of the month. To institutionalize its work, the Grouping called for the formation of Committees for the Defence of Democracy in different faculties. A programme was put forward for the Committees to adopt. Of the programme's ten points, five were related to the question of democracy within the university and five to democracy in the country at large.

Following these developments a government-instigated march was organized at Cairo University, where anti-Communist slogans were shouted and a leaflet on the same lines was distributed in massive numbers. In the course of a student meeting at the Cairo Faculty of Law, some government supporters (presumably belonging to the terror squads) used knives to settle the argument with their opponents, injuring three of them. The prosecution never completed its investigation of the incident, and the assailants remained free by virtue of their unacknowledged government backing. The incident helped the left's struggle for democracy within the university, however, and a call was advanced for a comprehensive student conference to be held on the anniversary of the January uprising, at which elections for an independent Union could take place.

To stem the rising tide of unrest, President Sadat, together with his inner cabinet known as the State Security Council, decided to arrest the ringleaders. In a speech given on the evening of 29 December he called for 'the practice of democracy without fear' and at the same time warned that 'as of that night' he would not allow the country's youth to be misled by 'the fanatical right or the adventurist left'. The words 'as of tonight' were in fact a code word to the minister of the interior to carry out the arrests at dawn.[97] Having done so, Sadat provoked further student unrest on a scale reminiscent of that prior to the Revolution.

The activist core which was arrested consisted of a leftist

majority, a few Nasserites and one Islamic fundamentalist, the president of the Youth of Islam. The arrest of the hard core resulted in the emergence of many offshoot groupings among its followers. A wave of protest broke out in five Egyptian universities and in a number of higher institutes. This took the form of mass meetings, sit-ins in various faculties, leaflets and wall-magazines and confrontations with the security forces around the university campuses, which resulted in serious disruption of studies.

A sit-in was organized in the main hall of Cairo University and residents of the university hostel protested by refusing meals. On 3 January there was a confrontation with the police outside the university. At Ain Shams University there was another sit-in and a hunger strike by students gathering in its central hall. Similar actions took place at Alexandria University, especially in its Polytechnic. At the southern University of Assiut, the newest of the universities built by the regime, there emerged a wave of protests unprecedented in its history. At al-Azhar University and at Cairo University's new regional branch in the Delta city of al-Mansoura meetings were held to protest at the arrest of students.

On 4 January the minister of higher education and rectors of the Universities published appeals in the press for students to be calm and concentrate on their studies. These went unheeded and after a week of disturbances the government resorted to its usual practice of bringing forward the date of the mid-year vacation. On 5 January Sadat asked parliament to form a 'Parliamentary Commission of Inquiry into Student Events'. To allow the commission to prepare a report, the vacation was extended for one more week.

The rallying point of student activities was the protest against the arrest of their colleagues. The right wing of the movement tried to confine it to a call for arrested students to be released. The Youth of Islam in Cairo Polytechnic, who could not understand why their leader Issam al-Ghazali had been arrested[98] with the bulk of his leftist rivals, took that attitude. Having tried unsuccessfully to organize a separate sit-in calling for his release,[99] they subsequently resorted to the painful task of closing ranks with their rivals, who tried to put 'the arrest' in its broader political context, and reiterated their national demands.

At the sit-in at Cairo University, students issued a declaration affirming their commitment to the 'proclamation' of January

1972, calling for the formation of Committees for the Defence of Democracy and offering their support to the Palestinian revolution, a stance which the fundamentalists considered a fudging of the issue. The fundamentalists therefore refrained from taking part and organized their own hunger-strike, which was quickly brought to an end by pressure from their teachers. At Ain Shams University the students who took part in the sit-in adopted a clearly militant position, reflecting, as they confessed to the commission, their 'total distrust of all state institutions' and demanding that the patriotism of the regime be judged on the basis of its attitude towards the question of democracy.

The official press did not report the events at the outset and when it began to do so it inevitably gave an adverse impression of what was going on. For example, *al-Ahram* of 3 January reported that 'some foreign radios and papers had capitalized on what a small minority of students had done and tried to use it to serve the enemy's purpose'. It gave the example of an American correspondent who was caught inside Ain Shams University taking photographs of student gatherings. It also accused students of beating up their teachers, a charge which was later upheld by the commission[100] but denied by the teachers themselves.[101]

The report of the eleven-man parliamentary commission, headed by the vice-Speaker, Dr al-Sayyid Ali al-Sayyid, was prepared in the three weeks of the vacation. Confirming student doubts about the impartiality of the commission,[102] its report was utterly condemnatory of the movement. After asserting that the events of that year were an extension of the preceding year's events, the commission followed the official line of ascribing the disturbances to:

> a small minority whose illegitimate activities were ignored by the vast majority of students . . . The commission takes an interest in pointing out that the total number of students in university faculties and higher institutes is two hundred and fifty thousand . . . while the number of students in custody under interrogation is about one hundred.

It quoted from a number of wall-magazine articles to prove that the wall-magazines as a whole were pernicious: 'They included articles violating moral and religious values . . . articles calling for violence and agitation . . . and articles exceedingly frivolous.' It also alleged that some wall-magazines were prepared outside and not inside the university, and remarked that 'the university campuses have become accessible to strangers who do harm to university traditions and to students'. Besides, it hinted at a connection between student activists and Sadat's rivals in the power struggle two years earlier, simply because some of their relatives were caught carrying student leaflets to them in prison.

The commission, however, acknowledged the political factors which had contributed to student unrest:

(1) The defeat of June 1967 . . .
(2) The political vacuum in the universities—the ineffectiveness of the ASU committees and the meagre student representation on them, and the weak link between students and teachers . . .
(3) The Student Union 'totally lost its power and its desired effectiveness. It could not lead and direct the student base because this latter looked at the Union as incapable of fulfilling even the purposes it was created for . . . Some members of its councils went along with views floated by events instead of guiding the base and strengthening its ties with it in order to promote mutual and honourable confidence and to face up to any deviant tendency. The delay in holding the Union elections was an opportunity for agitators to allege that the incumbent union would remain imposed on students.'
(4) The opposing ideological current: 'The stagnant political activity and the absence of the SYO from the university arena created the climate for the emergence of an opposing ideological current represented by the left in all its different shades, which attracted a minority of students by its neat organization . . . '
(5) The presence of ex-activists of the Socialist Vanguard . . .
(6) The absence of a defined information strategy . . .
(7) The long period of military service after graduation . . .

The commission ended its report by suggesting a number of solutions:

(1) Independence of the University (in the sense that 'communication between officials from outside the university

and its students should be through the university administration').

(2) Solving students' social problems (housing, books and welfare).

(3) Political activity in the university should be: through legitimate institutions not outside them; in non-study time; on the premises of the Union; and there should be opportunities for political discussion between teachers and students.

(4) Regulating the wall-magazines: 'Although some opinions favoured the abolition of these magazines . . . the commission is of the opinion that they should be given another chance to play their role in expressing students' views with due heed to religious, spiritual and patriotic values, and under the condition that a certain place should be assigned to them in each faculty, and that anyone who exceeds these limits should be severely punished.'

(5) Applying the University regulations thoroughly.

(6) Maintaining the system of teacher guides.

(7) Restoring the system of Families.

(8) Planning manpower to allow suitable employment for graduates.

(9) Revising the formation of the ASU committees to allow more student representation.

(10) Reforming the organization of the Union.

(11) Expanding regional universities to allow students to study where they live.

(12) Activating the teaching staff.

(13) Giving more attention to the teaching of the National Curricula and setting up a Higher Board for them.

The commission's report was discussed in parliament, where most of the MPs who took part in the debate condemned the activities of the 'deviant minority' and called for it to be severely punished. For one MP the wall-magazines were 'nothing more than sheer frivolity, rudeness and atheism'. For another they carried 'a plot to burn Cairo'. One MP noted that, 'Ninety per cent of students had the opportunity to study because of free education, being therefore more fortunate than the MPs themselves', while another suggested that 'the money spent to educate this corrupt minority at all levels of education should be recovered from their parents'.

Other MPs, however, were prepared to criticize the commission, either partially, like Dr al-Otaifi who asked why the reasons for the delay in holding the Union elections were not specified in its report, or wholly, like Ahmad Taha who considered the report merely administrative and judicial, not political, and criticized its emphasis on the involvement of the left without referring to the right.[103] The most courageous defence of the student movement came from the anti-corruption crusader MP Dr Mahmoud al-Qadi:

We should discuss this matter quietly and calmly, without hysteria or exaggeration . . . The student movement is a universal one, and in Europe, England, Japan and everywhere else they have more of it than we do. It is an ordinary matter and there would be nothing wrong with it even if a student were to ask us to prove the existence of Allah.[104] We would just have to prove it . . . We have fifty-two thousand students in one university; there will always be among them the hundred students referred to in the report. They might have different ideologies, or be deviant, or even insane. But they did exist, do exist and will exist in the future simply because it is a natural phenomenon.

Dr al-Qadi also criticized the decision to close the universities and advised Sadat not to put all his trust in the biased reports on the student movement.

The final touch to the work of the commission and parliament's discussion of its report was provided by Sadat himself in a major speech delivered in parliament on 31 January.[105] He began on a dramatic note by declaring that he was not going to reveal all the facts about the student disturbances but that one day he would uncover the staggering truth. He implicitly criticized the university administration for having failed to punish student activists during the previous year, thereby enabling them to continue their activities—'that should not have happened and should never happen in future', said the president. Answering Dr al-Qadi's criticism, he declared that the decision to close the universities was his own and he claimed to have done this despite advice given to him that this would affect the country's image abroad: 'I do not care for abroad. What I care for is our sons, the students, who do not know or understand what is going on. Only a small minority knew what they were doing.' In fact, the president did care about the country's image abroad.

In the same speech he referred repeatedly to the activities of correspondents of the foreign press:

> Foreign correspondents here are contacting Egyptians, journalists and others. They send telegrams stating that the situation in Egypt is grave. Even foreign broadcasting stations—the radio in London and elsewhere—the papers in Beirut and the Arab world, unfortunately, those with Egyptian correspondents, came out with such stories.

The president summed up his version of the events:

> There was a carefully designed plan which should have come into operation on 1 January (that is why I delivered a speech before you two days earlier). The plan was for a general conference of university students to be held which, on the basis of events of the preceding few months and the earlier summer preparations, would have been dominated by the adventurist left exactly as it was the previous year and with the same agitation . . . The conference was to start under a banner of withdrawing confidence in the Union, a gesture which would have been supported by general student opinion since they had made accusations against the Union. . . Next, the Union would be replaced by the National Democratic Grouping and the Committees for the Defence of Democracy; this would be a new formation! . . . Then there was to be a confrontation with the government to get people on their side. How was this to work? There was to be a clash with the police, and when that happened the people would give them 100 per cent support whatever the rights or wrongs of it . . . The culmination of the plan would be either the establishment of a new party which would totally negate the Alliance of People's Forces or it would end in incidents of killing and bloodshed, which would enable them to prove the bloody nature of the regime. Either way they could not lose.[106]

He denounced both the right and the left, who were unanimous in their opposition to the official political ideology of the Alliance of People's Forces: 'They do not want the 50 per cent representation of workers and peasants—the right says it is pointless, the left says there must be a dictatorship of the proletariat.' He paid particular attention to the left, portraying all its factions as anti-democratic: This is a very strange thing. Not just the adventurist left, but the left as a whole, is against the recti-fication of 15 May which is of special significance to the people. They want the suppression of liberties, the sequestration of property, the special measures and all those things that we abolished . . . ' The president also referred to a third element which took part in student disturbances, namely the ex-members of the Socialist Vanguard who kept up their links with its gaoled leaders, as distinct from 'the good people, who renounced their involvement'.

Sadat concluded his speech with a statement that served as an appeal to the student body as well as a pledge on its behalf:

> The patriotic student base is now required to fulfil its message and to participate positively and committedly in shaping its present and protecting its future. The student base itself will never again allow any section or group to lead it onto a deviant course or to control it while it is unaware. Moreover, the student base will assume a positive role in rebuffing such attempts which aim primarily to undermine the future of youth itself.

In practice, Sadat's appeal fell on deaf ears and his pledge was found to lack the consent even of those on whose behalf it was given.

When the universities reopened a few days later another wave of unrest broke out. Once again, there were many gatherings and confrontations with the police. At a demonstration by Cairo University students, the participants broke through the police cordon and reached al-Giza Square. Students occupied the square and were forcibly evacuated by the police, forty of whom were injured during the operation.[107] Other gatherings and demonstrations took place in the area around Ain Shams Uni-versity and in the city of Assiut.[108]. When the university admin-istration banned wall-magazines, students hung them on trees, laid them on the ground and carried them on their backs. The administration also began to take disciplinary measures against the activists, expelling eleven students from Cairo University. The students were undeterred; even the Union in some faculties[109] started to call for a speedy resolution of the case of the arrested students, the withdrawal of the police cordon and the lifting of restrictions on political activities within the universities. The Union of Cairo Faculty of Economics went so far as to criticize the commission's report and the press reporting of events.

In response, the commission was reconvened to report on the renewed strikes and parliament declared that 'student hearing sessions' would be held in the chamber. In the meantime, state officials appealed to students to end their strikes and prepare for the forthcoming examinations. Conscious of the government's growing isolation, the official press was especially eager to publish telegrams of loyalty to Sadat sent by various student organizations,[110] none of which wielded any significant influence in the student movement.

The government's isolation was enhanced by the catalytic effect of the student uprising on the professional unions and on university teachers, an important segment of the Egyptian intelligentsia. Both before and after the president's speech a number of professional unions issued statements and declarations sympathizing with the student movement and objecting to the official line of incriminating its activists.[111] A group of leading writers, led by the playwright Tawfiq al-Hakim, issued a statement expressing a similar view: 'Being the sensitive part of the nation, the most caring for the future, the young men see before them nothing but a bleak tomorrow.'[112]

The government's attitude towards the unions and the writers who sympathized with the student movement was in line with its attitude towards the student movement itself. It insisted that a deviant minority was deliberately making trouble inside the unions. As Sadat put it:

> In some professional unions there is an adventurist left . . . there is a hateful right . . . It is all hatred, deviation, and rebellion. This must be rectified. Any deviation from the line of the Revolution of 23 July is impermissible.[113]

The ASU Secretariat, headed by the notorious Muhammad Uthman Ismail, decided to expel scores of members[114] who had supported the student movement, either in their writings or through their union activities. The first list of these, totalling about one hundred and twenty, included the names of sixty-four members, some of whom were the country's most prominent writers and journalists. They were banned from writing in the press. The expulsion was counter-productive in that it sustained the argument of the government's opponents, both inside and outside the student movement,[115] that it was adopting an anti-democratic stance.

The impact of the 1972–73 student uprising on the teaching staff at the universities was of paramount importance, since it resulted in a break with the tradition, since 1954, of almost total political silence by university teachers. This by no means resulted in university teachers becoming a politically active group as they had been before the 1952 Revolution. Neither did it lead to the establishment of a common platform from which they could defend their professional interests and express their political views. It merely offered them an opportunity to change the terms of their relationship with the government—instead of having to submit to government pressure[116] and being forced to play a role in suppressing the activities of their students, they discovered that they could also exert pressure on the government. Those teachers who supported the government found themselves in a position to claim a higher price for their services, and those who opposed it felt more confident to express their views against the background of a politically active student movement.

A meeting was held in parliament attended by some three hundred university teachers.[117] Some of those present denounced the movement while others supported it. As far as Dr Kamel Laila of Ain Shams Law Faculty was concerned (he assumed the ministerial portfolio of higher education immediately afterwards), it was 'the work of a tiny incurable minority which was carrying out the instructions of some political organization'. Dr Laila exclaimed, 'Shall we engage in political debate all the year round and let students graduate fluent in politics and ignorant in medicine and engineering?!' Dr Zakariya al-Barri of Cairo Law Faculty (later minister of religious affairs) claimed that the government's handling of the student movement was inhibited because of its relations with the Eastern bloc. Other teachers demanded the return of the University Guard.

On the other hand, there were those who were either obviously sympathetic towards the movement or annoyed by government interference in their work as university teachers and administrators. Dr Ahmad Morsi of Cairo Arts Faculty argued:

Most questions posed by students are the same questions that are being asked outside the university. [He also noted with some incredulity:] Our young men are facing a world where there are many different political currents and we ask them to confine themselves to their studies and not participate in politics unless their teachers and the ASU, which has been absent from the university in the past, assign them a role. We also ask them to conduct their activities through the legitimate channels, which, if they do not satisfy their need to express themselves, they will rebel against.

Dr Ghareeb Fawzi of Cairo Polytechnic defended the students' wall-magazines: 'These magazines had done no harm and should not be feared.' Dr Hassan Fahmi, also of Cairo Polytechnic, noted that 'students' questions were usually answered in very general terms'. The veteran Professor Ibrahim Gaafar referred to the restrictions imposed by the university authorities on the wall-magazines as having been 'counter-productive'. Dr Ali al-Mufti, dean of Ain Shams Medicine Faculty, referred to the irony of his having imposed disciplinary penalties on some of his students and their nevertheless being arrested the same day.

Another meeting between government officials and some two hundred university teachers was held at the ASU headquarters in the presence of its secretary-general. The ideas expressed were similar to those at the meeting in parliament.[118]

An important initiative was taken by a group of university teachers who issued a moderately phrased declaration openly expressing sympathy with the student movement and criticism of the government:[119] 'We should not merely look at the accusations directed at particular students during the recent events but we should look at the student movement as a whole.' It explained the violence of student actions in the following terms, 'It was natural that many students felt that all channels were blocked and when such a feeling prevails it is difficult for the student movement to maintain quiet and orderly behaviour.'

To add to the pressure on Sadat's government, the country's judiciary, renowned for their liberal tradition, tended to take a lenient attitude towards the arrested students and frequently ordered their release on bail, to the embarrassment of the president, who used his constitutional right to object to the judgements, almost as a matter of course, and returned them to court. In most cases the original decisions were upheld at the second hearing, to which the president had no right of objection.[120] By the time the prosecution charges against the students had been published,[121] most of the arrested students had been released by the courts pending trial while others had already done their examinations, and some actually graduated, in prison. It was unusual (though in keeping with the general attitude of the judiciary) that when the core of student activists was finally brought to trial, the chief justice who was to try the first group of defendants opened the proceedings with a speech assuring his defendants of the court's impartiality and even of its patriotism.[122]

In the face of multiple pressures and in view of his plan to order the army to cross the Suez Canal, President Sadat, in his speech on Nasser's anniversary a few days before the October war of 1973, ordered a halt to be put to student trials, released those students still in prison and reinstated the journalists and writers who had previously been expelled from the ASU and from their jobs. This gesture, and the subsequent outbreak of war, eased the tension between students and government, and the students found themselves engaged in the civil defence committees within the universities or in their residential areas.[123]

The October war was followed by a period of calm in the universities. It also left the activists in a state of political perplexity. It took them some time to evaluate its impact, but in spite of some initial scepticism, this was not enough to provoke a large-scale debate at the universities in the period immediately after the war. The war[124] marked the beginning of a new era in the political, economic and social history of Egypt which prompted in the following years the resurgence of student activism in a measure and form responding to the changes that had taken place. When a multi-party system was eventually created, many activists of the 1972–73 student uprising continued to play an active part within the new order.

10
The Political and Social Role of Students

The attempts by the post-1952 regime to secure the support of the country's students through educational reforms and measures of organizational control and indoctrination at first achieved a considerable degree of success. But the government's firm intention to expand educational opportunities, primarily to the benefit of the middle class, created a civilian elite which was eager to express itself and acquire a share in power. The political monopoly of the military elite, and of the partly military and partly technocratic elite which in due course replaced it, however, remained unchallenged for thirteen years from 1954. Only the national defeat in 1967 served to strengthen the position of the civilian elite, making a historic turning-point which transformed the whispering about democracy into a many-stranded political movement and generated a degree of pressure from below which within one decade had transformed the entire political system.

The growing political activism in the ranks of university students was the clearest index of this change. The students, those oft-invoked 'Sons of the Revolution', turned out to be its prodigals. They discovered that their own hopes for a share in political power could not be realized without a direct confrontation with the regime.

Ironically, it was students from the university faculties of engineering, the main product of the expansionist policies of higher education and economic development of the Nasser years, who were in the forefront of student dissidence. It was precisely the students and graduates of these faculties, whom Kerr had described in 1965 as 'having a vested interest in what the regime was accomplishing and were hence its conservative supporters',[1] who became after 1967 its most vocal critics. The activists of the engineering students and the Engineers Union after 1967 proved that their initial support for the regime had been purely conditional. They found themselves denied any opportunity for effective political activity and accused by those in power of being bourgeois enemies of the ideology of the Alliance of People's Forces.[2] In explaining the comparative weight of engineering over law students in the student movement after 1952 an engineering student had claimed that the Co-ordination Bureau had chosen to place the secondary school graduates with the highest marks in the engineering faculties, 'causing them to be prominent in politics as they were prominent in science'.[3] In fact, the active role played by the law students before 1952 and by engineering students afterwards reflected their common concern to reform rather than destroy the political system. Only in the face of cumulative disappointment did these students choose actively to challenge the regime, either through the extra-parliamentary organizations, or, later, in the embryonic opposition movements which had gradually emerged.

Both before and after the Revolution of 1952 students enjoyed high status because of their middle-class origins. It was essentially this middle class which had implemented the economic and social projects of the liberal regime and its successor. Paradoxically, under the liberal regime the middle class, while by no means a ruling class, was allowed a considerable degree of freedom of political expression but under Nasser's regime, which came much closer to representing its class interest, its freedom of political association was sharply restricted by the ruling group.[4]

As an Egyptian scholar has written, 'Whether we like it or not, the sectors that influence decisions are the middle class, the technocrats, the army, the educated elite and university students. These are the sectors that have influence, though they do not necessarily make the decisions.'[5] In addressing the nation, Nasser was mainly seeking to persuade these groups. Despite the importance which he attached to control of the army,[6] he also recognized the importance of retaining control over the students from the early days of the Revolution and to an even greater extent after the defeat of 1967.[7] His successor also understood this need, considering students, together with workers, as tinder which his enemies had only to ignite to destroy the entire regime.[8]

President Sadat's minister of youth likewise explained his

government's sensitivity to student opposition:

> Students were about to create a security problem which would entail the use of force by the government. This was a situation which was bound to endanger the new political climate created after 1971 forming the *raison d'être* of a new era. [He added, more revealingly:] The presence of students in the streets could eventually have posed the threat of their association with other elements, unleashing social problems and capitalizing on people's economic grievances.[9]

Thus the preoccupation of Ismail Sidqi Pasha in 1946 remained very much in the minds of the government of 1972–73. Even under Nasser himself, when the loyalty of the peasant and working-class majority of the population was more secure, students were encouraged to remain within the boundaries of their educational institutions and not to mix with 'others'. In 1968 the Speaker of parliament, later to become President Sadat himself, addressed the turbulent engineering students: 'I have no objection to you expressing your views, but do it inside the university.'[10] In the same period the prominent journalist Heikal also endorsed the advice of the rector of Cairo University to his students:

> Here in the university you can discuss everything and express any opinion. But if you go into the streets you will lose your immunity, since you are no longer in the university precincts, and will not be able to ensure that events turn out as you want them to.[11]

The government's apprehension that students might associate with other social groups was coupled with a fear of the likely effect of their disturbances on the army. The sensitivity of the army's position in the period after 1967 was no longer a result of its earlier role as protector of the political system and recruiting ground for its ruling elite, but rather of the new task assigned to it (indispensable for maintaining the legitimacy of the regime), the liberation of the occupied territories. The fact that recent university graduates formed the backbone of the army in its period of reconstruction and that they might well prove responsive to student agitation was acutely alarming to the government.[12]

Whether the students were allowed to mix with others or not, the political reality of Egyptian student action after 1967 was that it formed a representative movement acting on behalf of a wide range of national forces in the face of territorial dismemberment and humiliating defeat, as well as acting on its own behalf to realize the more characteristically middle-class ambitions for political expression and participation. With the emergence of radical factions within the student movement in the early 1970s it could also claim to represent, to some extent, the ambitions of the country's lower classes, becoming in the eyes of one Egyptian scholar 'a legitimate representative of all classes in society and not merely a student movement'.[13] As he saw it, 'students bore the burden of a historical phase of a different quality . . . They were the organized vanguard, not just the youth of the university.'[14]

The support system given to the student initiatives both by the professional unions and by the intelligentsia at large makes it plain that the movement represented the ambitions of important sectors of the middle class, particularly the demand for the right to engage in independent political activity and the practical opportunity to take the first tentative steps towards the creation of an organized political opposition. In contrast with their position under the liberal regime, students were now creating wholly new political organizations rather than working within ones which were already established. The ideological divisions in the student body between Marxist, Nasserite and Islamic factions were a blueprint for the subsequent principal divisions in the Egyptian political spectrum as a whole.

Although the professionals and the intelligentsia were the prime beneficiaries of student initiatives, other groups also benefited from them. Among these were the working-class activists[15] who had shown a keen interest in student political activities ever since they joined the students in calling for a democratization of the political system in the aftermath of the 1967 defeat. In the early 1970s some of these men were accused of taking a direct part in student activities. Since the 1940s students had regarded the working class as an important political force and had consistently attempted to rally it to their support, despite sporadic attacks by individual students on the 50 per cent share of seats guaranteed to workers and peasants in parliament and other elected bodies. The main motives for these were provided by parliament's inability to restrain the executive, a problem which of course applied to the remainder of its members.

The policy of coercion applied to the student movement was accompanied by specific efforts to placate it. The language employed in these last appeals,[16] emotional and propagandistic, did not differ essentially from that employed before 1952. In this later period, however, students were flattered in an attempt to dampen their disruptive activities, while under the liberal regime they had often been flattered to incite them to act for the benefit of one or another of the contending political factions. In periods of upheaval after 1952 the government had no hesitation in accusing the students of complicity in foreign sabotage or espionage. But it combined these slurs, as its predecessor had done, with attempts to win over the leading figures in the movement by whatever means.

The principal difference between the two regimes was that under the liberal regime the student movement had been a subordinate, if slightly double-edged, instrument of governments and political parties while after 1952 it was seen as a direct threat to the regime as a whole. Under Nasser's doctrinaire rule, student unrest was seen as a threat to the ruling dogma and it did indeed provide a degree of pressure for political change. Under Sadat's somewhat more liberal rule, students continued to be seen as a threat simply because they put to the test the regime's liberal slogans and revealed their limits all too clearly. Even those in positions of power under Nasser and Sadat, like the journalist and statesman Muhammad Hasanain Heikal and the minister Dr Abul-Magd, who both advocated a flexible approach in dealing with student political activities,[17] shared this basic premise despite their tactical disagreements with harder-line colleagues and the greater restraint which they showed in commenting on student actions.

The students' sense of their own power after 1967 was influenced by the fact that they were virtually alone in challenging the existing authorities, and that even these authorities at times chose to praise their efforts. This led to some striking elitist proclamations. The declaration issued in Cairo Polytechnic during the student uprising of February 1968 spoke of 'imposing on the ruling power respect for liberties, and especially respect for you [students] in your capacity as the leading and most fully aware class in this country'.[18] A resolution of a student conference in Alexandria Faculty of Pharmacology during the same uprising called for student recommendations to be channelled 'from the university directly to the presidency'.[19] Students also took pleasure in mocking government officials whenever there was a chance to meet them.

This sense of their political position made the more active students confident of their ability to take the lead in solving the problems of their country. But the movement naturally also included students with a more modest sense of their own prospective contributions. In an article entitled, 'What is the Student Movement?', one student activist wrote in 1972:

> The student movement is not a subjective matter; rather, it is synonymous with national liberation. As long as the nationalist struggle continues, the political situation will remain inflammable and students will act as the spark . . .The student movement does not consist merely of strikes and demonstrations. These are forms of expression to which the movement sometimes resorts. What it is, rather, is a collective will which is permanent and uncrushable . . . The student movement in the short term is a safety valve against the manipulation of national rights and in the long run it is a consciousness that stimulates the whole country to strive towards progress and freedom.[20]

Student attempts at self-crititicism were usually postponed until after graduation. Faced with the comparatively immobile realities of life outside the university confines, some students were inclined to draw a gloomy picture of the movement to which they had been so enthusiastically committed. As one of them put it:

> We students flatter ourselves when we describe what we did as a 'student movement'. We have not as yet drawn the complete picture of the society we want. Student activism will remain impotent until students meet to discuss quietly and objectively the roots of the problem of Egyptian man. [Of the student wall-magazines, of which he was an editor, he wrote:] It is apparent that the articles in the university wall-magazines tended solely to criticize and attack. It never happened that an article praising a decision or an attitude of a government official was published. I even noticed that the ordinary student would not be interested in reading an article

unless its title incited him and satisfied his eagerness to criticize and curse.[21]

It is undoubtedly true that the student movement in Egypt failed
to draw up a complete picture of the kind of society to which it
aspired, a task which in any case should properly have required
the co-operation of a much broader segment of the society. In
this period the student movement acted more on behalf of other
social forces than in conjunction with them. Only when these
forces had developed their own consciousness and organization
could a wider range of possibilities for the future development of
Egyptian society be seriously considered and students act politically in closer concert with political organizations in the country
at large.

A more valid criticism which can be levelled at the student
body, however, concerns the superficiality with which it discussed the country's problems and the consequent callousness of
its propaganda activities. Here, too, students largely reflected
the weakness of the country's political climate as a whole: the
virtual absence of democratic traditions of discussion and
debate; and the profound unwillingness in practice, if not
always in theory, of different ideologies to co-operate, which led
Islamic fundamentalists to consider their Marxist colleagues as
foreign agents and student activism to be unrestrainedly attributed to foreign sabotage and espionage, while the head of state
did not hesitate to employ the rudest words in the Arabic dictionary to denounce the rudeness of his critics amongst the
students and elsewhere.

The demagoguery and intellectual superficiality of many
elements in the student movement, and, even worse, the fact
that many students were in no position even to form an opinion
of what was going on in the country, cannot be viewed in
isolation from the long years of official efforts to contain and
depoliticize the student movement, the educational techniques
which discouraged independent thinking and research,[22] and a
curriculum and official press which were themselves often
crudely propagandist in tone and content.

As a socio-political force, the Egyptian student movement
between 1967 and 1973 acted principally as an element of pressure on the ruling power to restore the country's self-esteem
through the recovery of its lost territories. In this respect at least,
students enjoyed the emotional support of the politically

inactive majority of the nation. The national reconstruction enforced by the defeat of 1967 brought to the fore the need to democratize the political system. Here, too, students played a pioneering role in stimulating other social forces, especially the middle class, of which they naturally formed an integral part. Finally, and perhaps most importantly, the student movement made a crucial contribution to major changes in the political system—changes which took place gradually in the years following the June war of 1967 and more rapidly in the aftermath of the October war of 1973.

Postscript: Student Activism 1974–84

Just as the aftermath of the June 1967 war marked a resurgence of student activism under the regime of the 1952 Revolution, so the aftermath of the October 1973 war heralded a turning point in the course of the student movement. The uprisings of 1972 and 1973 were followed by a brief period of calm, but the momentum of pre-war activism soon returned, and was sustained through most of the ensuing decade.

The liberation of Egyptian and Arab territory occupied by Israel remained the focus of student demands, but the shift in the regime's handling of this issue (culminating in a settlement with Israel) and its more general socio-economic and political tilt toward a liberal economy and a pro-Western international orientation policy kindled militant student activism and aroused sharper ideological divisions among the students.

The number of students rose rapidly, and post-secondary education proliferated throughout the country with the establishment of a number of provincial universities. A few major indicators for the beginning of the academic year 1983/84 give a brief portrait of university education:

* There were about half a million students in institutions of higher education.
* Eighty-six thousand new students were admitted.
* There were 13 universities in all, with a total of 142 faculties.
* The total university budget was E£370 million.
* The investment allocated for higher education in the five-year plan was E£585 million.
* The teaching staff totalled 36,000.
* Between seven and eight thousand new members of teaching staff had been appointed since 1973.
* The average teacher/student ratio was 1:19.
* Some fifty thousand students lived in university hostels.

* About E£2 million was allocated for student loans.[1]

Most of these indicators seem to have doubled over the past ten years. Nevertheless, certain aspects of government education policy were frequently criticized by students and teachers alike. In the early eighties the previous policy of allowing the bulk of secondary-school graduates access to higher education was effectively rolled back, as the government imposed a *de facto* freeze on the number of first-year students. Although the universities approved the admission of eighty-eight thousand students for the academic year 1984/85, the Higher Council for the Universities cut the figure to eighty-one thousand.[2]

Other practices of university education came in for criticism too. An example was the admission of the sons and daughters (and sometimes other relatives) of particular groups, like martyrs and university personnel, for whom the required marks were waived. One citizen actually initiated a court suit on the issue. The position of the teaching staff also became controversial on account of their insufficient numbers, the deteriorating quality of their training and lack of research ability, their living conditions (which force many to leave the country and others to turn to the lucrative business of selling textbooks they have written or giving private tuition to affluent students), and finally, the emergence of 'corrupt' practices such as allowing unworthy students to pass and translating or quoting academic references without citing them.[3]

The students naturally bore the brunt of the scarcity of resources allocated for higher education, and of the consequences of these increasingly prevalent practices as well. The problem of the provision of textbooks became acute. Moreover, the textbook itself remained the foremost source of learning in the university, which itself casts doubts on the quality of education. As one university teacher put it, Egyptian universities could do no more than 'produce a generation capable only of emulation and obedience'.[4] He attributed this to the poor conditions of staff and the techniques of learning through textbooks and formal lectures, as well as to the more general restrictions on independent student activity, whether academic or political. It is scarcely surprising that one survey of a thousand university students showed that 63 per cent of respondents considered higher education to be 'on the verge of collapse'.[5] In another survey 500 students were asked to define the aim of university study: 47% replied that it was 'to obtain a certificate and earn a living'; 20.2% said that it was 'to gain a higher position'; 27.2% said that they were genuinely interested in their course of study.[6] The same survey found that students held university education in low esteem:

12.8% thought that the universities were capable of creating conscious and cultured generations;

11.4% felt that they were capable of educating a responsible generation;

6% thought they were capable of developing political awareness among students;

18.4% said that the universities respond to the real needs of society;

82.8% said that the universities had to be improved.

Egyptian students' lack of initiative in acquiring knowledge, already noticeable at an earlier stage, continued to be evident over the decade 1973–83. In the previously mentioned survey, 94% of respondents said that they read weekly or monthly magazines, but only 38.8% read daily papers and a startlingly low percentage, virtually nil, read party political papers or books other than textbooks. When asked which items they preferred to read, 96.8% said that the sports pages were their favourites and 38% said they read political features (the equivalent figures for radio and television were 52% and 20% respectively). Another survey gave a somewhat more optimistic picture (61% of respondents saying that they enjoyed reading), but still rated political items as among the least preferred (17% read them, as opposed to the 28% who preferred religious items and the 26% who read scientific and cultural articles).[7] For radio and television (which 56% of respondents followed regularly and 36% occasionally), religious items were the favourites of 46%, entertainment was preferred by 35%, and politics by 25%.

The earlier survey (by Gama) also revealed a general mistrust of the media: 50.4% agreed that the media failed to play its role of making people politically aware, 66.6% said that the media paid insufficient attention to the problems of youth, and 93.8% said that their problems and needs were not expressed in the media. In the latter survey (Munir) only 33% said they listened to the official 'Youth Radio'.

For all its ills, however, the present system of university education is defended by its critics when any challenge is raised to two of its principles: equality of opportunity (the marks obtained in secondary-school examinations being the sole criterion for admission) and free tuition. Proposals to establish a fee-based private university sector, for example, have been made by proponents of the liberal economy, who favour a speedy extension of its principles to the educational arena. After a flurry of activity in 1973, they retreated in the face of public pressure. Towards the end of the Sadat era the project of establishing a private university system surfaced once again, but it was soon frozen for a second time. (Almost exactly a year before his assassination, Sadat promised to shelve the proposal for a year.) It has lately been advanced for the third time, now with more support from the establishment and against the background of a wide-ranging debate about the validity of free education in general.

Although the government managed to get away with its restrictions on the numbers admitted to universities, its sponsorship of private higher education is likely to provoke broader resistance, for the social consequences of the move are apparent: it would offer the sons and daughters of the affluent sections of the population further privileges. An indication of this is the ambivalent attitude of many Egyptians toward the country's only existing private (and foreign) university, the American University in Cairo (AUC). Whether or not private university education is introduced in Egypt, the fact remains that the middle classes receive the lion's share of higher education. In the Gama survey of students at the Faculty of Arts of Cairo University, 13.6% were classified as rich, 72.8% as middle class, and 10.6% as poor. Many university students from poor and lower-middle-class backgrounds endure material and financial hardships while studying. Apart from the onerous expenses for materials like textbooks, there is also the acute problem of transport, and the high cost of decent clothing has been a particular problem for female students.

Students are especially worried about their employment prospects after graduation. Although a few have been able to prosper rapidly in the free market (especially by working for foreign firms), the bulk of graduates, even in the prestigious faculties of medicine and engineering, rely on the government to provide them with jobs. The government has continued to do this as a statutory policy, although there have been sporadic threats to abolish it. Many students wait interminably for the government job to come through, and the introduction in 1973 of a statutory public service for those not enrolled in the army continues to arouse the sarcasm of graduates, who consider it no more than a means of keeping them busy while halting any independent search for employment. In the conditions of a free-market economy that offers quick prosperity for the few and little opportunity for the many, emigration from the country has become an increasingly common option. In the *Sabah al-Khair* survey, no less than 77.5% of students expressed willingness to emigrate.

Although these educational and living conditions aroused student grievances and prompted a number of strikes aimed at improving professional status and employment prospects,[8] they were really no more than background to the militant psychology of student activism between 1973 and 1984. Nationalist issues and the country's socio-political system remained the impetus of activism. This more recent activism has not taken the form of 'uprisings' or 'dramatic moments' as in the earlier period, but there has been a steady current of militant activity.

Soon after the October 1973 war, the students began reacting to the regime's tilt towards Washington in its search for a settlement with Israel. Since Sadat's foreign-policy shift was accompanied by a change in economic and political orientation at home, the students were driven to adopt sharper ideological attitudes, as the nationalist issue was mingled with the broader question of the economic and political system. Broadly speaking, five currents emerged on the campuses: the radical left, with its generally Marxist orientation; the Nasserist left; the Islamic fundamentalists, who gathered momentum and later managed to dominate the campuses; the right, who welcomed the regime's new orientation but urged Sadat to go further; and the supporters of the regime, who campaigned under the banner of the 'October triumph' but remained ill-organized because of the government's failure to reconstitute its Socialist Youth Organization in the universities. Within this array of currents, the prime issues remained the government's pro-American foreign policy, the free-market economy, and the multiparty system, while the opposite poles of the ideological spectrum were occupied by the radical left and the Islamic fundamentalists.

The radical left pioneered the opposition to the regime's fresh contacts with Washington just after the October war, organizing, for example, a photographic exhibition of the 'atrocities of American imperialism', presented at the Faculty of Economics and Politics at Cairo University at the beginning of the 1973/74 academic year. But in the euphoria of the war's immediate aftermath, it was difficult to attract support from the masses of students. Only when the initial 'contacts' had grown into a more sweeping pro-Western policy was it possible to recruit larger numbers of students to the leftist cause. Other events such as the arrest of a number of students in Port Said in December 1974 and the Helwan workers demonstrations in central Cairo in 1975 provoked student protests as well. Cairo University became the scene of heightened activism for about three months.

The left also pressed the demand for official recognition of 'the right to independent organization'. The left attained a measure of success when the official Student Union acknowledged this right, and the Club for Progressive Socialist Thought (CPST) was established in 1975. The leftist nucleus of the Society of Supporters of the Palestinian Revolution (SSPR) at Cairo Polytechnic continued to play an active role in this new forum, and provided its president, Ahmad Baha-eddin (Shaaban). The CPST's 'national democratic programme' listed three 'axes': democracy, the nationalist struggle, and the social struggle. The programme included detailed propositions for wide-ranging changes in many institutions, from the educational system to the army. Two of the Club's declarations (one signed jointly with other student societies) indicate the CPST's militant thrust: 'The Class of Millionaires and Not the War Is the Cause of the People's Hunger' and 'No to the Policy of Capitulation and People's Starvation'.

Among the activities of the CPST were celebrations of 21 February as Students' Day and 4 March as Martyrs' Day. Meetings were also held to support the Palestinian revolution, after which Committees for the Support of the Palestinian Revolution and the Lebanese Progressive Forces were established. In November 1976 plans were made for an event known as Week of the University and Society, with the participation of the CPST, the Club for Nasserist Thought (CNT), and the Islamic Society, a fundamentalist grouping. Representatives of the newly formed political parties (except the government party) accepted invitations to attend. When the Islamic Society pulled out, the CPST and CNT held the event jointly, marking a change in the hitherto tense relationship between the Marxist and Nasserist factions and kindling hopes for the emergence of a broader left front.

The Week of the University and Society concluded with a November Proclamation outlining student demands, which included lifting the limitation on the number of legal political parties, abolition of the laws inhibiting political freedom, and an end to the open-door economic policy, as well as to the 'capitulationist' foreign policy and the excessive powers of the president. A march was scheduled to convey these demands to parliament. When the CNT objected to the timing of the march, the CPST went ahead with it alone, on 25 November. Official press reports said that the demonstration began with about two thousand students and finished with no more than two hundred and fifty, thus failing to attract street support. With the exception of the weekly *Rose al-Youssef*, the press was uniformly hostile to the march, and *Rose al-Youssef* even commented that the prime achievement of the demonstration was to have exposed antagonism to the student movement on the part of the press. In the aftermath of the January 1977 food riots, Sadat claimed that the November march, conducted by 'an outcast clique', had been a prelude to the January events. The repression against the left after January 1977 weakened its position and overturned its leadership within the universities. The dominant place was subsequently assumed by the Islamic fundamentalists.

The rise of Islamic fundamentalism in Egyptian universities began in Cairo Polytechnic during the leftist-led uprising of 1972–73. It was here that the Society of the Youth of Islam was formed, and fundamentalism received an early impetus from its collaboration with pro-government circles. The fundamentalist groups were initially tainted by the prominent role played by Muhammad Uthman Ismail, organization secretary of the ruling Arab Socialist Union and later governor of Assiut, who used them to combat the left. A number of the activists of the Islamic Society, however, denied dealing with the government and considered those who did as non-representative of the mainstream Islamic current. The subsequent spread of Islamic fundamentalism and its confrontation with the government indicate that this current was genuine, despite the initial opportunism of some of its components.

From 1974 onwards, the fundamentalists gathered strength on the campuses. By 1976 they had become one of the three principal groupings of the student movement opposing the regime on clear ideological grounds. Between 1977 and 1981 they became the dominant force, managing to win increasing numbers of seats in Student Union elections, which they swept in a landslide in the academic year 1978/79. Their control of the Student Union gave the fundamentalists an opportunity to win even wider influence among the students and also helped them to bolster their own organization and to establish a countrywide communications network in a legal form. One indication of the measure of support they attained is given by the results of a survey of students at Cairo University's Faculty of Arts (conducted by S.I. Gama in 1979). Only 11.2% of respondents agreed that the religious groups were divisive, only 29.4% were against allowing them to exist on campus, and 33.2% felt that their ideas were helpful in developing religious awareness.

Sadat's visit to Israel in 1977 particularly antagonized the fundamentalists, and their control of the Student Union prompted the president to alter its constitution, to recreate the University Guard, and to denounce the fundamentalist current publicly. In addition to forbidding students to enter the universities wearing the distinctive clothing of some of the fundamentalists (and expelling others), the Sadat government also appealed to university teachers, Islamic scholars, and leading figures in the Muslim Brotherhood,[9] urging them to help stem the fundamentalist tide because of the excessive and sometimes violent behaviour of some fundamentalist groups.

The triumph of the Iranian revolution and the shah's reception in Egypt inflamed the situation. About six hundred students, mostly fundamentalists, were arrested in a major clampdown in September 1981, just one month before the assassination of Sadat. The strength of Islamic fundamentalism in Egyptian universities was curbed only with the general curbing of militant fundamentalism through outright repression, reform of the political system, and accommodation between the regime and the Muslim Brotherhood.

While the political programme of the fundamentalists, encapsulated in the utopian proposition of return to true Islam, is a subject of controversy and criticism, their ability to win wide support among students and to use the student movement to upset government plans is beyond doubt. The central obstacle to their creation of a coherent student movement was not so much their views, which many see as 'extreme', but their tactics against those who held different views or did not behave as good Muslims. Acts like forcing the separation of the sexes in lecture halls, breaking up the meetings of their opponents, tearing down their posters, and so on served to display fundamentalist muscle but alienated rising numbers of students, leaving the student movement as a source of disturbance rather than a real influence in national politics. The fact that some fundamentalists realized this and acted more democratically[10] does not alter the general picture or exonerate the fundamentalist current as a whole from responsibility for making a shambles of the universities and for causing the energies of activists to be wasted in internal squabbling.

Activism by all factions, especially the left, was badly affected by the repression that followed the food riots of January 1977. Although the students' direct role in the riots was minor, Sadat considered the students as indirectly responsible for them. In a meeting with the Higher Council for the Universities held shortly after January 1977, Sadat recalled the chronology of student disturbances since 1971 and concluded with a warning: 'I am saying that strikes, sit-ins, disruption of studies, and gangster actions on campuses are forbidden. The incendiary kindling of youth must not be manipulated. It should not happen at the universities . . . The mission of educational institutions is education. Political meetings should never be held in the universities. Those who wish to engage in politics should find a political party outside.'[11]

In a meeting with the national Student Union early in February Sadat reiterated his denunciation of the January riots and castigated the students for calling them 'a popular uprising'.[12] He defended his record as one of 'democracy', 'peace', and 'opening the economy to save the country from bankruptcy'. He rejected the 'dogma' of those who claimed that he had deviated from Nasser's path and refused to be considered a 'rightist'. After attacking the November march and urging his audience to condemn it, he turned to them and asked, 'Should political activity and expression be conducted through rudeness, my sons? . . . You cannot control the auditorium. That is why when I am asked to send a minister there I say "No".' He also asked whether the students would condone what was written in the wall-magazines. Finally, while claiming that democracy would be maintained, Sadat noted that 'democracy can have sharper teeth than any exceptional measures.' He urged the students to conduct politics through 'legitimate channels' (meaning the legal political parties), but contradicted himself by simultaneously calling upon them to be 'national', 'above parties', and 'for all of Egypt and not for one party or current'.

Sadat had support both within the university administration and without. Despite some student protests in February 1977, his strict policy against student activities began to be implemented on many campuses. The first casualty was the student press, especially the wall-magazines. Political meetings suffered too, particularly those to which outside speakers were invited. Worse still, at a later stage, when Islamic fundamentalists took over, the University Guard was returned to the campuses, eight years after its withdrawal, and a new constitution curbed the powers of the Student Union, which now became a faculty-by-faculty grouping whose council was composed of a joint committee of students, teachers, and administrators with students in the minority. All candidates wishing to stand for election to these new unions required security clearances. It is hardly surprising that in these circumstances students lost interest in the Union elections, independent groupings were established by militant activists, and Egyptian students abroad began to set up independent organizations opposed to the regime at home—an unprecedented action.[13]

In the aftermath of Sadat's assassination, the universities were placed under strict control, and the clampdown on fundamentalists effectively rooted Islamic militancy out of the universities. This control of the campuses, which included checking identity cards before allowing entrance to university grounds, affected other student groups as well and entailed a continuation of the previous restrictions on activities and interference in the elections to the Student Union. The elections for the academic year 1982/83, though held under the auspices of a new interior minister, saw classical methods of interference superimposed on the background of widespread lack of interest in these elections. A number of students who were forbidden to contest the elections took their cases to court. Fewer restrictions were imposed for the 1983/84 elections, and some of the candidates of a list calling for a change in the constitution of the Student Union actually won seats. At Ain Shams University a number of candidates who had been denied security clearances were reinstated at the behest of other candidates who collectively withdrew in their favour.

The quiet beginning of the academic year 1983/84 proved to be, as one reporter had speculated, the 'calm before a storm'. Protests erupted at the University of al-Mansoura after a member of the University Guard assaulted an engineering student on 29 December. The enraged students held a six-day strike and sent a delegation to the education minister carrying their demands, which centred on the abolition of the Guard and the repeal of the 1979 constitution of the Student Union. A petition listing the demands was signed by some twelve thousand students. After the meeting with the minister and a promise by the public prosecutor to investigate the assault by the Guard, the students held a mass meeting at which it was decided to conclude the strike, form Committees of Awareness of Student Rights, issue wall-magazines without seeking permission, and withdraw confidence in some Union representatives. A further meeting was planned for 21 February in anticipation of the government's promised response to their demands.

Although the Mansoura strike was not political in the strict sense, and reflected primarily the students' concern about their own rights on campus, it was nonetheless disturbing to the authorities and encouraging for the opposition,[14] since the question of university democracy has always been intertwined with that of democracy in the country at large. The opposition newspaper *al-Ahali* praised the students' self-restraint during the strike, hailing their refusal to resort to violence and their insistence on advancing their claims through legitimate channels. It also described the strike as 'an exclusively student movement of a strictly democratic character without outside incitement from parties'. This, the paper continued, was 'the basis of its solidity as a clear expression of a situation that should be changed' (11 January 1984).

More meetings and marches were held at Cairo University and elsewhere on 21 February and during the following three weeks. Student committees were formed at Alexandria University and a Committee for the Defence of Student Rights was established at Zagazig University. Wall-magazines were put up without permission from the University Guard, and student delegations confronted the rectors of Cairo and Alexandria universities, who, as staunch supporters of the government, were known for their unsympathetic attitude to student demands. Besides the declared support of the opposition parties, the students also received significant backing from an unexpected quarter: the faculty members. The Mansoura Teachers' Club issued an early statement of solidarity, and the General Conference of University Teachers' Clubs adopted resolutions sympathetic to the students' demands. During the same period, an independent slate of candidates defeated the slate of government supporters, led by Rector Hamdi himself, in a fiercely contested election to the board of Cairo University Teachers' Club. In April university teachers organized a symbolic one-day strike calling for reform of the university system.

The government responded by agreeing to study proposals for a new constitution for the Student Union and for reform of the general university regulations. But it remained adamant about the University Guard, refusing to withdraw the force from the campuses, on the unconvincing pretext that the Guard's task was solely to protect university installations against theft and arson. The government even rejected a compromise formula that would have allowed the Guard to remain on campus but placed it under the control of university administrators instead of the Interior Ministry.

The 1983/84 wave of student activism coincided with the run-up to the May 1984 parliamentary elections, held within the framework of a multiparty system and amid deafening democratic sloganeering by the regime. But the fact that university students were still fighting for basic democratic rights was a compelling indication of the limits of Egyptian democracy. The government insisted on holding the elections during examinations, which so alienated the students that many refused to take part in the voting, let alone the campaign. Although the political mechanisms of a liberal system deprived the student movement of its leading position in national politics, making it just one of various forces, the students' ability to confront the regime and to put its liberal politics to the test was not affected. This time the opposition was challenged as much as the government.

The deeper reasons for the alienation of the younger generation, students and non-students alike, lie in the socio-economic policies of the regime, which generate uncertain and often bleak prospects, unsuitable and underpaid employment, scarce and extremely expensive housing, costly marriage in a consumer society, and other difficulties like the miserable transport system, catastrophic in the case of the city of Cairo. The sudden emergence of a class of millionaires (or at least of well-to-do gamblers) produced by the operation of the free-market economy, with its accompanying corruption, adds another de-stabilizing dimension to the picture.

After the assassination of Sadat, a spate of writings on the 'crisis of the youth' appeared in the Egyptian, and more generally the Arab, press. Books on the subject were also published. The official magazine *al-Shabab wa 'Ulum al-Mustaqbal*, published monthly by *al-Ahram*, nonetheless managed to air some youth grievances. The influence of religion on the youth was an especially prominent subject, not surprisingly in view of the wave of Islamic fundamentalism and the assassination of Sadat. Most public discussion acknowledged a general 'crisis of belonging', a massive alienation of the younger generation. The differences lay in the degree of reform said to be required to resolve the problem. While some called for far-reaching changes in the social, political, and economic system, others argued that the involvement of youth in various 'community service' projects would be sufficient. Still others resorted to the classical device of patriotic sloganeering as a means of encouraging youth to identify with society.

Despite the turbulent picture that student activism sometimes offers, the fact remains that most Egyptian youth continue to be apathetic towards the country's politics. The extent of this apathy is perhaps the most telling indication of the measure of reform required if the younger generation is to be incorporated into the mechanisms of political life. In the Gama survey of students at the Cairo Faculty of Arts, the researcher concluded that 'belonging to political parties was more for the sons of the rich and middle classes and less for the sons of the poor and the very poor classes . . . as if participation in political activity has become a luxury or a risk that only those rich youth who have a sense of economic security could afford.'[15] The survey revealed many interesting trends:

81.2% of students surveyed were not on the electoral register;

84.2% were not members of any political parties or organizations;

81.4% said they never attended party activities;

11.6% said they attended such activities, but without joining the parties (while of party members, 80.6% belonged to the ruling National Democratic Party, 11.1% to the Socialist Labour Party, 5.6% to the Progressive National Unionist Party, and 2.7% to the Liberal Party);

54.8% said they had no inclination for political activity;

23.4% said they thought it useless to join a political party;

13.4% thought it would be risky to do so;

45% felt that the political atmosphere in the country was discouraging to democracy and free participation.

Another survey carried out by Alexandria University revealed that 91% of the youth do not participate in political activity, that there is widespread distrust of voting, and that participation of worker and peasant youth in political parties is higher than that of professional youth.[16]

Officials of the ruling party have varying views about the problem of youth participation in politics. Some hold that the low rate of participation is a result of the feeble infrastructure of democracy, others believe it to be the product of a mere 'misunderstanding', and still others appreciate the novelty of the democratic experiment but consider it an excuse for more, rather than fewer, restrictions on political activities. The opposition parties, for their part, blame the problem of apathy on the narrow scope of the democratic experiment, which is marked by limited freedom and the built-in hegemony of the ruling party. But most of the opposition parties would consider a common effort with the ruling party to mobilize young people, perhaps in the form of a national youth organization. It is difficult to imagine the ruling party adopting such a proposal, however, for it has no need of partners in controlling the state.

The scope of Egyptian democracy—a limited experiment in state liberalism in which it is impossible for the government party to be ousted—does not allow for any dramatic change in the level of youth participation. While a less restrictive democracy could undoubtedly improve the situation, more will depend on the direction of the regime's socio-economic policies and the prospects these offer the young generation. The political inclinations of university students will depend both on the measure and direction of socio-economic change and on the regime's flexibility (or lack of it) in responding to demands for democracy in the universities, along with its ability (or inability) to broaden democracy in the political system at large. The Egyptian student movement will preserve a patriotic dimension, with a clear anti-Israeli and anti-American bent. But patriotism may be more broadly defined to include Egypt's economic survival in the modern world. In an IMF-bound Third World, it is safe to predict more vigorous activity by the Egyptian student movement in the coming decade.

Notes

Chapter 1

1. Afaf Lutfi al-Sayyid Marsot, *Egypt's Liberal Experiment, 1922–1936* (University of California Press, 1977), p. 69.

2. Ahmad Baha al-Din, *Days of History*, 2nd edn (Books For All, Cairo, 1959) (in Arabic), p. 139.

3. One solution actively contemplated by Britain was to include Egypt ultimately in the British Empire. Anthony Eden described this as the 'only fundamental solution' in a conversation on 5 June 1936 with Miles Lampson, the British Resident in Egypt. The latter's more prudent approach was to proceed slowly but systematically in an endeavour to bind the material interests of the two countries more tightly together. (Marsot, *Liberal Experiment*, p. 174).

4. Yunnan Labib Rezq, *History of Egyptian Cabinets* (al-Ahram Centre for Political and Strategic Studies, Cairo, 1975) (in Arabic), pp. 474 and 481; Abd al-Azeem Ramadan, *The Development of the Nationalist Movement in Egypt, 1937–1948* (Arab World, Beirut, 1973) (in Arabic), vol. 2, p. 206.

5. Muhammad al-Tabi, *Secrets of Politics and Politicians — Egypt before the Revolution*, new edn (al-Hilal Books, Cairo, 1970) (in Arabic), pp. 350–2. Oddly enough, Mussolini had planned his parade in Alexandria and Cairo down to the menu for his first dinner in Cairo's Mena House Hotel! (Ibid., pp. 368–9).

6. The Board of Consultants of the Egyptian Council of Ministers prepared in 1947 a detailed report entitled 'Egypt's Services to the Allies during the Second World War' to be presented to the UN Security Council which was then discussing the Anglo-Egyptian dispute. The report included: *Politically*: Egypt declared martial law and abrogated its relations with the Axis countries. *Militarily*: Egypt became a strategic base for the Allies, a theatre for manoeuvres and operations and kept the Suez Canal open; the Egyptian army undertook the air defence and coast guard duties beside guarding the stores and the roads for the Allies; Egyptian ships were used for transporting the Allied troops; Egyptian authorities undertook the preparation of charts and surveying works; and residential districts were evacuated for the benefit of the Allies. Moreover, the Allies occupied freely or cheaply vast areas of Egyptian land — 597 feddans of agricultural area, 639 feddans of desert area and 17 million square metres in urban areas; and 1,000 km of railways, 1,735 km of inland routes, and 351 telephone lines were constructed for the benefit of the Allies. *Economically*: The Allies were given priority in the supply of goods and products, from wheat to cement (70 per cent of Egyptian production went to the Allies). Factories built for the benefit of the Allies were given facilitated licences. Egypt remained in the sterling area and

followed the war arrangements. Britain was given customs exemptions between 1939 and 1945 amounting to £62 million. Egypt's losses because of the war, air raids and additional budgetary expenditure amounted to £200 million. (Source: Asem al-Desouki, *Egypt in the Second World War 1939–1945* (Arab Institute for Research and Studies, Cairo, 1976) (in Arabic), pp. 345–50).

7. FO (Foreign Office) 141, 1063 (1945), 'The King's Birthday Parade'.

8. Ibid.

9. Asem al-Desouki, *Big Landowners and their Role in Egyptian Society, 1914–1952* (New Culture House, Cairo, 1975) (in Arabic), p. 248.

10. Lord Lloyd, the British Resident, once said that Fouad used to weep in front of him when reminded of his duties as King. (Al-Tabi, *Politics and Politicians*, pp. 127–8). See also the satirical poem by Beram al-Tunsi:

When there was no other King
The British poised you on the throne
To act like a King
And remain their pawn.

11. King Fouad inherited 800 feddans of agricultural land from his father. At the time of Fouad's death, this had increased to 39,000 feddans. (Mahmoud Zayid, *From Ahmad Urabi to Gamal Abdel-Nasser: Egypt's Modern Nationalist Movement* (United House for Publication, Beirut, 1973) (in Arabic), p. 40).

12. Al-Tabi, *Politics and Politicians*, pp. 96 and 194.

13. Ahmad Mortada al-Maraghi, *Oddities from Farouq's Reign* (al-Nahar House, Beirut, 1976) (in Arabic), pp. 6 and 35–42.

14. Rezq, *Egyptian Cabinets*, pp. 383–527.

15. Muhammad Zaki Abd al-Kader, *The Crisis of the Constitution* (Rose al-Youssef Books, no. 6, Cairo, 1955) (in Arabic), p. 125.

16. Ramadan, *Nationalist Movement*, vol. 1, p. 253.

17. Gamal Saleem, *The Political Police Rules Egypt, 1910–1952* (Cairo House for Arab Culture, Cairo, 1975) (in Arabic), p. 164.

18. Al-Tabi, *Politics and Politicians*, p. 200.

19. FO 141, 951 (1944), 'The Young Egypt Party'.

20. Fouad Sirag al-Din, *Why the New Party?* (al-Shorouk House, Cairo, 1977) (in Arabic), p. 74.

21. Zaheer Masood Quraishi, *Liberal Nationalism in Egypt – Rise and Fall of the Wafd Party* (Kitab Mahal, Delhi, 1967), pp. 83–4.

22. Albert Hourani, *Arabic Thought in the Liberal Age, 1798–1939* (Oxford University Press, London, 1962), p. 221.

23. L. Cantori, 'The Organisational Basis of an Elite Political Party: the Egyptian Wafd', unpublished PhD dissertation, University of Chicago, 1966, pp. 220–1.

24. Marius Deeb, *Party Politics in Egypt: the Wafd and its Rivals, 1919–1939* (Ithaca Press, London, 1979), p. 326.

25. Cited in ibid., p. 250.

26. P. Arminjon, 'L'Expérience constitutionelle de l'Egypte', *Revue de Paris*, no. 3 (1929), p. 597. Cited in George Kirk, 'The Corruption of the Wafd', *Middle Eastern Affairs* (Dec. 1963), p. 300.

27. FO 141, 543 (1936), 'Students: Political Activities and Strikes'; James P. Jankowski, 'The Egyptian Blue Shirts and the Egyptian Wafd, 1935–1938', *Middle Eastern Studies*, vol. VI, no. 1 (Jan. 1970).

28. FO 141, 1007 (1946), 'Political Situation'.

29. M.F. el-Khatib, 'The Working of Parliamentary Institutions in Egypt, 1924–1952', unpublished PhD dissertation, University of Edinburgh, 1954, p.

486, Table 1.

30. Ibid.

31. Quraishi, *Liberal Nationalism*, p. 158.

32. Salah Issa, *The Egyptian Bourgeoisie and the Method of Negotiation*, 2nd edn (National Culture Publications, Cairo, 1980) (in Arabic), p. 120.

33. Al-Desouki, *Egypt in the Second World War*, p. 34.

34. Deeb, *Party Politics*, passim.

35. Makram Ubaid Pasha was the most prominent Copt in the Wafd hierarchy. When he departed, the Wafd — supposedly a secular party — feared that the Copts might become alienated and so chose another Copt to succeed him as minister of finance. (Rezq, *Egyptian Cabinets*), p. 451.

36. Fouad Sirag al-Din Pasha, who came from a wealthy landowning family, was considered the leader of the party's right wing. He joined the Wafd in 1936 and swiftly rose to become secretary-general in 1942. (See: *May*, 1 June 1981; Tariq al-Bishri, *The Political Movement in Egypt, 1945–1952* (Public Agency for Books, Cairo, 1974) (in Arabic), pp. 305–6; Abd al-Kader, *Crisis*, pp. 163–4; FO 141, 1433 (1951), 'Political Situation'; Louis Awad, 'Ideology and Liberalism', *al-Musawwar*, 30 Dec. 1983.)

37. Al-Desouki, *Egypt in the Second World War*, p. 111. Al-Said contends that the confrontation with the Palace reflected the attitude of the Wafd leader Nahhas Pasha rather than that of the party as a whole, Nahhas being more liberal and constitutionalist than the Wafd's other leaders. (Rifat al-Said, *History of Leftist Organizations in Egypt, 1940–1950* (New Culture House, Cairo, 1976), p. 82). Ironically, in a meeting with the King in 1941 Nahhas Pasha swore his loyalty to the King on the Qur'an. (Al-Tabi, *Politics and Politicians*, p. 224).

38. Quraishi, *Liberal Nationalism*, p. 141. When, in 1930, al-Akkad told parliament that the House was ready to crush 'the highest head in the land' in defence of the constitution, the Speaker objected to his language and ordered that the words be struck from the record. When Ahmad Maher, in a conversation with Fathalla Barakat, said that should circumstances force the issue between the Wafd and the King, the Wafd would request the Assembly to depose the King, Barakat placed his hand over Maher's mouth. (Marsot, *Liberal Experiment*, p. 134).

39. Al-Tabi, *Politics and Politicians*, p. 60.

40. Ibid., pp. 261–7. At the beginning of the dispute, Nahhas Pasha accused Makram Ubaid of flattering the King in a 'language of slaves'. When Makram Ubaid argued that Nahhas himself used the same language, the latter replied that he used it in order to obtain the King's approval for certain measures designed for the benefit of the nation!

41. Sirag al-Din was accused, for example, of acceding to the King's wish to have his salary paid in sterling for a whole year and of agreeing to pay for £1 million worth of repairs to the King's private yacht from government funds. (*May*, 1 June 1981).

42. Shuhdi Atiyya al-Shafi, *The Development of the Egyptian Nationalist Movement, 1882–1956*, 1st edn (Egyptian House for Books, Cairo, 1957) (in Arabic), p. 111. Sirag al-Din has recently defended his position during this period by insisting that the proposed laws were the personal initiative of the deputy in question and that they did not have the agreement of the Wafd, and by stressing various examples of the Wafd's resisting the King's wishes — refusing to transfer an officer from his job at the King's request, refusing to invalidate a casino's licence at the King's request, and so on. (Sirag al-Din, *Why the New Party?*, pp. 42–53 and 62–3).

43. Al-Tabi, *Politics and Politicians*, p. 198.

44. Sirag al-Din, *Why the New Party?*, p. 40.

45. Al-Tabi, *Politics and Politicians*, pp. 254–5.

46. Ibid., p. 312.

47. M.S. Agwani, *Communism in the Arab East* (Asia Publishing House, London, 1969), p. 32.

48. Sirag al-Din, *Why the New Party?*, p. 91.

49. The King remained confident of the army's support throughout. His interest in the army was sufficiently keen for him to believe that he 'knew about its officers what their parents did not know'. (Al-Maraghi, *Oddities*, p. 16). He used to visit the Officers' Club and chat with the members. (Muhammad Hussein Heikal, *Memoirs in Egyptian Politics* (Egyptian Press, Cairo, 1953) (in Arabic), vol. II, p. 373).

50. Al-Maraghi, *Oddities*, pp. 159–62. Al-Maraghi approached the US government to obtain arms for his force. The Americans agreed, after withdrawing the precondition that Egypt should enter a formal alliance with them and replacing this with the requirement that the arms not be used against other countries, i.e. Israel.

51. Heikal, *Memoirs*, vol. II, p. 359.

52. Jean-Jacques Waardenburg, *Les Universités dans le Monde Arabe Actuel* (Mouton & Co., La Haye, 1966), vol. 2, p. 81, Table 110.

53. FO 141, 892 (1943), 'Education and Student Employment'.

54. FO 141, 1223 (1947), 'British Propaganda: Effendi Class' (C.W. Austin to Sir Ronald Campbell).

55. See, for example: Anwar Abdel-Malek, *Studies in National Culture*, 1st edn (al-Tali'a House, Beirut, 1967) (in Arabic); Anwar Abdel-Malek, *Arab Thought in the Battle of Renaissance* (al-Adab House, Beirut, 1974) (in Arabic); Abd al-Monem al-Ghazali, 'The Place of 21 February 1946 in History', *al-Tali'a* (Feb. 1966).

56. For information on the activities and leadership of the Partisans of Peace, see FO 141, 1434 (1951), 'Communism: Egypt'.

57. The Free Officers avoided drawing up a definite programme for their movement lest it intensify their differences and disrupt their unity of action. They confined themselves to affirming the general slogans of liberation and change. When they took power on 23 July 1952 they declared an extremely simple six-point programme. (See 'Testimony of Abd al-Latif al-Baghdadi' in Sabri Abul-Magd, 'The Years of Anger that Preceded the Revolution of 23 July 1952', *al-Musawwar*, 5 Nov. 1982.)

Chapter 2

1. The standard of students' command of both Arabic and foreign languages, however, was known to be poor. See Muhammad Hussein Heikal, *Memoirs in Egyptian Politics* (Egyptian Press, Cairo, 1953) (in Arabic), vol. II, p. 105; Malcolm Kerr, 'Egypt' in James S. Coleman (ed.), *Education and Political Development* (Princeton University Press, 1965), p. 180.

2. Joseph Szyliowicz, *Education and Modernisation in the Middle East* (Cornell University Press, 1973), p. 195. Data available for the years 1930–37 show that graduates of one trade school (Alexandria Intermediate School of Commerce) were distributed as follows:

	Government employees	Employed by business sector	Self-employed	Following higher education	Un-employed	Un-defined	Total
No.	201	98	23	4	165	40	531
%	37.7	18.5	4.3	0.6	31.1	7.8	100

Source: Abd al-Hamid Fahmi Matar, *Education and the Unemployed in Egypt* (Muhammad Ali Press, Alexandria, 1939) (in Arabic), p. 250.

3. Computed from data given in Jean-Jacques Waardenburg, *Les Universités dans le Monde Arabe Actuel* (Mouton & Co., La Haye, 1966), vol. 2, p. 80, Table 109.

4. Abu al-Futouh Ahmed Radwan, *Old and New Forces in Egyptian Education* (Teachers College, Columbia University, New York, 1951), pp. 100 and 110.

5. Cited in ibid.

6. Taha Hussein, *The Future of Culture in Egypt* (transl. from Arabic by Sidney Glazer) (American Council of Learned Societies, Washington DC, 1959), pp. 26–7.

7. Hasan al-Banna, *Imam Martyr Hasan al-Banna Speaks to the Youth of the Muslim World*, 1st edn (The Pen House, Damascus and Beirut, 1974) (in Arabic), p. 181.

8. Sayyid Qutb later changed his liberal interpretation of Islam and adopted a comparatively conservative line. He assumed the leadership of the banned Muslim Brotherhood in the 1960s and was executed by Nasser in 1965.

9. Sayyid Qutb, *Critique of the Book 'The Future of Culture in Egypt'* (collected and republished articles) (Saudi House for Publishing, Jeddah, 1969) (in Arabic), p. 36.

10. Ibid., p. 54.

11. Ismail al-Qabbani, *Studies on the Organization of Education in Egypt*, new edn (Egyptian Renaissance Bookshop, Cairo, 1958) (in Arabic), p. 150.

12. Radwan, *Old and New*, pp. 113 and 114.

13. In 1937 there were 7,500 unemployed secondary school-leavers and 3,500 unemployed university graduates. (Afaf Lutfi al-Sayyid Marsot, *Egypt's Liberal Experiment, 1922–1936* (University of California Press, 1977), p. 202).

14. Ibid., p. 118.

15. Radwan, *Old and New*, p. 125.

16. Ibid., pp. 125–6.

17. Kerr, 'Egypt', p. 182.

18. Mirrit Boutros Ghali, *The Policy of Tomorrow* (transl. from Arabic by Ismail R. el Farouqi) (American Council of Learned Societies, Washington DC, 1953), p. 79.

19. Taha Hussein, *Future of Culture*, p. 40.

20. Ibid., pp. 41–2.

21. Ibid., pp. 55–6.

22. Radwan, *Old and New*, p. 128.

23. Cited in ibid., p. 120.

24. Walter Laqueur, *Communism and Nationalism in the Middle East* (Routledge & Kegan Paul, London, 1957), p. 14; Marius Deeb, *Party Politics in Egypt: the Wafd and its Rivals, 1919–1939* (Ithaca Press, London, 1979), p. 151. According to Kerr, 'only those few who attended the better European secondary schools in Egypt are

likely to have come from privileged families'. (Kerr, 'Egypt', p. 179).

25. A.J. Craig, 'Egyptian Students', *Middle East Journal*, vol. VII, no. 3 (1953), p. 295.

26. Ibid., p. 293.

27. The university administration pressed students to pay fees on time. The police were sometimes called to prevent students who had not paid their fees from entering the university precinct. (Louis Awad, *The University and the New Society* (National House for Printing and Publication, Cairo, 1963) (in Arabic), p. 26.)

28. The students of the Faculty of Commerce demanded better employment prospects: first, by the government offering the graduates advances on similar lines to those given to students of the industrial schools; second, by making Arabic the official language in banks and commercial firms; third, by persuading the minister of finance not to reduce the initial salary given to graduates of the commercial schools; and finally, by giving government assistance to companies which offered to employ the greatest number of Egyptians. (Deeb, *Party Politics*, p. 346).

29. FO (Foreign Office) 141, 543 (1936), 'Students: Political Activities and Strikes'.

30. FO 407/219, no. 31 (1936), Lampson to Eden.

31. FO 141, 1223 (1947), 'British Propaganda: Effendi Class'.

32. FO 141, 892 (1943), 'Education and Student Employment'.

33. It used to be remarked of law students that in their first year they aspired to become prime minister, in their second year cabinet members, in their third year judges and by the time of their graduation they aimed simply to find whatever work they could. (Kerr, 'Egypt', p. 184).

34. Ibid., p. 187.

35. Laqueur, *Communism and Nationalism*, p. 15.

36. Groupe d'Etudes de l'Islam, 'L'Egypte Indépendente' (Paris, 1938), p. 80, in Raoul Makarius, *La Jeunesse Intellectuelle d'Egypte au Lendemain de la Deuxième Guerre Mondiale* (Mouton & Co., Paris, 1960), p. 40.

37. See L.J. Coverly, 'The Egyptian Undergraduate and Politics', *Journal of Education*, vol. LXXIX (June 1947), pp. 334–6.

Chapter 3

1. About the earlier period of student activism in Egypt see, for example, Muhammad Abu al-Asaad, *Educational Policy under the British Occupation, 1882–1922* (Arab Renaissance House, Cairo, 1983) (in Arabic), pp. 244–64.

2. Yunnan Labib Rezq, *History of Egyptian Cabinets* (al-Ahram Centre for Political and Strategic Studies, Cairo, 1975) (in Arabic), p. 377.

3. FO (Foreign Office), 407/219, no. 31 (1936), Lampson to Eden.

4. Before he died al-Garrahi wrote a letter with his own blood to the British prime minister. His name has been kept alive in an Egyptian folk song, 'Abd al-Hakam Kept the Flag Flying'. (See Salah Issa, 'Injustices are to be Avenged', *al-Ahali*, 6 Oct. 1982.) Another student victim, Ali Taha Affifi who died on 15 November, has also been immortalized: he is one of the principal characters in the novel *Cairo 30*, written by the famous Egyptian novelist Naguib Mahfouz and subsequently made into a film. See also Salah Issa, 'Abd al-Hakam Kept the Flag Flying', *al-Shabab*, no. 1, 5 Dec. 1972.

5. FO 407/219, no. 31 (1936).

6. Abd al-Rahman al-Rafi, *In the Aftermath of the Egyptian Revolution* (Egyptian Renaissance Bookshop, Cairo, 1949 and 1951) (in Arabic), vol. II, p. 202.

7. Muhammad Hussein Heikal, *Memoirs in Egyptian Politics* (Egyptian Renaissance Bookshop, Cairo, 1951) (in Arabic), vol. I, p. 384.

8. Ibid., p. 385.

9. FO 407/219, no. 31 (1936).

10. FO 141, 618 (1935), 'Students: Political Activities and Strikes'.

11. At the time, Ahmad Hussein of Young Egypt considered the student uprising 'a triumph for the spirit of Young Egypt'. (See Ahmad Hussein, *My Faith* (al-Raghaeb Press, Cairo, 1936) (in Arabic), p. 234.) More recently, he has referred to it as 'the immediate result of Young Egypt's struggle' since many of the uprising's leaders, and indeed its first martyrs, were members of his organization. (Ahmad Hussein, 'Memoirs', *al-Shaab*, 18 Aug. 1981).

12. On the spread of semi-Fascist organizations among the students, Bashatli Effendi noted, 'Students in Egypt are great newspaper readers and there is no doubt that Italian propaganda in papers like *al-Ahram* and *al-Balagh* has had its effect on them, encouraging them to form groups on Fascist lines.'

13. Marius Deeb, *Party Politics in Egypt: the Wafd and its Rivals, 1919–1939* (Ithaca Press, London, 1979), pp. 63–4.

14. Salah Issa, *Stories from Egypt* (Arab World, Beirut, 1973) (in Arabic), p. 271.

15. The anti-Wafdist students claimed to have the support of 70 per cent of university students in 1936. Sir Miles Lampson's opinion was that '30 per cent would probably be nearer the mark'. (FO 141, 543 (1936), 'Students: Political Activities and Strikes').

16. FO 407/219, no. 31 (1936).

17. Abd al-Azeem Ramadan, *The Development of the Nationalist Movement in Egypt, 1937 to 1948* (Arab World, Beirut, 1973) (in Arabic), vol. I, p. 172. Kelly wrote to Eden, 'The Wafd is now in fact feeling the other edge of the weapon which it itself forged. The students, who for so long have been sedulously incited by the Wafd to oppose authority, appear to be running true to form and to be preparing to oppose the Wafd itself now that it is in power.' (FO 407/221, Part CXXII, no. 107 (1937), Lampson to Eden).

18. Ramadan, *Nationalist Movement*, p. 98. The first squadron was formed by the medical student Muhammad Bilal from among his faculty colleagues.

19. FO 141, 543 (1936).

20. Ibid.

21. Author's interview with Abd al-Monem al-Ghazali (April 1979). Al-Ghazali testified that every kind of inducement, including money and violence, was used to impose Yassin Sirag al-Din as leader of the Wafdist students instead of Hafiz Shieha. The latter had the backing of the actual leader of the Wafdist students, Mustafa Musa, who later became the official leader for many years. Musa was the most famous student leader at the time and was elected to parliament while still a student.

22. Interview with al-Ghazali.

23. FO 141, 1077 (1946), 'Political Situation'.

24. Author's interview with Muhammad Farid Abd al-Khaleq (Aug. 1981). See also Hasan al-Banna, *Imam Martyr Hasan al-Banna Speaks to the Youth of the Muslim World*, 1st edn (The Pen House, Damascus and Beirut, 1974) (in Arabic), *passim*.

25. Zakariya Suleiman Bayoumi, *The Muslim Brotherhood and Islamic Societies*

in Egyptian Political Life (Wahba Bookshop, Cairo, 1979) (in Arabic), p. 309.

26. FO 141, 1077 (1946).

27. Bayoumi, *Muslim Brotherhood*, p. 271; Jean and Simonne Lacouture, *Egypt in Transition* (Methuen, London, 1958), p. 247. I.M. Husaini attributes their comparatively limited success at al-Azhar to their failure to treat the existing spiritual crisis and to address the educated Sunni mind. (Ishak Musa Husaini, *The Moslem Brethren: the Greatest of Modern Islamic Movements* (Khayat's College Book Cooperative, Beirut, 1956), p. 106).

28. Author's interview with Dr Hassan Hathout (Sept. 1979). In a meeting with a group of university students in 1937, al-Banna reminisced, 'I recall that blessed moment when I sat down with six of your colleagues four years ago to discuss the duty of university students towards Islam. By the end of the second year they were forty . . . By the end of the third year they were three hundred . . . And now, in your fourth year, you increase and never decrease.' (Hasan al-Banna, *Memoirs of the Advocate and Advocacy*, 3rd edn (Islamic Bureau, Beirut, 1974) (in Arabic), pp. 229–30).

29. Husaini, *Moslem Brethren*, pp. 106–7.

30. According to Abd al-Khaleq, the Muslim Brotherhood's involvement in the political struggles in the immediate post-war years far exceeded their initial intentions. They had planned to wait until they had succeeded in creating a new generation brought up on the teachings of Islam. They were forced into this increasing involvement by the intensification of the nationalist struggle. (Interview).

31. Interview with Dr Hathout.

32. Salah Issa's estimate (based on Ahmad Hussein's defence of the Brotherhood before the court after it was banned by the al-Nokrashi government in 1948). (See *al-Hadaf*, 23 June 1977).

33. Abd al-Azeem Ramadan's estimate (based on Scouting Activities Report prepared by A. Abdeen, vice-leader of the Brotherhood's Rover Scouts). See Ramadan, *Nationalist Movement*, vol. I, p. 127.

34. Rifat al-Said, *Hasan al-Banna: When, How and Why?* (Madbouli Bookshop, Cairo, 1977) (in Arabic), p. 144.

35. Lacouture, *Egypt in Transition*, p. 247. A British scholar studying at Cairo noted that this claim was 'an absurd exaggeration'. (A.J. Craig, 'Egyptian Students', *Middle East Journal*, vol. VII, no. 3 (1953), p. 294).

36. Husaini, *Moslem Brethren*, p. 66. According to the *New York Times* of 1 Dec. 1951, the result was:

11/13 for the Faculty of Science;
9/12 for the Faculty of Commerce;
with the additional result:
8/15 for the Faculty of Veterinary Science.

37. Interviews with Dr Hathout and Abd al-Khaleq.

38. According to a British Embassy file, 'Agent said that Mumin was a man over 30 years of age and only qualified as a student on the grounds that though he was a graduate in engineering he was at present a student member of the journalistic section of the university.' (FO 141, 1187 (1947), 'Political Situation'). Mumin was expelled from the Brotherhood at the end of 1951 for demanding its democratization. (A. Ramadan, *al-Hadaf*, 9 Dec. 1980).

39. See his book, *The Voice of Egypt* (Arab Book Press, Cairo, 1951) (in Arabic).

40. Rifat al-Said, *History of Leftist Organizations in Egypt, 1940–1950* (New Culture House, Cairo, 1976) (in Arabic), p. 265. A British Embassy report alleged that Communism was spreading fast in the Faculty of Commerce because a

Marxist professor there was secretly indoctrinating students. It also alleged that the female students at the Faculty of Arts were particularly inclined towards Communism. See Mahmoud Mitwalli, *Egypt and the Communist Movement during the Second World War* (Arab Attitude House, Cairo, 1979) (in Arabic), p. 50.

41. Al-Said, *Leftist Organizations*, p. 322; author's interviews with Saad Zahran (Sept. 1981) and al-Ghazali. Iskra also had a number of female students, among whom were Fatima Zaki, Suraya Adham and Latifa al-Zayat.

42. Al-Said, *Leftist Organizations*, p. 348–50. When the University of Khartoum was closed in 1946 many Sudanese students travelled to Egypt. Among them were some who later became leading figures in the Sudanese Communist Party, including its secretary-general Abd al-Khalig Mahgoub. (See Salah El Din El Zein El Tayeb, *The Students' Movement in the Sudan, 1940–1970* (Khartoum University Press, 1971), pp. 40–1).

43. Author's interview with Dr Ahmad Shawqi al-Fangari (June 1978). A British Embassy report noted, ' . . . the Egyptian government were now really scared about the threat of Communism in the University'. (FO 141, 1434 (1951), 'Communism: Egypt').

44. Saad Zahran (interview) reported that he had stepped down from the post of representative of the leftist group in the committee which organized the strikes of February 1946 in order to let his female colleague Latifa al-Zayat take his place, as a symbolic encouragement of female students to take part in political activities.

45. Al-Said, *Leftist Organizations*, p. 376. The New Dawn group, which did not join the unified grouping of 1947, came under pressure from its own students in 1951 to alter its stance towards unity. Its leadership responded harshly by dissolving the organization's student section. (Interview with Sadek Saad in ibid.).

46. Interview with Mustafa Taiba in Abd al-Azeem Ramadan, *Nasser and the Crisis of March 1954* (Rose al-Youssef Press, Cairo, 1976) (in Arabic), p. 371.

47. Walter Laqueur, *Communism and Nationalism in the Middle East* (Routledge & Kegan Paul, London, 1957), p. 55. In 1948 HADITU called for a demonstration to commemorate the 21 February 1946 student uprising: only sixty students turned up. (Al-Said, *Leftist Organizations*, p. 416).

48. Notable among these was Khalid Mohieddin who studied at Cairo University's Faculty of Commerce while he was an officr. (See Ahmad Hamroush, *The Story of the Revolution of 23 July* (Arab Institute for Research and Publishing, Beirut, 1976) (in Arabic), p. 144).

49. Ahmad Hussein, 'Memoirs', *al-Shaab*, 23 June 1981.

50. FO 141, 498 (1934), 'Students: Political Activities and Strikes'. Young Wafdists labelled Ahmad Hussein 'the robber of the piastre'. (Ahmad Hussein, 'Memoirs', *al-Shaab*, 28 July 1981).

51. FO 141, 498 (1934).

52. Ahmad Hussein, *My Faith*, p. 234.

53. Later vice-president of Egypt.

54. Shukri was reported to have been seriously injured in the demonstrations and to have narrowly escaped death. He was therefore called 'the living martyr'. In 1950 he became the first Socialist MP; he is now chairman of the Socialist Labour Party and an MP.

55. FO 141, 618 (1935). As an indication of the strength of Young Egypt among students, the report added, 'Saladin Zohni, a student of the school of law and right hand of Me. Sanhouri, is reported to have secretly approached Mohamed Subeih of the Young Egypt Society on the subject of the Wafdist Student Committees joining the Society.'

56. FO 141, 951 (1945), 'The Young Egypt Party'.

57. FO 141, 1005 (1945), 'Political Situation'.

58. Cited in Rifat al-Said, *Ahmad Hussein: Words and Attitudes* (al-Arabi for Publication, Cairo, 1979) (in Arabic), p. 20.

59. Ibid., p. 201. These included such slogans as 'Young men of 1945, be like the young men of 1919.'

60. In the words of one of its activists, the Nationalist party was 'an ideally militant and straightforward party which held to its principles . . . It was a genuine school for patriotic upbringing rather than political training.' (Author's interview with Maher Muhammad Ali (Sept. 1981)).

61. Among the female activists of the Nationalist party were Aisha Rateb and Leila Takla (both of whom became ministers in President Sadat's cabinet), Aziza Heikal, Nemat Badr and Nahed Rushdi.

62. According to Maher Muhammed Ali (interview), the Nationalist party activists received no perquisites through their work for the party since, unlike other parties, it never held office.

63. Among these were student members of the Peasant party, the Workers' party and Egypt's Front. (Interview with Maher Muhammad Ali).

64. The largest of the religious groups was the Young Muslim Men's Association (YMMA).

65. G.E. von Grunebaum, 'The Political Role of the University in the Near East as Illustrated by Egypt' in G.E. von Grunebaum (ed.), *Modern Islam: The Search for Cultural Identity* (University of California Press, 1962), p. 195. See also Abu al-Asaad, *Educational Policy*.

66. Groupe d'Etudes de l'Islam, 'L'Egypte Indépendente' (Paris, 1938) in Raoul Makarius, *La Jeunesse Intellectuelle d'Egypte au Lendemain de la Deuxième Guerre Mondiale* (Mouton & Co., Paris, 1960), p. 12.

67. Abd al-Hamid Fahmi Matar, *Education and the Unemployed in Egypt* (Muhammad Ali Press, Alexandria, 1939) (in Arabic), p. 29.

68. Craig, 'Egyptian Students', p. 293. Crag noted, 'Many, perhaps most, of the demonstrations by Egyptian students which are reported in the press concern not the university undergraduates but pupils at the secondary schools. These pupils are not necessarily young boys . . . ' Another British commentator observed, 'The word "student" must be understood to include boys at the secondary schools who are usually the most prominent when political demonstrations are afloat.' (H. Deighton, 'Higher Education in Egypt', *Times Educational Supplement*, 25 Jan. 1947).

69. See, for example, Farouq Muneeb, 'Unforgettable Incident', *al-Arab*, 6 Oct. 1983.

70. FO 141, 1187 (1947).

71. Ibid.

72. FO 141, 961 (1944), 'Military Training of Egyptian Students'.

73. FO 141, 543 (1936).

74. Interview with Zahran.

75. Interview with Abd al-Khaleq.

76. When at a later stage there was a squabble between the Brotherhood and Young Egypt, the latter's magazine accused Hasan al-Banna of being an instrument of the British, Sidqi Pasha and Jewish capitalism. (Ahmad al-Misri, 'The Muslim Brothers', *al-Tadamun*, no. 30 (July–Aug. 1979), p. 46).

77. Ramadan, *al-Hadaf*, 20 Nov. 1980. In Port Said bullets and bombs were used in a battle between the Wafdists and the Muslim Brethren. (Tariq al-Bishri, *The Political Movement in Egypt, 1945–1952* (Public Agency for Books, Cairo, 1974)

(in Arabic), p. 77).

78. Interview with Abd al-Khaleq.

79. Interviews with Dr al-Fangari and Zahran.

80. Interview with Abd al-Khaleq.

81. Interview with Dr Hathout.

82. Abd al-Motal al-Gabri, *Why Was Imam Martyr Hasan al-Banna Assassinated?* (al-Itisam House, Cairo, 1977) (in Arabic), p. 99.

83. *Egypt News*, vol. I, no. 2 (3 Jan. 1948). Enclosed in FO 141, 1272 (1948), 'Arab Societies: The Democratic Movement for National Liberation'.

84. Both the Communists and the Brethren were known as 'enemies of all governments'. (Interview with Dr Hathout).

85. In 1952 the elections for the Union of the Faculty of Law at Cairo University showed the Muslim Brotherhood and the United Front (Wafdist-Communist front, with the latter in the commanding position) to be of about equal strength. (Laqueur, *Communism and Nationalism*, p. 16. Based on *al-Misri*, 6 Jan. 1953).

86. Interview with al-Ghazali.

87. Interview with Abd al-Khaleq. The Wafd was then reported (by the oriental secretary at the British Embassy) to 'have taken the Brothers into their pay'. (FO 141, 951 (1944)). A number of Wafd leaders, including Sirag al-Din Pasha, visited the headquarters of the Brotherhood, where they delivered amicable speeches and were admitted as honorary members. (Bayoumi, *Muslim Brotherhood*, p. 227).

88. Interview with Abd al-Khaleq; Fouad Nosehi, *Young Egypt — The Socialist Party* (Alamiyya Press, Cairo, 1978) (in Arabic), p. 16; Zaheer Masood Quraishi, *Liberal Nationalism in Egypt — Rise and Fall of the Wafd Party* (Kitab Mahal, Delhi, 1967), p. 190; Husaini, *Moslem Brethren*, pp. 144–7.

89. Interviews with Dr al-Fangari and Maher Muhammad Ali.

90. Interview with Abd al-Khaleq; Jean-Pierre Thieck, 'La Journée du 21 Février dans l'Histoire du Mouvement National Egyptien', unpublished PhD dissertation, Paris, 1975.

91. FO 141, 543 (1936).

Chapter 4

1. FO (Foreign Office) 141, 1005 (1) (1945) 'Political Situation'.

2. Al-Ghazali estimates the attendance at up to fifty, but Zahran denies that it ever exceeded twenty. (Author's interviews with Abd al-Monem al-Ghazali (April 1979) and Saad Zahran (Sept. 1981)).

3. Interview with al-Ghazali.

4. Richard P. Mitchell, *The Society of the Moslem Brothers* (Oxford University Press, London, 1969), p. 44; Zakariya Suleiman Bayoumi, *The Muslim Brotherhood and Islamic Societies in Egyptian Political Life* (Wahba Bookshop, Cairo, 1979) (in Arabic), p. 103. According to Zahran (interview), this meeting, which was inaugurated by Fouad Mohieddin, was attended by collaborators of other political parties and the government, with the deliberate aim of disrupting it. Within an hour the meeting duly ended in uproar.

5. FO 141, 1009 (1946), 'Public Security'. The strike continued the following day in Cairo and Alexandria and was accompanied by anti-Jewish demonstrations. (See Amin Said, *Political History of Egypt* (Revival of Arab Books House, Cairo, 1959) (in Arabic), p. 283).

6. Interview with al-Ghazali.

7. Led by Mustafa Mumin of the Muslim Brotherhood (Mitchell, *Moslem Brothers*, p 44).

8. The police force was led by a British officer, Fitzpatrick, who was killed by students a few years later. (See Jean-Pierre Thieck, 'La Journée du 21 Février 1946 dans l'Histoire du Movement National Egyptien', unpublished PhD dissertation, Paris, 1975; author's interview with Dr Ahmad Shawqi al-Fangari (June 1978)).

9. Abd al-Rahman al-Rafi, *In the Aftermath of the Egyptian Revolution* (Egyptian Renaissance Bookshop, Cairo, 1949 and 1951) (in Arabic), vol. III, p. 181.

10. Shuhdi Atiyya al-Shafi, *The Development of the Egyptian Nationalist Movement, 1882–1956*, 1st edn (Egyptian House for Books, Cairo, 1957) (in Arabic), p. 97. The author states that seven people were killed in these demonstrations. A number of students injured in Cairo were received by the Wafd leader Nahhas Pasha, who delivered a speech in support of the students. (Author's interview with Maher Muhammad Ali (Sept. 1981)).

11. The ceremony took place under the strictest security as rumours spread of an attempt to bomb the King's procession. Only a few students were trusted by the security personnel and allowed to attend. (Muhammad Hussein Heikal, *Memoirs in Egyptian Politics* (Egyptian Press, Cairo, 1953) (in Arabic), vol. II, p. 315). According to al-Ghazali, the King's reception by the students included more vigorous forms of protest—burning his portrait, shouting 'No God but God', throwing dust at the royal torch and uprooting trees in the path of the King's procession. (Abd al-Monem al-Ghazali, 'The Place of 21 February 1946 in History', *al-Tali'a* (Feb. 1966), pp. 52-3). The scale of student participation in these acts, however, is unclear from al-Ghazali's emotional accounts and cannot be traced in other sources.

12. Tariq al-Bishri, *The Political Movement in Egypt, 1945*-1952 (Public Agency for Books, Cairo, 1974) (in Arabic), p. 100.

13. Thieck, 'Journée du 21 Février', pp. 115-16. Thieck estimates the number of demonstrators at some fifteen thousand for Cairo University, rising to forty thousand when they were joined by the students from al-Azhar.

14. *Al-Tali'a* (Feb. 1976). Students contacted the Congress of Egyptian Trade Unions, the Preparatory Committee for the Confederation of Egyptian Trade Unions and various other trade unions, especially in the Cairo industrial suburb of Shubra al-Khaima, where workers had already started to form their own National Committees. (See also al-Bishri, *Political Movement*, p. 100).

15. Anwar Abdel-Malek, *Egypt: Military Society* (transl. from French by Charles Lam Markmann) (Random House, New York, 1968), p. 24; Mos'ad Oweis, 'Towards a Political Organization for the Youth' in Kamal S. Darwish *et al.*, *Political Education of the Youth* (al-Maaref House, Alexandria, 1973) (in Arabic), pp. 84-5; al-Shafi, *Egyptian Nationalist Movement*, pp. 98-9.

16. Al-Shafi (*Egyptian Nationalist Movement*, p. 99) estimates forty to one hundred thousand. Al-Ghazali's estimate ('Place of 21 February', *al-Tali'a* (Feb. 1966), p. 55) is over one hundred and fofty thousand, of whom fifteen to forty thousand were workers, especially from the industrial area of Shubra al-Khaima. A third estimate (*al-Tali'a* (Feb. 1976)) puts the figure as high as two hundred and fifty thousand.

17. This is the opening stanza of a longer song written by Abd al-Wahed Boseila of the Faculty of Science.

18. Al-Rafi, *Aftermath*, vol. III, p. 186.

19. Some sources claimed that the Brotherhood participated in these demonstrations. According to Mitchell *(Moslem Brothers,* p. 45), 'On the day of the strike the Moslem Brothers were, of course, out in full force, with the major focus of their independent activity in Alexandria. Whatever Banna might have promised Sidqi, it clearly could not have included the diversion of the national fervour of his followers.' Al-Ghazali implicitly admitted that participation when he referred to the abortive attempt by the Brotherhood's Rover Scouts to divert the course of the demonstrations in Cairo to the Royal Palace in order to submit a petition to the King. ('Place of 21 February', *al-Tali'a* (Feb. 1966), p. 56).

20. Al-Shafi, *Egyptian Nationalist Movement,* p. 100.

21. This call seems to have been in response to pressure from the Muslim Brotherhood. (Thieck, 'Journée du 21 Février', p. 124). Later in 1948 the British Embassy reported, 'In Mansoura, the Moslem Brethren, through their members who are employed in the Post Office and other government departments, are intercepting mail which is addressed in European languages.' (FO 141, 1245 (1948), 'Political Situation'). At one point in the course of the student movement, the Brethren also burnt English books in public. (Abd al-Motal al-Gabri, *Why Was Imam Martyr Hasan al-Banna Assassinated?* (al-Itisan House, Cairo, 1977), p. 99).

22. Al-Shafi, *Egyptian Nationalist Movement,* pp. 102-3. The divisions within the student body, however, had some effect on the organization of the strike in Cairo. (*Al-Tali'a* (Feb. 1976)).

23. FO 141, 1009 (1946).

24. Thieck, 'Journée du 21 Février'.

25. Interview with Zahran.

26. To the students of the period these committees were reminiscent of the committees of 1919. (Thieck, 'Journée du 21 Fevrier', p. 96).

27. Mitchell, *Moslem Brothers,* p. 44. The separate committee of the Wafdist students, which had an identical name, collectively joined the ECS. (Thieck, 'Journée du 21 Février', p. 97).

28. Abd al-Azeem Ramadan, 'The Muslim Brotherhood: the Most Dangerous Religious Movement in Modern History', *al-Hadaf,* 20 Oct. 1980. The Brethren accused their rivals of using a 'Communist terminology' in their statements: 'liberation struggle', 'economic evaluation', 'people's struggle' and 'alliance of workers and students'.

29. Interview with Zahran.

30. Abdel-Malek, *Egypt: Military Society,* pp. 23 and 25.

31. Michel Kamel, 'The Development of the Movement of National and Social Struggle in Egypt', *Dirasat Arabiyya,* no. 11, year 16 (Sept. 1980), p.4.

32. Tortured in prison until he died in June 1960, Shohdi al-Shafi became the most celebrated martyr of the Egyptian Communist movement.

33. Al-Shafi, *Egyptian Nationalist Movement,* pp. 108-9.

34. A statement from the Preparatory Committee for the Confederation of Egyptian Trade Unions to the NCWS. Cited in Taha Said Uthman, 'Memoirs and Documents in the History of the Working Class', *al-Kateb,* no. 134, year XII (May 1972), pp. 153-8.

35. Ibid.

36. L.J. Coverly, 'The Egyptian Undergraduate and Politics', *Journal of Education,* vol. LXXIX (June 1947), p. 336.

37. Interview with Ahmad Sadek Saad in Rifat al-Said, *History of Leftist Organizations in Egypt, 1940–1950* (New Culture House, Cairo, 1976) (in Arabic), pp. 276-7.

38. Bayoumi, *Muslim Brotherhood*, p. 283; Thieck, 'Journée du 21 Février', p. 126; Rifat al-Said, *Ahmad Hussein: Words and Attitudes* (al-Arabi for Publication, Cairo, 1979) (in Arabic), p. 202. The Muslim Brotherhood was criticized by another Islamic society, the Youth of Muhammad, for 'forming that committee at the behest of the government in order to undermine the nationalist movement'. (Bayoumi, *Muslim Brotherhood*, p. 283).

39. Al-Ghazali, 'Place of 21 February', p. 59.

40. Bayoumi, *Muslim Brotherhood*, p. 105.

41. Ibid., pp. 104-5.

42. Al-Bishri, *Political Movement*, p. 85; Thieck, 'Journée du 21 Février', p. 97.

43. Al-Shafi, *Egyptian Nationalist Movement*, pp. 107-8. See also Heikal, *Memoirs*, vol. II, pp. 321-2.

44. Kamal Abd al-Halim.

45. P. J. Vatikiotis, *The Modern History of Egypt* (Weidenfeld & Nicolson, London, 1969), p. 363; Marcel Colombe, 'Deux Années d'Histoire de l'Egypte (8 Octobre 1944 – 9 Décembre 1946)', *Politique Etrangère*, vol. 12e, part 2 (May 1947), p. 213. It was reported that earlier, on 7 May 1946, bombs were thrown at Mustafa Pasha Barracks in Alexandria, injuring four British soldiers, and a basket with sixty hand grenades was seized. On 17 July more bombs were thrown at the British Club in Alexandria, injuring twenty-eight people. (See Said, *Political History*, p. 293).

46. Mustafa Mumin travelled to the meetings of the Security Council on behalf of a student Front of Publicity for the Nile Valley which consisted mainly of students belonging to the Muslim Brotherhood and the Nationalist party. Two university rectors, Dr Abd al-Wahab Azzam and Mansour Fahmi Pasha, were chosen as its presidents and its members included a number of teachers. (Interview with Maher Muhammad Ali).

47. A British Embassy reported noted, 'Agent told me that the reopening of the universities was being awaited with some interest and anxiety, for Mostafa Mumin, the student leader, was thought to be out to provoke demonstrations against Nokrashy . . . It was he who had tried to shout Nokrashy down at Lake Success. The students hate Nokrashy, he said, anyway, largely because of the incident of the Abbas Bridge. They now say he is not the man to lead the revolution the nation is preparing for.' (FO 141, 1187 (1947), 'Political Situation').

48. A British Embassy report noted, 'The University will re-open . . . the blacklisted elements will be removed but the opposition parties, the Communists, the Nationalists, the Brothers, have decided to contact the students in order to organise disorder and riots, regardless of the cost, until the downfall of Nokrashi and his Cabinet.' (FO 141, 127 (1948), 'Arab Societies: Ikhwan Al-Muslimene').

49. Four days later the Wafd leader also announced his government's rejection of the US proposals for collective defence in the Middle East. (Abdel-Malek, *Egypt: Military Society*, p. 31.) See also FO 141, 1442 (1951), 'USA-Great Britain: Middle East Policy'.

50. There was no unified command for the battalions as each group obeyed its own leader. (Abdel-Malek, *Egypt: Military Society*, p. 31; al-Bishri, *Political Movement*, p. 507).

51. Mitchell, *Moslem Brothers*, pp. 94-5. The author also noted, 'The students, demonstrating their "victory" over the government attempt to crush the liberation battalions, regularly rode around the campus in an amphibious-type jeep and, in front of the administration building, sprayed their machine guns around its famous dome. Similar reports of armed students testing explosives and

spraying arms fire around the campus came from Alexandria University. The students involved were in the vast majority from the Moslem Brothers.

'At the same time, however, in what appeared to be the other side of a bargain, the University demonstrations and opinion at large were brought under control. Hilali needed quiet while he pushed on with his programme of reform, and also attempted to re-establish negotiations with the British; at the University he was given assistance by the Brothers. In control of the student unions the Brothers were in a position to direct university activity.'

Chapter 5

1. FO (Foreign Office), 371/45921 no. 3 (1944). Earlier in 1943 the King was injured in a car accident and student well-wishers demonstrated in sympathy. (FO 371/41237, no. 207 (1944)).

2. FO 207/219, no. 31 (1936), Lampson to Eden.

3. Shaikh Mustafa al-Maraghi, Shaikh of al-Azhar and a supporter of the Palace, was described by Heikal as 'an influential man in all the country's affairs—its politics, its government and its ruling'. (Muhammad Hussein Heikal, *Memoirs in Egyptian Politics* (Egyptian Press, Cairo, 1953) (in Arabic), vol. II, p. 112.

4. FO 141, 874 (1943), 'Al-Azhar'.

5. Ibid. The ambassador minuted: 'I have authorised my view being made known to Hassanein Pasha [of the Palace] confidentially—namely that this is a row between the Government and the Azhar into which Palace would be ill advised to get drawn in, as they would probably end up by burning their fingers.'

6. Jean-Pierre Thieck, 'La Journée du 21 Février 1946 dans l'Histoire du Mouvement National Egyptien', unpublished PhD dissertation, Paris, 1975. At this point the King resorted to the secondary school students in a desperate effort to restore his declining popularity within the university. On 15 July 1946 all newspapers announced the establishment in every Egyptian school of groups of 'torch-bearers' on the occasion of King Farouq's birthday 'as part of the Royalist propaganda'. (FO 141, 1007 (1946), 'Political Situation').

7. Abd al-Rahman al-Rafi, *Prelude to the Revolution of 23 July 1952*, 2nd edn (Egyptian Renaissance Bookshop, Cairo, 1964) (in Arabic), pp. 77–8 and 88–9; Fouad Sirag al-Din, *Why the New Party?* (al-Shorouk House, Cairo, 1977), p. 60. Sirag al-Din reports that some school and university students even shouted republican slogans. (Ibid., p. 85).

8. FO 141, 543 (1936), 'Students: Political Activities and Strikes'.

9. Enclosed in FO 407/219, no.31 (1936).

10. Enclosed in FO 141, 543 (1936).

11. Sylvia G. Haim, 'State and University in Egypt' in Max Horkheimer and Chauncy D. Harris (eds.), *Universität und Moderne Gesellschaft* (Frankfurt am Main veranstalteten Seminar, 1959), p. 108.

12. In 1937 students hostile to the Wafd protested against an alleged leak of the examination papers to Wafd supporters. To avoid a scandal the Wafd government ordered new examinations to be prepared. After the results were announced, those students affected demonstrated again in front of the parliament building demanding that the minimum pass mark be lowered by 10 per cent. The government made some minor concessions to meet these demands. (FO 407/221,

part CXXII, nos. 102 and 103 (1937), Lampson to Eden).

13. Taha Hussein, *The Future of Culture in Egypt* (Dar al-Maaref Press, Cairo, 1938) (in Arabic), p. 129.

14. FO 141, 1187 (1947), 'Political Situation'.

15. FO 407/219, no.31 (1936).

16. Ibid.

17. Author's interview with Maher Muhammad Ali (Sept. 1981).

18. Abd al-Monem al-Ghazali, 'The Place of 21 February 1946 in History', *al-Tali'a* (Feb. 1966), p. 52. A British Embassy report noted: 'On December 10th 1948 Abdel Hadi called on the Ambassador . . . Abdel Hadi's reference to Selim Zaki (the Commandant of the Cairo City Police who was killed by a hand grenade last week) arises from the stories that have been circulating that the police had fired first upon the students.' (FO 142, 1271 (1948)). Ibrahim Abd al-Hadi was minister of the interior and, as prime minister, introduced into Egypt the techniques of systematic torture of political prisoners.

19. Author's interview with Dr Ahmad Shawqi al-Fangari (June 1978).

20. FO 141, 618 (1935), 'Students: Political Activities and Strikes'.

21. FO 141, 543 (1936).

22. Ibid.

23. Author's interview with Saad Zahran (Sept. 1981).

24. Ahmad Amin, 'The University and Politics' in Fayd al-Khater, *The Outpouring of Mind*, 2nd edn (Egyptian Renaissance Bookshop, Cairo, 1953), vol. VI, p. 134. An Embassy report gave this example: 'The university will reopen next Saturday . . . The opposition parties . . . have decided to contact the students in order to organise disorder and riots until the downfall of Nokrashi and his Cabinet.' (FO 141. 1271 (1943), 'Arab Societies: Ikhwan Al-Muslimene'). When the Opposition leader Dr Heikal went to the university for a meeting with its rector amid student turmoil during the Wafd's term of office from 1936 to 1937, he was accused by the Wafd newspapers of inciting students against the government. (Heikal, *Memoirs*, vol. II, pp. 51–2).

25. Heikal, *Memoirs*, vol. II, p. 314; Mahmoud Zayid, *From Ahmad Urabi to Gamal Abdel-Nasser* (United House for Publication, Beirut, 1973) (in Arabic), pp. 41 and 187. Heikal described the summer of 1945: 'When students finished their exams and went back to their families there remained no semblance of activity to be feared in the capital.' (*Memoirs*, vol. II, p. 312).

26. FO 407/219, no.31 (1936). Muhammad Mahmoud Pasha even promised a delegation of ten students to give them high posts in the government (FO 141, 543 (1936)).

27. Quoted in Ahmad Abd al-Rahim Mostafa, *Development of Political Thought in Modern Egypt* (Arab Institute for Research and Studies, Cairo, 1973) (in Arabic), p. 80. Abd al-Rahman al-Rafi, a famous historian and political opponent of the Wafd, sharply criticized the Wafd's policy towards students: 'The Wafd's corruption spread to the students. It diffused amongst them the spirit of utilitarianism and opportunism. Students were led to seek material gains and to aspire for the privileges of exercising political power after graduation. This type of student cannot be a good citizen but represents instead a life-long parasite who cannot be of any use to his country.' (Abd al-Rahman al-Rafi, *In the Aftermath of the Egyptian Revolution* (Egyptian Renaissance Bookshop, Cairo, 1949 and 1951), vol. III, pp. 156–7). See also the comments of the writer Ahmad Amin: 'It is utterly wrong that a rector, or dean or teacher should plunge into political partisanship so that it affects his behaviour—he would favour students

from his party and maltreat those from others, and he might behave likewise with his fellow-teachers who are subject to his decision on questions of promotion and demotion . . . This would destroy the independence of the university and would spoil the manners of students and teachers alike.' (Amin, 'University and Politics'). Many student activists have denied the accusation that they received educational facilities in return for their political activities, arguing that they had been obliged to be academically successful to gain the respect of their followers and that their political involvement was an incentive to read and gain theoretical and practical knowledge about politics. (Interview with Maher Muhammad Ali). Party leaders frequently advised the student activists of their party to perform well in their academic studies. (See *Rose al-Youssef*, 5 March 1934; author's interview with Muhammad Farid Abd al-Khaleq (Aug. 1981)).

28. Heikal, *Memoirs*, vol. II, p. 110.

29. Dr al-Fangari reports proposing that party leaders ought to lead the demonstrations against the British. A student activist of the Wafd objected to this proposal on the grounds that 'We would prefer to lose a thousand martyrs than to lose one party leader.' (Interview).

30. FO 407/219, no. 31 (1936).

31. FO 141, 543 (1936).

32. FO 141, 618 (1935).

33. FO 141, 543 (1936).

34. FO 407/221, part CXXII, no. 107 (1937).

35. The following examples were reported:

During the student uprising of 1935–36 a group of students smashed the windows of the offices of *Rose al-Youssef* magazine. The following day they went to the offices of the magazine of the Constitutional Liberal Party *al-Siyasa*. One of the party's leaders, Dr Heikal, mounted a table to talk to them. When one of the students asked him a question he promised to answer under one condition—that the student should admit that he was convinced by the answer if he found it convincing, and that Dr Heikal himself should acknowledge that he was convinced by the student's response if this was indeed the case. After Heikal had finished speaking the students applauded without further argument. (Muhammad Hussein Heikal, *Memoirs in Egyptian Politics* (Egyptian Renaissance Bookshop, Cairo, 1951) (in Arabic), vol. I, p. 387).

On 23 December 1944 the Saadist prime minister, Dr Ahmad Maher, made a sudden and unguarded visit to the university and publicly urged the students to call off their strike. (Yunnan Labib Rezq, *History of Egyptian Cabinets* (al-Ahram Centre for Political and Strategic Studies, Cairo, 1975), p. 467).

During the 1951–52 guerrilla war demonstrating engineering students made their way to the Ministry of the Interior and shouted imprecations at the minister, Sirag al-Din Pasha, who ordered the police not to intervene. On the same evening, one of the students went back to apologize to the minister on behalf of his colleagues, who had realized that they had been wrong to shout abuse at a minister who had allowed them to demonstrate on his doorstep. (Sirag al-Din, *Why the New Party?*).

36. *Rose al-Youssef*, 5 Feb. 1951. Cited in ibid., 5 July 1976.

37. Tariq al-Bishri, *The Political Movement in Egypt, 1945–1952* (Public Agency for Books, Cairo, 1974), pp. 374–5; Abd al-Azeem Ramadan, 'The Muslim Brotherhood: the Most Dangerous Religious Movement in Modern History', *al-Hadaf*, 4 Dec. 1980.

38. Asem al-Desouki, *Egypt in the Second World War, 1939–1945* (Arab Institute

for Research and Studies, Cairo, 1976) (in Arabic), p. 321.

39. FO 141, 1271 (1948).

40. Interview with Dr al-Fangari.

41. FO 141, 1256 (1948).

42. Thieck, 'Journée du 21 Février', p. 97.

43. Ahmad Baha al-Din, *Days of History*, 2nd edn (Books for All, Cairo, 1959) (in Arabic), p. 84; L. Cantori, 'The Organisational Basis of an Elite Political Party: the Egyptian Wafd', unpublished PhD dissertation, University of Chicago, 1966, p. 190.

44. Marius Deeb, *Party Politics in Egypt: the Wafd and its Rivals 1919–1939* (Ithaca Press, London, 1979), pp. 63–4.

45. Abd al-Azeem Ramadan, *The Development of the Nationalist Movement in Egypt, 1937–1948* (Arab World, Beirut, 1973) (in Arabic), vol. I, p. 114.

46. Cited in al-Bishri, *Political Movement*, p. 36.

47. Ibid., p. 156.

48. The Ministry of the Interior authorities saw little danger in propagandist literature if 'its distribution did not have wider circulation outside student circles'. (See FO 141, 842 (1942), 'Young Egypt').

49. Thieck, 'Journée du 21 Février', pp. 109–10 and 122.

50. Ibid., p. 110.

51. Ibid.

52. Ibid., p. 92.

53. In 1924 a student committee at Alexandria helped the government to suppress the workers' strikes of that year. (See Rifat al-Said, *History of the Socialist Movement in Egypt, 1900–1925*, 2nd edn (al-Farabi House, Beirut, 1975) (in Arabic), p. 272). Students were also reported to have established in the 1920s a 'national guard' to prevent 'the riff-raff' from intruding into their demonstrations. (See Salah Issa, *The Egyptian Bourgeoisie and the Method of Negotiation*, 2nd edn (National Culture Publications, Cairo, 1980) (in Arabic), p. 96). The hostility between the student Blue Shirt squads and the worker Youth Committees of the Wafd in the 1930s should also be remembered. (James P. Jankowski, 'The Egyptian Blue Shirts and the Egyptian Wafd, 1935–1938', *Middle Eastern Studies*, vol. VI, no. 1 (Jan. 1970), p. 84).

54. According to Saad Zahran, student contacts with the working class during the 1946 uprising largely enabled students to act independently of political parties. Hence they did not have to repeat in 1946 their course of action in 1935, when they had resorted to the political parties to form a united front. (Interview).

55. Cited in Taha Saad Uthman, 'Memoirs and Documents in the History of the Working Class', *al-Kateb*, no. 134, year XII (May 1972), p. 158.

56. Ibid.

57. Ibid., p. 155.

58. In defending his party against the accusation that it had been infiltrated by Communists, the leader of the Wafd Opposition in parliament said that the Wafd 'had as many capitalist members as any other party'. (Al-Bishri, *Political Movement*, pp. 124 and 209).

59. FO 141, 543 (1936).

60. A.J. Craig, 'Egyptian Students', *Middle East Journal*, vol. VII, no. 3 (1953), p. 294.

61. In an attempt to woo the support of the landed interests in parliament for his proposed laws to combat Communism, the industrialist Sidqi Pasha argued that, 'Students will try to spoil the relations between landowners and peasants in

the villages . . . This is a serious danger to the social system.' (Al-Bishri, *Political Movement*, p. 124; Asem al-Desouki, *Big Landowners and their Role in Egyptian Society, 1914-1952* (New Culture House, Cairo. 1975) (in Arabic) pp. 282–3).

62. FO 407/219, no.31 (1936).

63. See the incident when al-Azhar shaikhs were arrested for 'not controlling their students'. (FO 141, 874 (1943)).

64. Heikal, *Memoirs*, vol. II, p. 131. Heikal's recommendation to the teachers was to give advice to their students or else to continue giving their lectures regardless of the limited numbers present.

65. A report in the *Times Educational Supplement* noted: 'A large proportion of the students in the secondary schools and universities are the children of the vast army of government officials. In demonstrating they are to some extent expressing the discontent which is rife among their parents, and since most of them will follow their fathers in the same treadmill, the values of their qualifications as expressed in salaries and bonuses is of vital importance to them.' ('Sports of Students . . . Politics in Egypt', *Times Educational Supplement*, 7 Sept. 1951).

66. FO 407/219, no.31 (1936).

67. FO 141, 543 (1936).

68. Author's interview with Dr Hassan Hathout (Sept. 1979).

69. Interview with Maher Muhammad Ali.

70. Al-Bishri, *Political Movement*, p. 515.

71. Owen Holloway, 'University Students of the Middle East', *Journal of the Royal Central Asian Society*, vol. XXXVIII (Jan. 1951), p. 10. Craig confirmed this: 'In a land where illiteracy is still the rule, the educated wield a measure of authority disproportionate to their numbers.' (Craig, 'Egyptian Students', p. 295). According to Marsot, 'Students became a corps d'élite in the country, their importance in social and political life outmatched their real contributions.' (Afaf Lutfi al-Sayyid Marsot, *Egypt's Liberal Experiment, 1922–1936* (University of California Press, 1977), p. 202).

Chapter 6

1. Jean-Jacques Waardenburg, *Les Universités dans Le Monde Arabe Actuel* (Mouton & Co., La Haye, 1966), vol. II, p. 80, Table 109.

2. M.G.R. Nuweir, 'Towards a New Educational Policy for Youth', *al-Tali'a* (Feb. 1966), p. 48.

3. Georgie D.M. Hyde, *Education in Modern Egypt . . . Ideals and Realities* (Routledge & Kegan Paul, London, 1978), p. 74.

4. Rushdi Labib *et al.*, *History and System of Education in Egypt* (Anglo-Egyptian Bookshop, Cairo, 1968) (in Arabic), p. 220.

5. Ibid., p. 219.

6. Louis Awad, *The University and the New Society* (National House for Printing and Publication, Cairo, 1963) (in Arabic), p. 18.

7. William R. Polk, 'The Nature of Modernisation—the Middle East and North Africa', *Foreign Affairs* (Oct. 1965), p. 104.

8. Mukhtar Hamza, *Development of Educational Trends in the Service of Economic and Social Development*, Planning Theses Series, no. 63 (National Planning Committee, Cairo, 1960), p. 22, Table 11.

9. Labib *et al.*, *History of Education*, p. 213.

10. Joseph Szyliowicz, *Education and Modernisation in the Middle East* (Cornell

University Press, 1973), p. 264.

11. Labib *et al.*, *History of Education*, p. 213.

12. Szyliowicz, *Education and Modernisation*, p. 265.

13. Peter Dodd, 'Youth and Women's Emancipation in the U.A.R.', *Middle East Journal*, no. 22 (Spring 1968), p. 171.

14. *Al-Tali'a* (Oct. 1968), p. 21.

15. Thirty-two per cent, according to Szyliowicz, *Education and Modernisation*, p. 278.

16. Labib *et al.*, *History of Education*, p. 281.

17. It was even suggested that the figures showing numerical expansion were inaccurate. In 1968 *al-Tali'a* magazine commented, 'An honest survey should be carried out to define the actual situation, especially in the countryside, to reach the truth beyond the inaccurate figures.' (*Al-Tali'a* (Oct. 1968), p. 19).

18. In answering student protests, the minister of education gave the following example to prove the necessity of raising the standard of education: in 1967/68 the number of students who sat for the general secondary examination was 130, 804. The number of those who passed was 69, 339. Of these 19,536 obtained less than 50 per cent of the marks. (*Al-Ahram*, 3 Dec. 1968).

19. Paradoxically, the graduates of general secondary education were given priority over the graduates of technical secondary education in admissions to the higher technical institutes. (M.E. Ismail, 'Social Analysis of Youth Problems in Our Contemporary Society' in *al-Tali'a* (Feb. 1966), p. 36).

20. Hyde, *Education in Modern Egypt*, p. 93. See also Mahmud Faksh, 'Education and Political Modernisation and Change in Egypt', unpublished PhD dissertation, University of Connecticut, 1972, pp. 116–17.

21. *Al-Ahram*, 3 June 1977.

22. See Table 6.1 above.

23. Labib *et al.*, *History of Education*, p. 217.

24. Arab Republic of Egypt—State Information Service, *Egyptian Education* (July 1973), p. 52 (Table). A few hundred more students were enrolled at the American University in Cairo, which escaped the deterioration of Egyptian-US relations in the 1960s. Hyde refers to the position of this university in the following terms: 'It kept its head when all around were losing theirs, maintaining complete independence through a period of great political and social change which saw the struggle for national independence marked by riots of the masses against the classes whom it educated . . . ' (Hyde, *Education in Modern Egypt*, p. 173). See also Raymond A. Hinnebusch, 'Children of the Elite: Political Attitudes of the Westernized Bourgeoisie in Contemporary Egypt', *Middle East Journal*, vol. XXXVI, no. 41 (Autumn 1982), pp. 535–61.

25. Saad El-Din, 'La Nouvelle Fonction des Universités d'Egypte', *Civilisations*, vol. V, no. 3 (1955), p. 3.

26. A Student Bank was established in 1961–62 with an initial capital of E£60,000 (Waardenburg, *Universités*, vol. I, p. 240).

27. *Al-Akhbar*, 2 Feb. 1977.

28. Towards the end of the 1950s, well before education was made completely free in 1962, about 71 per cent of university students were actually exempted from fees on grounds of low family income or because they had obtained a mark of more than 75 per cent in the secondary examinations. In some faculties the percentage of students exempted from fees was as high as 91 per cent. (Saad El-Din, 'Nouvelle Fonction', p. 348). The average fee at ten university faculties in 1959 was E£18.00, as compared with E£30.50 in 1939. (See Jean-Jacques

Waardenburg, *Les Universités dans le Monde Arabe Actuel* (Mouton & Co., La Haye, 1966) vol. II, p. 102, Table 136).

29. In a sample survey, carried out in 1961–62, of factors affecting educational choice, only 43 per cent of respondents from vocational secondary schools and 49 per cent of respondents from the universities attributed their educational choice to personal satisfaction. (Mokhtar Hamza, 'Analysis of the Employment Situation amongst the Educated Classes in the UAR', *National Review of Social Sciences* (henceforth *NRSS*), vol. IX, no. 1 (Jan. 1967), p. 16).

30. *Al-Tali'a* (Oct. 1968), p. 25.

31. According to Binder, the school system played a more important role in the socialization effort directed to the middle class than the economic achievements of the regime. (Leonard Binder, 'Egypt: The Integrative Revolution' in Lucien W. Pye and Sidney Verba (eds.), *Political Culture and Political Development* (Princeton University Press, 1965), p. 416).

32. Mohamed Emad-edin Ismail, 'Relationship between the Parents' Socio-Economic Level and their Aspirations Regarding their Children's Future', *NRSS*, vol. I, no.3 (Sept. 1964), p. 147.

33. Emad-edin Sultan, 'Problems of University Students', *NRSS*, vol. VIII, no.1 (Jan. 1971), p. 13, Table 5.

34. Emad-edin Sultan, 'The Needs of the Students of Higher Institutes', *NRSS*, vol. VI, no. 1 (Jan. 1969), pp. 18 and 79–80.

35. According to Professor Rashad Rushdi, this system was not welcomed by the university staff when it was introduced in 1953. However, 'the minister of education considered that a conspiracy and imposed the system on the university'. (Rashad Rushdi, 'Who is Responsible for the Loss of the University?', *al-Akhbar*, 6 Feb. 1977).

36. Awad, *University and New Society*, p. 124, Table 14. Awad considers the system of external students 'a democratic system that deviated from its original purpose' (p. 130).

37. Hamza, 'Analysis of the Employment Situation', p. 3.

38. Malcolm Kerr, 'Egypt' in James S. Coleman (ed.), *Education and Political Development* (Princeton University Press, 1965), pp. 169 and 187.

39. Between 1955 and 1960 the percentage of students in the scientific section of secondary education rose from 63.2 per cent to 80.3 per cent. (Hamza, *Development of Educational Trends*, p. 25, Table 14). In higher education between 1952/53 and 1972/73 the number of students in scientific faculties increased by 721 per cent while those in theoretical faculties increased by 322 per cent. (See Table 6.6 above).

40. Louis Awad, *Our Culture at the Crossroads* (al-Adab House, Beirut, 1974) (in Arabic), p. 40.

41. Awad, *University and New Society*, p. 52.

42. Waardenburg, *Universités*, vol. I, p. 62.

43. Ibid.

44. Sikas Sanyal *et al.*, *University Education and the Labour Market in the Arab Republic of Egypt* (UNESCO—International Institute of Educational Planning, Pergamon Press, Oxford, 1982), p. 255, Table 4.25; data in Table 6.4 above.

45. It is also worth mentioning that teachers at the Jordanian University were not allowed to take employment other than their teaching jobs inside the university, unlike the situation at the Egyptian universities, where many teachers are dubbed 'taxi professors' because they have to rush from one lecture in one university to another in a different institution!

46. Mahmoud El-Zayadi, 'The Effect of Different University Structures on Student Adaptability—A Comparative Study between Two Groups of Students from Ain Shams University and the Jordanian University', *NRSS*, vol. IV, no. 1 (Jan. 1967), pp. 53–64.

47. Szyliowicz, *Education and Modernisation*, p. 289.

48. Awad, *University and New Society*, p. 139. See also Rushdi Said, 'The Universities and Scientific Research', *al-Ahram*, 2 Jan. 1962.

49. Amir Iskandar, 'An Opinion in Culture: Education is the Beginning of Cultural Change', *al-Balagh*, no. 160, 3 Feb. 1975.

50. Waardenburg, *Universités*, vol. I, pp. 55–6.

51. Ibid., p. 87. It should be noted, however, that a definition of what constitutes a university is a controversial issue in the academic circles of advanced Western universities, despite the general agreement about its broad educational purposes. See, for example, H. Livingstone, *The University: An Organisational Analysis* (Blackie & Sons, Glasgow, 1974), pp. 7–40.

52. Waardenburg, *Universités*, p. 84; Latifa al-Zayat, 'Arab Intellect is Paralysed', *Rose al-Youssef*, 18 April 1977.

53. Awad, *University and New Society*, pp. 40–41. See also Nadia Gamal-eddin, 'On Youth Problems in Egypt', *al-Ahram al-Iktisadi*, 29 Sept. 1983.

54. Gamal al-Otaifi, 'The Crisis of Culture as Illustrated by the Experience of the Information Institute', *al-Ahram*, 25 Jan. 1971.

55. A student magazine, in an article entitled 'The Crisis of Basic Literacy', admitted that out of every 200 university graduates in Egypt only one had an interest in reading serious books. (*Al-Rababa*, no.30 (30 Oct. 1972), p. 30).

According to Kerr, the Egyptian graduate 'has little taste for independent reading, and being unable to afford expensive foreign books (which he finds difficult anyway), his knowledge of the outside world comes either through the limited and unreliable medium of Arabic translations or through the propaganda-rigged Cairo press . . . In forming his political views the Egyptian secondary or university graduate is often as exclusively dependent on local propaganda as the man with only a few years of primary education.' (Kerr, 'Egypt', p. 181).

56. Al-Otaifi, 'Crisis of Culture'.

57. Louis Awad, 'Examples from the Illiteracy of the Educated', *al-Ahram*, 26 Jan. 1971.

58. The introduction of the National Charter into schools as part of the curriculum was castigated by an opponent of the revolutionary regime in the following terms: 'A holy book!, the book of revolutionary thought. More copies were printed than copies of the Qur'an and the Bible in several generations . . . It was taught at schools and in the universities and became a curriculum to pass or fail . . . The Qur'an was not honoured in the same manner!' (Ibrahim Abdu, *Democracy between the Alley Patrons and the Councils of Clowns*, 2nd edn (Arab Record Publishers, Cairo, 1979) (in Arabic), p. 153).

59. The National Charter, Chapter 5. Nasser dealt with this issue in the following terms: 'The new culture which we want is a reflection of the new order . . . The culture we want is the culture of the people, hostile to imperialism, to political, economic and social exploitation . . . The cultural revolution places itself at the service of the political and social revolutions.' (Science Day Speech, 18 Dec. 1961).

60. Ibid.

61. Szyliowicz, *Education and Modernisation*, p. 281. When asked why the

historical chapters almost entirely ignored four centuries of Ottoman rule in the Arab East, the co-author of the texts disarmingly explained that the Ottoman age was a dark period in Arab history and that he and his colleagues had decided to treat only the brighter periods! (Kerr, 'Egypt', p. 182).

62. Louis Awad, 'Maniton is Sullen', *al-Ahram*, 19 March 1971.

63. Awad, *Our Culture*, p. 36.

64. Ibid., p. 39. For a more recent analysis of political issues in textbooks see Nadia H. Salem, 'Political Education of the Arab Child—Content Analysis of Textbooks', *al-Mustaqbal al-Arabi*, no. 51 (May 1983), pp. 54–68.

65. *Al-Tali'a* (Oct. 1968), pp. 37 and 39.

66. Ibid., p. 47. The same argument applies at the university level. In Sultan's survey of the problems of university students, about 50 per cent of students at the three major universities who responded agreed with the following statement: 'Part of the curricula does not keep pace with social development.' (Sultan, 'Problems', p. 8). In this context, some authors of school textbooks were criticized as 'remnants of the *ancien régime*'. See, for example, Abd al-Hay Diyab, *Intellectual Feudalism and its Effect* (al-Shaab, Cairo, 1969) (in Arabic), p. 67.

67. Binder, *Egypt*, p. 413; Mahmud A. Faksh, 'The Consequences of the Introduction and Spread of Modern Education: Education and National Integration in Egypt', *Middle Eastern Studies*, vol. XVI, no.2 (May 1980), p. 51; *al-Tali'a* (Feb. 1966), p. 34.

68. Hyde, *Education in Modern Egypt*. According to Professor Rashad Rushdi, 'Public opinion at the university totally rejected this idea but had to submit under the pressure of the power centres.' (Rushdi, 'Who is Responsible?').

69. A considerable proportion of students found no use in taking these courses. In Sultan's survey about one third of the sampled students at the three major universities agreed with the statement: 'I resent the inclusion of the national courses in the curriculum', while about half of the male, and over one third of the female students agreed with the statement: 'I feel uneasy about the socialist studies' failure to achieve their goal.' (Sultan, 'Problems', pp. 18–19, Table 7).

70. Louis Awad, 'Cultural and Intellectual Development in Egypt since 1952' in P.J. Vatikiotis (ed.), *Egypt since the Revolution* (George Allen & Unwin, London, 1968).

71. Speech of 25 Nov. 1961.

72. Mahmoud A. Shafshak, 'The Role of the University in Egyptian Elite Recruitment: A Comparative Study of Al-Azhar and Cairo Universities', *NRSS*, vol. V, no.3 (1968), p. 429. Some of the differences between al-Azhar and Cairo University students in the early 1960s were the following: 20 per cent of al-Azhar students were married as opposed to only 1 per cent at Cairo University; 100 per cent of the al-Azhar students were Muslims, while the corresponding percentage at Cairo was 84 per cent (the rest being 15 per cent Copts and 1 per cent Christians of other sects); and al-Azhar's pan-Islamic ideals and sympathies were directed towards the Muslim world while Cairo's were pan-Arab nationalist and orientated towards the Arab world. In addition, there were differences in the social origins of the students at the two universities (see Table 6.8 above).

73. Sultan, 'Needs', p. 29. About the more liberal attitudes of students at the American University in a more recent period see Hinnebusch, 'Children of the Elite'.

74. Hamza, 'Analysis of the Employment Situation', pp. 17 and 19.

75. *Al-Akhbar*, 31 Jan. 1977.

76. Awad, 'Cultural and Intellectual Development', pp. 155–6.

77. The same argument was advanced over the students' support for the Revolution. *Al-Daawa* (organ of the Muslim Brotherhood) wrote in 1952, 'The army knows perfectly well that the university students have paved the way and created the atmosphere for the deposition of the King.' (*Al-Daawa* (Sept. 1952) in Walter Laqueur, *Communism and Nationalism in the Middle East* (Routledge & Kegan Paul, London, 1957), p. 16).

78. Dr Abd al-Monem al-Sharkawi, *al-Ahram*, 3 June 1977.

79. G.E. von Grunebaum, 'The Political Role of the University as Illustrated by Egypt' in G.E. von Grunebaum (ed.), *Modern Islam: The Search for Cultural Identity* (University of California Press, 1962), p. 195; *Rose al-Youssef*, 17 Feb. 1975; Hassan Muhammad Hassan, 'The Attitude of the Ruling Power towards Student Political Activity', paper presented at the Seminar on Democracy and Education, al-Ahram Centre for Political and Strategic Studies, Cairo, 2–5 April 1984. About forty teachers were sacked, covering various political tendencies— liberals, Islamic fundamentalists, leftists, and so on.

80. K.M. Khalid, 'The Brothers, the Communists and the Revolution', *al-Gumhuriyya*, 20 March 1954. Cited in Karam Shalabi, *Twenty Days that Shocked Egypt—A Documentary Study of the March Crisis* (Usama Publishing and Printing House, Cairo, 1976) (in Arabic), p. 67.

81. Interview with Abd al-Monem al-Ghazali in Abd al-Azeem Ramadan, *Nasser and the Crisis of March 1954* (Rose al-Youssef Press, Cairo, 1976) (in Arabic), pp. 349–50. Al-Ghazali mentioned that the Front succeeded in reinstating Dr Abd al-Wahab Moroe as rector of Cairo University after he had been officially asked to resign. The decision was taken after a meeting between a student Front delegation and the Revolutionary Command Council.

82. Rifat al-Said, *Organizations of the Egyptian Left, 1950–1957* (New Culture House, Cairo, 1983) (in Arabic), p. 170.

83. Interview.

84. In 1953 a Brotherhood leader, Said Ramadan, alleged that 85 per cent of university students were supporters of the Muslim Brotherhood (Christina Phelps Harris, *Nationalism and Revolution in Egypt: The Role of the Muslim Brotherhood*, Publication of the Hoover Institution on War, Revolution and Peace (Mouton & Co., The Hague, 1964), p. 159). The accuracy of this statement is open to dispute in view of the fact that representatives of the above-mentioned Front defeated the Brethren in the Student Union elections in some faculties of the university. (See al-Ghazali in Ramadan, *Nasser and Crisis of March*, pp. 349–50). At that time the Brotherhood students were led by Hasan Douh: 'An extraordinary leader and orator who was very active, always drawing up petitions, organising meetings and censuring students' behaviour and ready for any form of violence.' (Jean and Simonne Lacouture, *Egypt in Transition* (Methuen, London, 1958), pp. 247–8). Hasan Douh was defeated in the Law Faculty elections at Cairo University although Nasser himself visited the university and spoke in his support. The winner was the Wafdist Ahmad al-Khatib, who was supported by the Front. (Al-Said, *Organizations of the Egyptian Left, 1950–1957*, p. 72).

85. Interview with Saleh Abu Rukayek in Ramadan, *Nasser and Crisis of March*, p. 145.

86. Muhammad Mahfouz, 'A Roamer', *al-Arab*, 14 April 1982.

87. Fouad Zakariya, 'Apathy, Football . . . ', *al-Tali'a* (Feb. 1966), p. 42.

88. See Sultan, 'Needs', pp. 18–19, Table 7; Sultan, 'Problems', pp. 45 and 96. For a more recent study asserting the generally liberal attitudes of the students of the American University, see Hinnebusch, 'Children of the Elite'.

89. According to Zakariya, 'This was a purge that effectively degraded the

university . . . it replaced its academic hierarchy with an administrative one which carried with it the vices of bureaucracy and its ignoble values.' (Fouad Zakariya, 'The Independence of the University', *Rose al-Youssef*, 25 Aug. 1975).

90. Ibid; Waardenburg, *Universités*, vol. I, p. 54.

91. Latifa al-Zayat, 'Arab Intellect is Paralysed', *Rose al-Youssef*, 18 April 1977.

92. Zakariya, *Rose al-Youssef*, 25 Aug. 1975.

93. Zakariya claims that ten years after the 1954 confrontation he met one of the students who used to lead the demonstrators shouting against 'the rule of majors and lieutenants'. The student admitted to having done so for security officials who wanted to find out who his followers were! (Author's interview with Professor Fouad Zakariya (June 1978)). After the student uprising of 1968, Nasser replied to a student delegation's demand that he withdraw intelligence agents from the university by promising only to avoid using outside agents.

94. Interview with Zakariya.

95. An opposite account of Dr Laila's alleged popularity among students is given in Muhammad al-Tameel, 'Interview with Dr M.K. Laila', *October*, 13 Nov. 1983.

96. Zakariya divided university teachers into various categories according to their attitudes towards the student movement: '(1) Those who stood against the movement because they were: a) ideological opponents; b) class opponents; c) narrow-minded teachers whose academic disciplines gave them no chance to follow public affairs; d) hypocrites and opportunists who unashamedly acted in accordance with government wishes regardless of their own personal opinion. This last is the most important group to emerge after the Revolution. (2) The apathetic, who formed a large group whose members were not interested in anything unless it was related to personal interests. This was the fruit of many years of insufficient political and social consciousness, which encouraged the pursuit of selfish ends and the avoidance of risks. They used to smile and withdraw from any meeting when a discussion of public issues started, while they were always amongst the most enthusiastic when the discussion turned to salaries, rewards and promotions. (3) The undeclared but sympathetic, who did not manifest their sympathy by action. (4) The positive supporters, mainly leftists and liberals, who were not necessarily hostile to the regime but who supported the student movement on patriotic and moral grounds. The younger members of the teaching staff represented a considerable proportion of this group.' (Interview). See also Hassan M. Hassan, 'The Attitude of the Ruling Power towards Student Political Activity', paper presented at the seminar on Democracy and Education, al-Ahram Centre for Political and Strategic Studies, 2–5 April 1984, p. 12.

97. *Rose al-Youssef*, 17 Feb. 1975. Dr Asfour went as far as to claim for the university staff the prerogatives of judges and MPs for immunity from prosecution for the expression of political views.

98. *Rose al-Youssef*, 25 Aug. 1975.

99. 'Statement of the Teaching Staff in Egyptian Universities' in A Group of Egyptian Militants, *The New National Democratic Movement in Egypt: An Analysis and Documentary* (Ibn Khaldun House, Beirut, 1973) (in Arabic), p. 177.

100. Louis Awad, 'The University Guard Once Again', *al-Ahram*, 19 Feb. 1977; Adel Montasser, 'La Répression Anti-Démocratique en Egypte', *Les Temps Modernes*, nos. 173–7 (August-September 1960), pp. 426–7; Binder, *Egypt*, p. 415.

101. Public Agency for Official Publications, *Ordinance of Universities in the UAR* (Cairo, 1970), pp. 100–3.

102. Recommendations of the Committee of Ordinance Review and Student

Problems, The Student Seminar, 1972. In *The Student Uprising in Egypt, January 1972* (Ibn Khaldun House, Beirut, 1972) (in Arabic), pp. 98–9.

103. A veteran Student Union leader who observed the whole period in question listed a dozen organizations in all, political, non-political and security. (Author's interview with Helmi Nahnoush (Dec. 1978)). See also Hassan, 'Attitude of Ruling Power', pp. 15–16.

104. Abd al-Majid Farid, 'Pages from Nasser's Secret Files', weekly series, *23rd July*, 22 Oct. 1980; General Union of Students of the United Arab Republic (GUSUAR), *Nasser's Speech in the Camp of the Socialist Youth Organization* (Alamiya Press, Cairo, n.d.) [1965] (in Arabic), pp. 15–19.

105. Salah al-Sharnoubi in Fawzi Bishri, *al-Tali'a* (May 1969), p. 50. Another leading member of the SYO confirmed: 'Although the social composition of the university had changed after education was made free, so that it could serve as a fertile soil for producing socialist leaders, it could prove equally fertile for producing class ambitions, and therefore readily produce the opposite effect.' (Ahmad Yousef, p. 34). Before the establishment of the SYO an earlier attempt had been made in 1961 to incorporate university teachers and students within the general framework of the ASU. Binder refers to the strong university representation among the 250-member Preparatory Council which determined the representative formula of the founding body of the ASU, the Congress of Popular Forces, as an indication that 'in the reaction to the separation of Syria and the apprehension lest the former privileged class move for power, the government sought to mobilize all middle-class forces, and particularly the professors and students at the universities, who might provide support for the reactionaries if not quickly mollified'. (Binder, 'Egypt', p. 437).

106. Dr Mufid Shehab in ibid., pp. 25 and 40.

107. Dr Ibrahim Saad al-Din in ibid., p. 43.

108. One of the founders of the SYO observed that, in the early years of the organization, they had found the youth of the production units intellectually and organizationally superior to those of the university, despite the educational gap between the two groups. He also noticed that secondary school students were more prepared for political activity than the university students. (Dr M. al-Khafif, 'Organizing the Youth Politically', *al-Tali'a* (Feb. 1966), p. 29).

109. Presumably this is what an anti-SYO Student Union leader meant when he labelled some of the SYO activists as 'adolescent'. (Interview with Nahnoush). See also GUSARE, *Students and the Development of Society*, prepared by Abd al-Hamid al-Gazzar (Cairo, Feb. 1972), p. 18.

110. Muhammad Galal Kishk, *What do Egyptian Students Want?*, 1st edn (no pub., Beirut, 1968) (in Arabic), pp. 45–6; *al-Tali'a* (May 1969), pp. 25–6. In this respect the case of the members of the regime's underground Socialist Vanguard was even more blatant. Its exposed members were known to have close ties with the minister of the interior, who happened at the time to be the Vanguard's secretary, thus fusing political leadership with policing. It appears that this is what President Sadat was referring to when he said, 'During the time of the "centres of power" in the 1960s I was informed of unacceptable deeds like a university student entering his dean's office without permission, to telephone the minister of the interior with whom he was in direct communication!' (*Al-Akhbar*, 31 Jan. 1977).

111. Cited in Kishk, *What do Egyptian Students Want?*, p. 98.

112. Kamal S. Darwish *et al.*, *The Political Education of the Youth* (al-Maaref House, Alexandria, 1973) (in Arabic), pp. 147–8.

113. Usually the minister of higher education.

114. *The Constitution of the Student Union of the UAR* (Cairo University Press, 1969); Public Agency for Official Publications, *Ordinance of Universities in the UAR* (Cairo, 1970), pp. 263–85.

115. Ibid.

116. The General Union of Students of the United Arab Republic (GUSUAR) was a founding member of the first pan-Arab student union, the General Union of Arab Students, established in the 1960s. There was an earlier attempt to establish such a union—though on a limited scale and ultimately unsuccessful—in March 1936, when contacts between Egyptian and Iraqi students were established by the Wafdist Professor Sanhouri, who was then teaching at Baghdad. (See FO 141, 543 (1936), 'Students: Political Activities and Strikes').

117. The Union Council in every faculty or institute was composed of the secretary and vice-secretary of each of these committees who were in turn elected by the elected representatives of each grade. In other words, the Council was not directly elected by students and its various committees were formed before the Council itself was established. See, for example, Dr G. al-Otaifi, 'Discussion in Parliament', *al-Ahram*, 29 Jan. 1973.

118. Administrative and Financial Ordinance of the GUSUAR in ibid.

119. Contrary to Hyde, who believed that Union membership was not compulsory. (Hyde, *Education in Modern Egypt*, p. 55).

120. Helmi Nahnoush's speech at the National Congress of the ASU in Kishk, *What do Students Want?*, p. 102.

121. M. al-Khafif, *al-Tali'a* (Feb. 1966), p. 27.

122. National Committee of Cairo University Students, A Student Declaration, 1972. In *Student Uprising in Egypt*, p. 39.

123. Interview with Nahnoush.

124. For the historical background to the Vanguard, see Gamal Saleem, 'Secret Organizations under Nasser', *al-Ahrar*, 27 Sept. 1982.

125. Recommendations of the ASU Conference at the Faculty of Economics and Politics on the Obstacles to Political Activity at the University, 1971. In *Student Uprising in Egypt*, p. 60.

126. Dekmejian, 'Student Activism' in Faksh, 'Education and Political Modernisation'. One year after the confrontation of 1954 Nasser began to gain popularity in the student body after he had taken an active part in the First Conference of Non-Aligned Nations held at Bandung in Indonesia. Students at schools and universities formed Bandung Committees in support of Nasser. (Al-Said, *Organizations of the Egyptian Left, 1950–1957*, p. 293).

127. Kerr, 'Egypt', p. 189.

128. Ghali Shukri, *Counter-Revolution in Egypt* (al-Tali'a House, Beirut, 1978) (in Arabic), pp. 107 and 109. Well before the military disaster an Egyptian writer noted: 'The young men of today did not witness the forms of exploitation and corruption we lived through in pre-revolutionary Egypt. To them, the great achievements of the Revolution are ordinary matters . . . When they take a walk along the Nile they see the buildings of the Arab League, the Hilton Hotel and the ASU headquarters. We used to see the British barracks!' (Al-Khafif, *al-Tali'a* (Feb. 1966), p. 26).

Chapter 7

1. Abd al-Azeem Ramadan, *Nasser and the Crisis of March 1954* (Rose al-Youssef Press, Cairo, 1976) (in Arabic), p. 186.

2. Leonard Binder, 'Egypt: The Integrative Revolution' in Lucien W. Pye and Sidney Verba (eds.), *Political Culture and Political Development* (Princeton University Press, 1965), p. 402.

3. A peculiar incident occurred in 1965, when a number of cadres in the SYO, shortly before it was officially inaugurated, were arrested and interrogated for extreme leftist (i.e. Marxist) views, and accused of having connections with a foreign power, China. They were not officially tried or convicted but, as Rageeb al-Banna put it, 'it is the idea of having a political organization that was convicted well before it was born'. (Rageeb al-Banna, 'While We Open the File of the Youth', *al-Ahram*, 6 Dec. 1981). See also: A Group of Egyptian Militants, *The New National Democratic Movement in Egypt: An Analysis and Documentary* (Ibn Khaldun House, Beirut, 1973) (in Arabic), p. 63; Ghali Shukri, *Counter-Revolution in Egypt* (Dar al-Tali'a, Beirut, 1978) (in Arabic), p. 108.

4. Amos Perlmutter, 'Egypt and the Myth of the New Middle Class: A Comparative Analysis', *Comparative Studies in Society and History*, vol. X, no. 1 (Oct. 1967), p. 63.

5. Malcolm Kerr, 'Egypt' in James S. Coleman (ed.), *Education and Political Development* (Princeton University Press, 1965). Even after the 1967 defeat some Arab intellectuals preserved the tendency to self-reproach. According to Dr Burham Dajani, 'We have to ask ourselves why we were defeated and why the Arab nation was defeated under our intellectual leadership.' (See A. Hilal Dessouki, 'Arab Intellectuals and Al-Nakba: The Search for Fundamentalism', *Middle Eastern Studies*, vol. IX (May 1973), p. 188). See also: Menahem Milson, 'Medieval and Modern Intellectual Traditions in the Arab World', *Daedalus* (Summer 1972), pp. 17–37; Nikki Keddie, 'Intellectuals in the Modern Middle East', *Daedalus* (Summer 1972), pp. 39–57.

6. When in the Committee of National Guidance of the National Union (1958–61) a university teacher suggested that such issues as Arab nationalism and socialism should be left to 'professors' to discuss, he was rebuffed for treating the university as an ivory tower. (See Jean Tusan, 'L'Union Nationale de la R.A.U.' (translated excerpt from Muhammad Kamel Hitta, *Al-Ittihad al-Qawmi* (Cairo University Press, 1960)), *Orient*, no. 20 (1961), pp. 205–6). The problem at that time was that the leftist intellectuals could not put forward the contrary point of view simply because they had been imprisoned by Nasser during the clampdown of 1958–59.

7. Muhammad Hasanain Heikal, 'About the Experiment and Democracy in Our Age', *al-Ahram*, 15 Nov. 1968.

8. As a press institution *al-Ahram* was a forum for intellectual debate, within limits, where a number of periodicals were published, representing the views of intellectuals of different political persuasions. Most famous among these was *al-Tali'a* (The Vanguard), the sole platform open to Egyptian Marxists after their organizations had been disbanded.

9. Joseph Szyliowicz, *Education and Modernisation in the Middle East* (Cornell University Press, 1973), p. 296.

10. Fouad Zakariya, 'Apathy, Football . . . ', *al-Tali'a* (Feb. 1966), p. 41.

11. Mustafa al-Fiki in *al-Tali'a* (May 1969), p. 44.

12. Cited in Muhammad Galal Kishk, *What do Egyptian Students Want?*, 1st edn (no pub., Beirut, 1968) (in Arabic), p. 95.

13. Ibid., p. 96. A similar line of argument was common in the case of university teachers. According to Professor Ahmad Badr of the Faculty of Arts at Cairo University, he asked a colleague, a political scientist, to write to the country's leadership to express his disagreement with Heikal's views concerning

the pre-emptive war, published in *al-Ahram* just before the six-day war. His colleague refrained from doing so for fear of reprisals. Thus, 'It is fear', Professor Badr maintains, 'that led us to defeat.' (*Al-Ahram*, 3 June 1977).

14. Abd al-Majid Farid, 'Pages from Nasser's Secret Files', weekly series, *23rd July*, no. 24 (13 Aug. 1979).

15. Cited in Kishk, *What do Egyptian Students Want?*, pp. 104–5.

16. Ibid.

17. Shukri, *Counter-Revolution*, p. 130.

18. Farid, 'Nasser's Secret Files'.

19. At the same cabinet meeting, precisely one week before the Programme of 30 March was issued, Nasser interpreted the slogan of 'freedom' raised by students in their demonstrations as follows: 'It means we should educate them, offer them jobs after graduation, get them married and provide them with accommodation.'!

20. *Al-Ahram*, 15 Oct. 1968.

21. Ibid., 16 Oct. 1968.

22. Ibid., 17 Oct. 1968.

23. Ibid., 19 Oct. 1968.

24. Ibid., 17 Oct. 1968.

25. I.S. Abdalla, 'In the Name of Science and Without Irritation', *al-Ahram*, 20 Oct. 1968.

26. G. al-Otaifi, 'A Last Word on Public Freedom and the Freedom of Scientific Research', *al-Ahram*, 21 Oct. 1968.

27. Kishk, *What do Egyptian Students Want?*, p. 97.

28. Mahmoud Hussein, *The Arabs at Present* (transl. from the French by Ibrahim al-Helw) (al-Tali'a House, Beirut, 1974) (in Arabic), p. 13.

29. Farid, 'Nasser's Secret Files', 6 Aug. 1979.

30. R. Hrair Dekmejian, *Egypt under Nasser* (University of London Press, 1972). In his answer to the demonstrations of February against the negligent air force officers Heikal justified this attitude: 'If a leader knows that the evaluation of his judgement will not be left to the military traditions and rules but to the demonstrations and the strong feelings of the public, regardless of their sincerity, such a leader would most probably be unable to make a move!' (*Al-Ahram*, 1 March 1968).

31. Dekmejian, *Egypt under Nasser*, p. 257. After the defeat Nasser admitted, in a famous saying, that he had 'relied upon the Intelligence but that the Intelligence had failed him. What should I do? Put the Intelligence under the supervision of another Intelligence?'

32. Ibid., pp. 264–5.

33. Kishk, *What do Egyptian Students Want?*, p. 86.

34. Ibid., p. 12.

35. Dekmejian, *Egypt under Nasser*, p. 235.

36. Dessouki, 'Arab Intellectuals', pp. 188–92.

37. Mahmud A. Faksh, 'The Consequences of the Introduction and Spread of Modern Education and National Integration in Egypt', *Middle Eastern Studies*, vol. XVI, no. 2 (May 1980), p. 84.

38. Recommendations of the ASU Conference on the Obstacles to Political Activity in the University, Faculty of Economics, Cairo University, 1971. In *The Student Uprising in Egypt, January 1972* (Ibn Khaldun House, Beirut, 1972) (in Arabic), p. 60.

Chapter 8

1. Muhammad Abd al-Salam, *Rough Years — Memoirs of a Public Prosecutor*, 2nd edn (al-Shorouk House, Cairo, 1975) (in Arabic), pp. 121–3.

2. Wael Uthman, *Secrets of the Student Movement — Cairo Polytechnic, 1968–1975* (Makdour Printers, Cairo, 1976) (in Arabic), p. 24. President Sadat admitted this incident much later and blamed his rivals in power: 'Their aim was to prove that my views were of no significance or weight, that neither I as Speaker nor the parliament itself had real power.' ('Papers of President Sadat', *October*, no. 24, 10 April 1977).

3. The summons to the sit-in read: 'Let every free man among you know that freedom is to be taken not to be given, to be extorted not to be donated. Since we do not have enough power to impose our demands we have found that the only way to let the people hear our voice . . . and to force the ruling power to respect freedoms and to respect you in particular is to resort to passive resistance in the form of a full-scale sit-in.' (In Uthman, *Secrets*, p. 28).

4. Ibid., p. 33.

5. Musa Sabri, *Documents of the October War*, 1st edn (Modern Egyptian Bureau, Cairo, 1974) (in Arabic), p. 117. The arrested students were released ten days after this meeting (Uthman, *Secrets*, p. 33) but the minister of the interior kept some of them in custody without permission from the public prosecutor, who was informed about the incident by the rector of Ain Shams University, later minister of education, Dr Helmi Mourad. (Abd al-Salam, *Rough Years*, p. 130).

6. *Al-Ahram*, 25 Feb. 1968.

7. Ibid., 1 March 1968.

8. Uthman, *Secrets*, p. 29.

9. Abd al-Salam, *Rough Years*, pp. 123–6.

10. Those present at the meeting were: Abd al-Hamid Hassan for Cairo University, Helmi Nahnoush for Ain Shams University, Atef al-Shater for Alexandria University, Muhammad Awad for Assiut University, Mansour Satour for al-Azhar and Muhammad al-Nazer for the higher institutes. Nahnoush commented that only Abd al-Hamid Hassan reached Nasser's heart and found a common understanding with him. (Interview). This was borne out by an article Hassan wrote in a student paper after the meeting praising Nasser. Hassan was labelled an opportunist by many students. One student portrayed his attitude in 1968 thus: 'While students of various persuasions were writing an honourable page in Egyptian history and playing a heroic symphony, he was playing a discordant note of great hypocrisy!' (Uthman, *Secrets*, p. 35). In fact, Hassan became an elected MP (not appointed as I. Abdu asserts: Ibrahim Abdu, *Democracy between the Alley Patrons and the Councils of Clowns*, 2nd edn (Arab Record Publishers, Cairo, 1979) (in Arabic), p. 165) and in his thirties, was appointed minister of youth by President Sadat (not by Nasser as Abdu has claimed).

11. The questions discussed included such topics as the war and the defeat of 1967, the previous war in Yemen, the ASU, the SYO, the security bodies, relations with the USSR, relations with the Arabs, and so on.

12. Author's interview with Professor Fouad Zakariya (June 1978).

13. *Al-Ahram*, 4 March 1968.

14. Ibid., 29 Feb. 1968.

15. Ibid., 27 Feb. 1968.

16. Ibid., 28 Feb. 1968. The minister of the interior claimed in parliament that

the fact that the number of policemen injured in the riots was far higher than that of demonstrators injured (57:21) proved that his men had carried out their orders to minimize the confrontation. (Ibid., 27 Feb. 1968).

17. The Ministry of the Interior's order banning demonstrations, *al-Ahram*, 25 Feb. 1968.

18. Ibid.

19. The public prosecutor of the period later affirmed that no foreign hand had been proved to have been behind the uprising. (Abd al-Salam, *Rough Years*, p. 127).

20. *Al-Ahram*, 28 Feb. 1968.

21. Ibid., 29 Feb. 1968.

22. Muhammad Hasanain Heikal, 'About the Trial, the Demonstrations and the Retrial', ibid., 1 March 1968.

23. Ibid., 29 Feb. 1968.

24. Ibid.

25. Sabri, *Documents*, p. 116.

26. Speech of 3 March 1968, *al-Ahram*, 4 March 1968.

27. Ibid.

28. Ibid.

29. Ibid.

30. Muhammad Galal Kishk, *What do Egyptian Students Want?*, 1st edn (no pub., Beirut, 1968) (in Arabic), p. 21.

31. Uthman, *Secrets*, pp. 31–4.

32. R. Hrair Dekmejian, *Egypt under Nasser* (University of London Press, 1972), p. 258; Abd al-Majid Farid, 'Pages from Nasser's Secret Files', weekly series, *23rd July*, 17 Sept. 1979. The percentage of ministers with a military background was reduced to 39.4 per cent in this cabinet, while it was 65.4 per cent in the war cabinet and 55.2 per cent in the pre-war cabinet. (Dekmejian, *Egypt under Nasser*, p. 259, Table 24).

33. Uthman, *Secrets*, p. 39.

34. *Al-Ahram*, 22 Nov. 1968.

35. *Al-Ahram*'s first account of the events (22 Nov. 1968) gave the number as only four.

36. Thirty, according to *al-Ahram*'s early account (22 Nov. 1968).

37. 'Report of the Minister of Justice to the National Congress of the ASU', *al-Ahram*, 3 Dec. 1968.

38. *Al-Ahram*, 22 Nov. 1968.

39. Ibid., 23 Nov. 1968.

40. Makram Muhammad Ahmad, 'The Students of al-Mansoura', ibid., 25 Nov. 1968; Makram Muhammad Ahmad, 'A Light of Truth on the Student Movement in Egypt', ibid., 26 Nov. 1968.

41. Makram Muhammad Ahmad, 'Light of Truth'.

42. Makram Muhammad Ahmad, 'Students of al-Mansoura'.

43. Makram Muhammad Ahmad and Ihsan Bakr, 'The Real Picture of What Happened in Alexandria', *al-Ahram*, 28 Nov. 1968.

44. The meeting was attended by a number of students who were later to lead the uprising and were officially charged with that offence by the public prosecutor. They included: Atef al-Shater, president of the Student Union of the Polytechnic and of Alexandria University; Ahmad Hussein Hilal, vice-president of the Polytechnic Union; Muhammad Nagi Abu al-Maati, member of the Polytechnic Union; and Muhammad Khayrat Saad al-Shater, a student at the Polytechnic. (The last two were the students who brought the report from al-

Mansoura.) See *al-Ahram*, 3, 12 and 31 Dec. 1968.

45. One of the first students to shout was Taymour al-Mallawani (according to the justice minister's report). Taymour's slogan was, 'Shaarawi *saffah* [murderer] . . . The blood of students is not *mubah* [to be spilt].'

46. 'Report of the Minister of Justice'.

47. On that day some of the students in the Polytechnic sit-in seized a senior police officer outside the faculty and dragged him inside. He was rescued by some of the teaching staff. ('Report of the Minister of Justice').

48. Ibid. These official figures are more convincing than the exaggerated totals given by other sources which estimated the number of casualties in hundreds. See, for example, Mahmoud Hussein, *L'Egypte 1967–1973* (Maspero, Paris, 1975), pp. 50–5.

49. 'Report of the Justice Minister'.

50. 'Report of the Minister of the Interior to the National Congress of the ASU', *al-Ahram*, 3 Dec. 1968.

51. *Al-Ahram*, 28 Nov. 1968.

52. Ibid., 29 Nov. 1968.

53. Ibid., 6 Dec. 1968.

54. Ibid., 30 Nov. 1968.

55. Muhammad Hasanain Heikal, 'The Cause of this Generation', *al-Ahram*, 28 Jan. 1972.

56. Farid, 'Nasser's Secret Files', 17 Sept. 1979.

57. See *al-Ahram*, 22 Nov. to 6 Dec. 1968.

58. See full coverage of the session in *al-Ahram*, 3 and 4 December 1968.

59. It was not until seven years later that a different account was given by Dr al-Burullusi, in which he blamed the director of security in Alexandria for provoking students and affirmed that, 'The motives of the November uprising were the same motives as those of the February one—the state of anxiety and distress that followed the defeat of 1967.' ('Testimony of the Elderly Minister Abd al-Wahab al-Burullusi . . . Thus was Nasser's Cabinet', *Rose al-Youssef*, 29 Sept. 1975).

60. For example, Dr M. Fathalla al-Khatib, the dean of Cairo Faculty of Economics and Politics whose Edinburgh PhD thesis in the 1950s was on 'The Working of Parliamentary Institutions in Egypt', said: 'It is well known in the study of politics that strikes and demonstrations are not natural forms of expression and should not be resorted to even under unusual conditions . . . there are many official and popular organs through which people may express their opinions in society.'

61. These included the president and vice-president of the Union at the national level, who tried to persuade their colleagues in al-Mansoura and Alexandria to refrain from action. They, and the president of the Union of Cairo Polytechnic, were praised by the minister of the interior in the Congress: 'They made an enormous effort to clarify the facts in Alexandria and Cairo but unfortunately failed in their endeavour because they were overwhelmed by the agitators.'

62. *Akhbar al-Youm*, 23 Nov. 1974.

63. *Al-Ahram*, 28 Nov. 1968.

64. M. Heikal, 'Youth Between Fire and Ice', ibid., 6 Dec. 1968.

65. Ali Hamdi al-Gammal, 'People's Talk,' ibid., 5 Dec. 1968.

66. Ibid., 6 Dec. 1968.

67. This conclusion is contrary to what Dekmejian (*Egypt under Nasser*, p. 265) and Joseph Szyliowicz (*Education and Modernisation in the Middle East* (Cornell

University Press, 1973), p. 298) thought. Their reference to students having been 'given a greater voice in university affairs' and having been 'encouraged for involvement in the political process' is more appropriate to the uprising of February than to that of November 1968.

68. Mahmoud Hussein, *L'Egypte 1967_1973*, p. 50.

Chapter 9

1. Where no source is given for information included in this chapter, it is derived from the author's personal observation.

2. According to an activist of the period, 'The wall-magazines were based on a simple equation: a big sheet of paper + writing brush + courageous ideas = the sparking off of a creative intellectual debate within the universities which helped to develop student awareness.' (Ahmad Baha Shaaban, 'The Egyptian Student Movement and the Palestinian Revolution', *al-Thakafa*, no. 7 (July 1977), p. 61). See also 'New Press at University Walls', *al-Gumhuriyya*, 13 Jan. 1972.

3. Some of the wall-magazines were issued regularly with standard artwork, while others were issued only occasionally. The paper produced by the author, for example, was called *The Rough Copy*. A caption explained its title: 'I'll not let anybody censor me, nor will I censor myself, I'll publish my rough copy as it is.' It also had a margin which quoted Spinoza on man's freedom. Its first article in December 1971 was entitled, 'O God . . . You are the Decisive One', referring to the president's failure to keep his promise of making 1971 the year of decision for regaining the occupied territories.

4. A few printed student magazines slipped through the tight censorship. These included a small pamphlet-like magazine of satire and caricature called *Whips*, which was published by a group of Cairo Polytechnic students, and a more stylish magazine named after the folk musical instrument *al-Rababa*, published by students of the American University in Cairo. The latter was a vehicle for their liberal political and social opinions and was open to students from other universities to publish articles. It included some pages in English which explicitly supported the cause of the Palestinians.

5. Wael Uthman, *Secrets of the Student Movement—Cairo Polytechnic, 1968–1975* (Madkour Printers, Cairo, 1976) (in Arabic), p. 39.

6. Among these were: The Society of Political Studies and Abd al-Hakam al-Garrahi Family at Cairo University Faculty of Economics; Egypt's Family at Cairo University Faculty of Arts; al-Salam [Peace] Family at Ain Shams Faculty of Engineering; Zuhour al-Salam [Flowers of Peace] Family at Ain Shams Faculty of Law, among others.

7. Author's interview with Dr Ahmad Kamal Abul-Magd (June 1978).

8. In this year Magdi Hussein of the Economics Faculty at Cairo University was the first candidate for the Cairo Union presidency to put forward an explicitly political programme in his manifesto.

9. In this contest the two leftist candidates for the presidency and vice-presidency of Cairo Union lost by a margin of two votes. Leftist students, however, had some individual gains, including the Secretariat of the Committee of Cultural and Political Activities at the University of Cairo. At the Faculty of Arts in Cairo University and the Faculty of Medicine in Ain Shams University they had a majority on the Union Council.

10. *Al-Ahram*, 14 Jan. 1972.

11. David Hirst and Irene Beeson, *Sadat* (Faber & Faber, London, 1981), p. 126. (David Hirst was at this time the *Guardian's* correspondent in Cairo. He remained there until he was expelled by the Egyptian government following his reporting of the upheaval of January 1977. President Sadat called his reporting 'gutter press'.)

12. Paul Martin, *The Times*, 22 Jan. 1972.

13. Anthony McDermott, *Guardian*, 21 Jan. 1972.

14. Hirst and Beeson, *Sadat*, p. 127.

15. Henceforth referred to as minister of youth.

16. The first wall-magazine to comment on the president's speech seems to have been the one issued by the arts student Zein-elabiedin Fouad.

17. A placard in the Economics Faculty read: 'The fog: a local product . . . not an import from Bangladesh!'

18. The slogan was coined on the spur of the moment and written on the blackboard in the auditorium where the meeting was held. It read: 'Total Democracy for Students . . . Total Sacrifice for the Country'. In later versions the word 'people' replaced 'students'.

19. The hottest debate took place with the delegation from Cairo Polytechnic. At the general secretary's meeting with the delegation from Cairo Economics Faculty, which was attended by other ASU officials including the minister of youth Dr Abul-Magd, the discussion was interrupted several times by phone calls from President Sadat. When Sayyid Mara'i told the delegation that the president was distressed about what was going on, a member of the delegation replied that he should be happy to see students so concerned with their country's destiny and making such vigorous attempts to participate in shaping it. At the same meeting the general secretary informed the delegates that the president would not be available for the proposed inter-university conference because, as a religious man, he would be observing the Muslim custom of visiting the graves of his relatives. This transparent excuse greatly offended the students.

20. The highly charged atmosphere of the time encouraged a fervour and freedom in political discussion of which the students had no previous experience: 'In those tremendous days the national question, the humiliating occupation, and the nightmare of the enemy strangling the nation were at the centre of the ferment. The national question, and Palestine at its heart, was present heavily at every moment of the sit-in, present as never before. The dream of people struggling with weapons in their hands as the only force that can challenge and triumph haunted the restless nights of these young men and women standing firm in the face of a government with all the power and the repressive ability of its machinery.' (Ahmad Baha Shaaban, 'The Egyptian Student Movement and the Palestinian Revolution', *al-Thakafa*, no. 7 (July 1977), p. 50).

21. *Al-Ahram*, 21 Jan. 1972.

22. See, for example: Musa Sabri, *al-Akhbar*, 21 and 30 Jan. 1972; Ihsan Abd al-Kuddous, *al-Akhbar*, 20 Jan. 1972; Abd al-Rahman al-Sharkawi, *Rose al-Youssef*, 24 Jan. 1972. The only magazine which was prepared to defend the movement was the Marxist monthly *al-Tali'a*, which held a discussion with a group of student leaders on their release from prison and promised to publish the full text. It was unable to keep its promise, however, owing to press censorship.

23. *Al-Ahram*, 20 Jan. 1972.

24. Minutes of Students' Meeting in Parliament, 23 Jan. 1972. In *The Student Uprising in Egypt, January 1972* (Ibn Khaldun House, Beirut, 1972) (in Arabic), p.

134.

25. Ibid., pp. 134–5.

26. Some students accused Dr al-Otaifi of deception. As far as this particular incident is concerned, it is not clear whether he was aware from the beginning that nothing would be published or whether he was informed of this by a last-minute presidential telephone call.

27. The delegation consisted mainly of members of the official Student Union who lost their influence in the course of the uprising. The delegation had been hastily assembled in order to discredit the delegation from the meeting and sit-in. But the ex-president of Cairo University Union, Hussein Samir Abd al-Nabi, was careful not to weaken the solidarity of the movement, opening the discussion by affirming: 'We have come to declare our support for our colleagues and also to declare our disagreement with their approach.'

28. The proposal to organize a march to central Cairo was postponed on the second day of the sit-in after a delegation of two students met the interior minister, Mamdouh Salem, and failed to obtain permission to proceed with a march.

29. Many people suggested that the decision to send the forces was made by President Sadat rather than by Minister Salem. The vice-premier of Salem's cabinet, Muhammad Abd al-Salam al-Zayat, testified that the decision was made by Sadat himself. He also stated that the president had actually threatened to send the Presidential Guard in the face of Premier Salem's reluctance to send the security forces. See M.A. al-Zayat, 'The Circle of Violence and Political Decision', *al-Ahali*, 23 March 1983.

30. Of all the riots under Sadat's government, he singled out this particular uprising for repeated condemnation in his speeches and press interviews up until his death in 1981. See, for example: Speech of 31 Jan. 1977; Interview, *May*, 22 May 1981; Interview, *May*, 13 July 1981.

31. The scene inspired several Cairo poets who witnessed it. The well-known poet Amal Dunkul wrote a poem called 'Stone Cake', referring to the cake-like column in Liberation Square.

32. Paul Martin, *The Times*, 25 Jan. 1972. A statement prepared by five of the country's leading writers noted, 'Despite our rejection of some excessive pronouncements in the student movement we salute the peaceful spirit that characterized it and the lack of either violence or subversion, proving that our sons the students have reached the age of social maturity.' (Ghali Shukri, *Counter-Revolution in Egypt* (al-Tali'a House, Beirut, 1978) (in Arabic), p. 142).

33. *Al-Ahram*, 25 Jan. 1972.

34. Ibid., 26 Jan. 1972.

35. Declaration of the Arts Faculty Conference, 18 Jan. 1972. In *Student Uprising in Egypt*, p. 52.

36. Ahmad Younis, the head of the peasants' Co-operative Union and one of the three MPs who had gone to the university, volunteered to attack the uprising, revealing that he had seen the president of the HNCCUS putting a sinister 'red-coloured' scarf around his head!

37. Dr Hassan al-Sherif, a Chicago PhD-holder, co-owner of the biggest accountancy firm in Egypt at the time, and later minister of social security.

38. *Al-Ahram*, 25 and 26 Jan. 1972.

39. Tawfiq al-Hakim, Naguib Mahfouz, Hussein Fawzi, Dr Louis Awad and Ahmad Baha al-Din.

40. In Shukri, *Counter-Revolution*, p. 142.

41. *Student Uprising in Egypt*, pp. 114–15.

42. Interview with Dr Abul-Magd.

43. The government was concerned about foreign influences on the uprising. The arrested students were questioned by the prosecutor about a North Korean connection. Despite the clear hostility of the uprising towards Israel the possibility of an Israeli connection was also investigated, on the strength of a photograph of one of the student leaders in Hyde Park which happened to feature an Israeli flag in the background. Serious debate on the merits of publishing this photograph as evidence went on even at the highest levels of the government. (Interview with Dr Abul-Magd).

44. See, for example: the Declarations of the 21 February Meetings in the Faculties of Economics and Arts in Cairo University in *Student Uprising in Egypt*, pp. 87–91; Shaaban, 'Egyptian Student Movement', p. 54.

45. Declaration of the Conference of the Arts Faculty on 21 February. In *Student Uprisings in Egypt*, p. 90.

46. Interview with Dr Abul-Magd.

47. Uthman, *Secrets*, p. 61. In 1971 military training courses were provided for 70,000 students. (Georgie Hyde, *Education in Modern Egypt . . . Ideals and Realities* (Routledge & Kegan Paul, London, 1978), p. 152). But students complained that they provided no serious training for military action.

48. Foreign correspondents in Cairo at the time received little direct assistance from students, who did not want to lay themselves open to accusations that they were distorting the country's image abroad, if not betraying it. Once, when three foreign correspondents succeeded in slipping into the University Hall, they were asked by students to leave at once.

49. Paul Martin, *The Times*, 22 Jan. 1972.

50. Amnon Kapeliuk, 'Student Unrest in Egypt', *New Outlook*, vol. XV (Feb. 1972), p. 29.

51. *Student Uprising in Egypt*, p. 49.

52. 'The HNCCUS, A Student Declaration' in ibid., p. 40. The *Guardian* correspondent noted, 'Together with the call to arms, inextricably bound up with it is the call for reform and far-reaching changes in the ruling system. This is basically a call for democracy—democracy for students and everyone else.' (David Hirst, *Guardian*, 25 Jan. 1972).

53. In this respect prominent editors of the official press were attacked by name. Muhammad Hasanain Heikal of *al-Ahram* and Musa Sabri of *al-Akhbar* topped the list of student enemies in the press, greatly to their mutual horror. Although Sabri's touch was more demagogic, and Heikal's pretensions were more intellectual, in the eyes of the students both wrote grossly misleading articles. As David Hirst noted, 'It is because they regard Heykal as a defeatist and the symbol of long years of intellectual repression that they have focused most of their opprobrium on him.' (*Guardian*, 25 Jan. 1972).

54. Minutes of Students' Meeting in Parliament. In *Student Uprising in Egypt*, p. 127.

55. *Al-Ahram*, 26 Jan. 1972.

56. Interview with Dr Abul-Magd.

57. Dorsey, '1968 Revisited', p. 14.

58. Shaaban, 'Egyptian Student Movement', p. 57.

59. See, for example: Statement of the Conference of the Economics Faculty at Cairo University, 21 February 1972 in *Student Uprising in Egypt*, p. 81; Statement of the Union of the Faculty of Commerce at Alexandria University, 20 February

1972 (original copy).

60. Shukri, *Counter-Revolution*, pp. 114 and 254.

61. The Egyptian Communist, no. 11 (July 1976).

62. Uthman, *Secrets*, p. 6. Uthman also admitted, 'I felt that there was a danger that the Communists might succeed in capturing the leadership of the movement. Therefore I tried to expose their real political tendency to the students, and repeated my warning against their intellectual domination. It was not easy, however, to convince the ordinary student that those pretending to be patriots were foreign agents. So I tried to portray them as a group trying to impose its views on students . . . The majority of students still believed in the patriotism of the leadership of the movement, and it looked as if I stood against the patriotic current in the university.' (pp. 57 and 78).

63. Declaration from the HNCCUS. In *Student Uprising in Egypt*, pp. 47–8. When President Sadat expelled the Soviet experts from Egypt a few months later, the pro-Nasser grouping at Ain Shams University expressed their doubts on the decision at their Union meeting. See A Group of Egyptian Militants, *The New National Democratic Movement in Egypt—An Analysis and Documentation* (Ibn Khaldun Publishing House, Beirut, 1973) (in Arabic), pp. 87–9.

64. See, for example: Mahmoud Hussein, *'L'Egypte 1967–1973* (Maspero, Paris, 1975), *passim*; Mahmoud Hussein *et al.*, *La Révolte des Etudiants Egyptiens, janvier 1972* (Maspero, Paris, 1972), *passim*; Shukri, *Counter-Revolution*, p. 114; *Student Uprising in Egypt*, p. 22.

65. President Sadat's speech, *al-Akhbar*, 31 Jan. 1977.

66. Shaaban, 'Egyptian Student Movement', p. 61. In a meeting with Dr Abul-Magd after the events he expressed this view strongly.

67. Declaration from the HNCCUS. In *Student Uprising in Egypt*, p. 46.

68. *Guardian*, 25 Jan. 1972.

69. Shaaban, Egyptian Student Movement', p. 62. David Hirst wrote: 'The students want their own freely-elected leadership and, for the first time for 20 years they seem, for the moment, to have something like one. They demand official recognition of the National Student Movement [wrong translation of the HNCCUS] headed by one, Ahmed Abdulla, which has unofficially emerged supplanting or absorbing the official students' union.' (*Guardian*, 25 Jan. 1972).

70. Interview.

71. Interview with Dr Abul-Magd.

72. David Hirst, *Guardian*, 25 Jan. 1972.

73. Dr Hassan al-Sherif, vice-rector of Cairo University and the Guide of its Union Council, said at a meeting with President Sadat: 'Very often I convened the Cairo Union for five or six meetings in the course of one month in order to contain the movement which I first started to discern in December. These meetings lasted for some five hours. However, we could not agree upon the right line to take in the face of the developments.' (*Al-Ahram*, 26 Jan. 1977).

74. See ibid., 21, 22 and 23 Jan. 1972.

75. Ibid., 26 Jan. 1972.

76. Ibid., 25 Jan. 1972.

77. Interview with the president of the Union of a higher institute in Cairo (wished to remain anonymous); Text of the Union Statement of 24 January in GUSARE, *Student Unions of the Present Phase* (1972), p. 69.

78. *Al-Ahram*, 26 Jan. 1972.

79. One of those who attended the conference admitted: 'The meeting concentrated on the question of the Union elections and there was no talk of politics.

When some leftist members hung up a political wall-magazine, we tore it down.' (Interview with the president of a higher institute). It is also worth noting that some leaders of the January uprising, who travelled from Cairo to Alexandria where the conference was held, were refused entry to it.

80. One writer described it as: 'The first phase of the revolutionary response of the Arab people to the conspiracy [of surrendering Palestine in return for Sinai], and a heavy blow to the American influence in the Arab World.' (Zuhair El-Haj. In Hussein *et al.*, *La Révolte des Etudiants Egyptiens*, pp. 27–8).

81. Interview.

82. There was an early unsuccessful attempt to form a Union of the country's writers in the heat of the student uprising. See Shukri, *Counter-Revolution*, pp. 135–41.

83. Referring to this gathering, and the radical political programme put forward by the Nasserites, President Sadat said in a speech to parliament: 'A strange line has emerged—an attack has been made on the regime on the grounds that it is no longer Nasserite . . . The dean of Cairo Economics Faculty went and talked to students. He found the discussion to be leading in the direction that Nasser's thought was Marxist. Aha! that must be the reason why we gave up Nasserism! The dean stood up to them and said that if they wanted to talk about Nasser's thought that was one thing, but if they wanted to talk about Marxism that was another.' (*Al-Ahram*, 1 Feb. 1973).

84. Interview with the president of the Union of a higher institute in Cairo, who noted: 'Because there were in the camp students from different universities and of different political tendencies, especially the Marxist left, it was necessary to bring in the Karaté squad of the students of the higher institutes to control it. At the camp there were fierce discussions between the leftist students and state officials like the governor of Alexandria, the minister of youth, and others. We had to bring in the Karaté squad because we were told that the Communist students would spoil the camp, as was actually proved by their verbal attacks on state officials.'

85. See, for example: Shukri, *Counter-Revolution*, p. 121; Group of Egyptian Militants, *New National Democratic Movement*, pp. 8–9 and 72. M.A. al-Zayat dates back the formation of these sqads to December 1971. He was then the First Secretary of the ASU Central Committee and was informed that a number of MPs from Assiut were behind this. (See M.A. al-Zayat, 'The Circle of Violence and Political Decision', *al-Ahali*, 23 March 1983).

86. A student activist described Dr Abul-Magd: 'A quiet and placid man . . . an intellectual who frequently cites his experience in the Muslim Brotherhood. He is undoubtedly the most intelligent state official we have met, who acquired an ability to convince and expertise in political tactic.' (Uthman, *Secrets*, p. 105).

87. Interview.

88. Uthman, *Secrets*, pp. 120 and 68.

89. Ibid., pp. 115, 117 and 91. To ingratiate themselves with the Muslim fundamentalists, leading officials of the ASU, including its secretary-general, emphasized the ideological grounds for co-operation: the secretary-general asserted that the ASU ideology was in total agreement with Islamic thought (ibid., p. 102); Dr Abul-Magd recalled his own experience in the Muslim Brotherhood, affirming that the government was opposed only to Marxist thought (ibid., p. 195); and the organization's secretary swore by the Qur'an that he was most loyal to Islam (ibid., p. 129).

90. One of the Brotherhood's activists noted, 'What would student opinion be about a new society which advocated Islam and used knives to support that advocacy?' (ibid., p. 91). However, the same activist later regretted that the events had proved to him that 'some people deserve not only beating but also killing' (ibid., p. 118).

91. An example of this is an article in the *Rough Copy* entitled 'Our Crippled Government' which accused the government of being unable to raise the standard of living of the vast majority of the population and failing to liberate the occupied territories. It also accused it of inventing new ways to destroy the student movement.

92. 'The Prosecution Charge, Case no. 902 for the Year 1972', *al-Ahram*, 19 June 1973. The content of the wall-magazines was the subject of many questions during the interrogation of the students accused in this case. One magazine's quoting from Spinoza even came under interrogation:

Q. It appears that the article entitled 'Tractatus Theologico-Politicus' scoffs at the government and denounces it for repressing freedom!

A. This is Spinoza's view—ask him about it.

Q. Assuming it is a quotation from Spinoza, does its publication not mean some kind of agitation against the government, provoking its animosity by describing it as a repressor of freedom?

A. This is a broad political phrase. To invoke the historical literature of philosophers is more than a mere attempt at agitation. (Text of the Interrogation of the First Defendant, Case no. 902 for the year 1972).

93. Ibid.

94. Declaration of Students of Cairo Polytechnic 30 Oct. 1972. In Group of Egyptian Militants, *New National Democratic Movement*, p. 102.

95. A clandestine leftist report noted: 'Some childish and naive ideas are put forward calling upon us to do the enemy's job by inviting the Communist students to carry knives and engage in a holy war. Those who say these things are, despite their goodwill and indignation, falling into the trap of transforming the people's political struggle into a duel between an isolated vanguard and the regime. What a peculiar ditch they invite us to fall into! . . . With their isolationist and adventurist tactics they cannot see that thousands of students in the simplest and most peaceful manner condemning gangster tactics is a thousand times more effective than a bout of beating up their enemies.' (Samir Muhammad Kamel, 'Notes on Mass Action in the Ranks of Students', *al-Shuyu'i al-Misri*, no. 9 (May 1976), p. 50).

96. A number of lawyers, mostly leftists, were known to be sympathetic to the student movement and undertook the legal representation of the activists. Among these were: Ahmad Nabil al-Hilali, Zaki Mourad, Ahmad Megahed, Adel Amin, Dr Galal Ragab, Abdulla al-Zoghbi, and others.

97. Speech of 14 May 1980. The number of activists arrested on that day was fifty-two (of whom thirteen were non-students, i.e. journalists, poets, lawyers, etc., who attended some student activities and were accused of inciting them). Later on, when the level of turbulence had escalated, hundreds of students were arrested and interrogated in different parts of the country. When official charges were laid in June there were some one hundred defendants distributed among four separate cases—two in Cairo, one in Alexandria and one in Assiut. The prosecution had a difficult time with some defendants who refused to answer questions unless in the presence of their lawyers during the early stages of the interrogation. They later backed down on the advice of their own lawyers. The

insistence of the prosecution that the lawyers should not be present led many students to believe that it was heading towards a trumped-up case.

98. Issam al-Ghazali was an engineering student and a talented classical poet. Some members of his family had been activists of the Muslim Brotherhood. He was renowned for his attacks on his Marxist colleagues in poetry and prose. Only in gaol did he discover there could be a common cause between them. Despite attempts by some of them to isolate him as an enemy, others treated him as a patriot with a different ideology.

99. Uthman, *Secrets*, p. 94. Uthman's description of their attempt is a self-evident reason for failure: 'Our meeting ended with a sit-in, in which only thirty-five students, half of whom were security agents, took part. The Communists refused to join us. It was a shock to me that, contrary to my expectations, the Muslims who liked Issam and his poems did not take part in the sit-in. I could not understand what was wrong with the students. We did not meet to form committees or to withdraw our confidence in anyone. We did not meet to discuss our relations with Russia or America . . . We met in search of the truth, the truth behind the arrest of our colleagues. Is this a demand which any one could turn down? And if students do not want to get involved in that sort of situation, when will they get involved?'

100. 'Report of the Minister of Justice', *al-Ahram*, 28 Jan. 1973.

101. Statement of Members of the Teaching Staff at Cairo and Ain Shams Universities. In Group of Egyptian Militants, *New National Democratic Movement*, p. 178.

102. On the basis of these doubts the arrested students refused to be interviewed by the commission while in gaol. From the windows of their cells they shouted, 'The inquiry should take place in the university not in gaol'. Students ridiculed the commission by saying that it had the function of *takhatti* (ignoring) facts, rather than that of *takassi* (inquiring) into them. Some students met the commission and advised it to set up another commission of inquiry, to look into the ills of parliament itself. (Uthman, *Secrets*, p. 104).

103. The cursory mention of the right in the report read as follows: 'Various groupings emerged during the events, which took different organizational forms and different names like the religious societies and the regional societies. While these rival factions competed, the right stood aloof, apparently pleased at what was happening, fueling the conflict and looking to reap the rewards.'

104. The question of asking for the existence of Allah to be proved, which was never a major or even a minor issue for the student movement at any point in time, was mentioned in the report as the reason for the knife attack on a girl student who had uttered that heresy. When asked to elaborate, the head of the commission gave the following answer: 'As regards the "knife incident" in particular, I, together with my colleagues, did not want to discuss it. But since it has been raised, I would like to say first of all that we object to violence and object to its use in the ranks of our students and young men or in our society. But what provoked it was a discussion between a group of male students and a group of female students after the end of a student meeting at the Cairo Faculty of Law. When a girl student boldly asked, "You say that your God can be found everywhere, can I pull Him out of my pocket?", one male student could not control his emotions and struck her with a knife. Although we deplore the use of such weapons, we deplore most of all insults to the beliefs with which this country survived.'

105. See *al-Ahram*, 1 Feb. 1973.

106. Some years later, with the benefit of further information, or in his final revelation, President Sadat said that the plan was drawn up under orders from Beirut. (Speech, *al-Akhbar*, 31 Jan. 1977). Although it is true that Beirut was a centre of expatriate Egyptian opposition to President Sadat's regime, it became so well after 1972–73. The only indirect tie between student events in Egypt and Beirut at the time was that some sympathizers of the student movement in Egypt had formed an *ad hoc* solidarity committee to support it, without direct links of any significance (see: Group of Egyptian Militants, *New National Democratic Movement*, p. 70). Some years later President Sadat was confident enough to do what he did not do at the time—to denounce Communist activists in the movement as 'Moscow agents who incited students to clash with the police by alleging that the police had killed some students in the course of demonstrations', something which had never happened in his regime: 'No student was killed, injured or arrested by military or administrative orders over the whole eleven-year period.' (Speech, *al-Akhbar*, 31 Jan. 1977; Speech, *al-Akhbar*, 29 Jan. 1980; Interview, *May*, 22 June 1981).

107. Report of the Minister of the Interior to Parliament, *al-Ahram*, 13 Feb. 1973. The minister alleged in this report that there were no injuries among students.

108. Report of the Minister of Higher Education to Parliament, *al-Ahram*, 13 Feb. 1973. At that time the events in Assiut reached a higher level of confrontation between students and the police. Unconfirmed reports spoke of the death of a police officer. In central Cairo a demonstration of the mothers of the arrested students took place.

109. The Union at the national level, where it was most amenable to government control, remained silent until it issued a statement on the occasion of Students' Day, 21 February, calling on students to involve themselves in their studies 'in order to foil the enemy's plan and its attempt at psychological warfare'. The theme of the statement was the attempt of the Israeli Student Union indirectly to approach its Egyptian counterpart. This approach was rejected: 'The Israeli Union has a wrong perception about the motives of the student movement in Egypt, where there is no contradiction between students, the sons of the Revolution and the Alliance of People's Forces, and the patriotic leadership of the country.' (*Al-Ahram*, 21 Feb. 1973).

110. See for example *al-Ahram*, 17 Feb. 1973, in which a number of telegrams, coming mainly from official educational bodies rather than 'student organizations' proper, were published. There were also telegrams from non-student bodies, including a Dervish Society!

111. See Shukri, *Counter-Revolution*, pp. 117–18 and 160–1.

112. Ibid., p. 147.

113. In subsequent speeches and interviews President Sadat repeatedly denounced his opponents in these unions. (See, for example, Speech, 31 Jan 1977; Speech, 8 Aug. 1979; Interview, *May*, 13 July 1981). The president singled out the unions of the engineers, lawyers and journalists. About the latter he said, 'There are times when I think concentration camps should be reopened. Like when I heard that the Journalists' Union had met and had sent me a warning that the university wall-magazines should be classified as "press", when in fact they were really poison.' (*Al-Akhbar*, 8 Aug. 1979).

114. In defending himself against the accusation that the expulsion was his decision, Muhammad Uthman Ismail later said that his responsibility was only to provide the ASU with information about the political activities of its members.

When asked about the source of his information he answered, 'Various security bodies'. (*Rose al-Youssef*, 20 Jan. 1975). The expulsion was clearly President Sadat's decision. He later admitted, 'I dismissed 120 journalists, besides the students . . . I dismissed them as an example. At that time I did not want the media to praise me in poems. All I wanted was for these people to stand by their country . . . by your country not by me. Your country that was being distorted abroad . . . I dismissed them, but I did not deprive them of their living. I just stopped them from writing in the papers. Their salaries were not stopped. My aim was not to take revenge.' (Speech of 30 Jan. 1977).

115. The expulsion was taken by the university activists as proof that their movement wielded influence outside the university. They included it in the list of student grievances. However, the Islamic fundamentalists tried to separate the issue of expulsion from that of student demands: 'The approach of the Youth of Islam at the time was not to get involved in the battle of the left against the government and to prove that our presence in the movement was for the students' sake only. That was undoubtedly an intelligent tactic for the Society to adopt.' (Uthman, *Secrets*, pp. 107–8).

116. Professor Zakariya described the position of a university rector under government pressure: 'Dr Ismail Ghanim, the rector of Ain Shams University, was, despite his ties with the government, sympathetic towards the student movement and the teachers who supported it . . . It was easy for the "dissidents" of the teaching staff who met him to realize what tension the man was enduring—on the one hand under pressure from government (especially from the Ministry of the Interior, of which he was a part, and on the other, from his conscience, which understood and appreciated the reasons behind student and teacher rebellion.' (Interview).

117. See *al-Ahram*, 16 Feb. 1973. A number of teachers, mainly the Guides of the Union in different faculties, were questioned by the prosecution about the events. Most of them, especially Dr Kamel Laila, took an anti-movement stance. The one teacher who strongly supported it was Dr Abd al-Hamid al-Ghazali, associate professor at Cairo Faculty of Economics and the Guide of its Union. Dr al-Ghazali, a Glasgow PhD-holder and an Islamic fundamentalist who co-operated with the left on the basis of the common national cause, was one of the two teachers (the other being Dr Nader Firgani of the same faculty) who were arrested with students at their sit-in of January 1972.

118. Professor Zakariya was present and recalls the following impression of the ASU meeting: 'I remember that few of those present were speaking sincerely about the main issue. Some were combining talk about it with talk about themselves. Others were trying to lead the discussion on to the demands of the teaching staff about their working conditions. There were also those who expressed the views of the Ministry of the Interior in an intellectual style. However, the meeting did not lack some brave and positive words and in the end a phrasing committee, of which I was a member, was formed to propose a communiqué which included some positive resolutions, though diluted owing to the endeavour of Dr Kamal Abul-Magd and the attitude of some hesitant colleagues.' (Interview).

119. Text of declaration in Group of Egyptian Militants, *New National Democratic Movement*, pp. 175–81. The story behind this declaration is told by Professor Zakariya: 'The declaration was the outcome of discussions which started in some faculties of Ain Shams University and were then continued in its Teaching Staff Club. In the course of these discussions there was at least one

meeting between the rector and a number of teachers sympathetic to the student movement. I drafted the declaration and some amendments were introduced on the draft. It was then read in the Club and a handwritten copy was prepared and signed by those present. Before the process of collecting signatures was completed we decided to take the declaration and go to parliament. There was not much competition for the right to go. Eventually, I went together with Dr Abd al-Monem Tallima [of Cairo Faculty of Arts] and Dr Reda al-Edel [of Ain Shams Faculty of Commerce]. We were supposed to meet the speaker but we met the vice-speaker Dr al-Sayyid Ali al-Sayyid [also head of the commission of inquiry into student events] who was accompanied by two other members, Albert Barsoum [member of the commission and later a minister] and Mamoun Mishali [member of the commission]. Our dialogue with them was a dialogue of the deaf. There was no agreement on anything . . . The pivotal point of our argument was that students were sincerely advocating the preparation of the country for a real battle not for a rhetorical one. The argument of the other side was an advocacy of total silence and that any voice raised in opposition at that time was the voice of traitors . . . In the course of our discussion the word "left" was mentioned, causing the three MPs to feel so disgusted that one of them, Mishali, said he wished the word could be removed from the dictionary of the Arabic language! In the ensuing process of collecting signatures the number of signatories was relatively high as compared with what was usual at the university.' (Interview). According to Dr Reda al-Edel, the number of signatories was between ninety and one hundred teachers, mainly from Ain Shams University and, in collecting signatures: 'There were teachers whom we never asked to sign because we knew they would not, those who refused to sign on the pretext that the phrasing was inappropriate and those who refused with the excuse that they did not like to involve themselves in politics. Strangely, some of those who refused to sign were known to have definite political views, like two leftist professors in Ain Shams University.' (Interview).

120. There were strong rumours at the time that the president felt deeply unhappy about the attitude of the judiciary, and expressed to his intimates his particular disappointment that the judiciary did not appreciate that it was he who had released them from the political pressures they had been subject to under Nasser.

121. See *al-Ahram*, 19 and 20 June 1973.

122. While the hearing was taking place in the High Court of Justice in central Cairo there was a heavy presence of plain-clothes police and a reserve of armed police at the rear of the court in anticipation of trouble. This was just what happened. Scores of students organized a demonstration and the Central Guard was called in to disperse them.

123. According to Hyde, about one hundred and twenty-three thousand young people took part in civil defence activities, one hundred and twenty-seven thousand donated blood, nineteen thousand engaged in public service activities and five thousand participated in the war effort in other ways. (Hyde, *Education in Modern Egypt*, p. 166). Nevertheless, students complained about the level of preparation of the home front and the limited role they were allowed to play through civil defence activities. However, some of the activists of the student movement became deeply involved in these activities and were granted official certificates of worthy service.

124. The only survey exploring the attitudes of the country's young men towards the October war was a questionnaire distributed among 200 Egyptian

postgraduate students in the US. It produced some interesting results. See Saad al-Din Ibrahim, 'Questionnaire on the Views of Egyptian Young Men in America Regarding the October War', *Dirasat Arabiyya*, vol. X, no. 9 (July 1974), pp. 10–25.

Chapter 10

1. Malcolm Kerr, 'Egypt' in James S. Coleman (ed.), *Education and Political Development* (Princeton University Press, 1965), p. 190.

2. Wael Uthman, *Secrets of the Student Movement—Cairo Polytechnic, 1968–1975* (Madkour Printers, Cairo, 1976) (in Arabic), p. 45. At a meeting in 1969 between Nasser's minister of youth, Dr Safiy al-Din Abul-Ez and a delegation from the Economics Faculty of Cairo University, the minister referred to the fact that the number of cars parked outside the Engineering Faculties was higher than outside any other faculty proof of the class situation of the engineering students.

3. Ibid., p. 39–40.

4. According to G.M. Hasanain, the conflict between the 'bureaucratic bourgeoisie' and the 'urban petty bougeoisie' was reflected in the student movement, especially after 1967. See Gamal Magdi Hasanain, *Class Structure in Egypt 1952–1970* (al-Thakafa House for Printing and Publication, Cairo, 1981) (in Arabic), p. 136.

5. Saad al-Din Ibrahim, 'Questionnaire on the Views of Egyptian Young Men in America Regarding the October War', *Dirasat Arabiyya*, vol. X, no. 9 (July 1974), p. 11.

6. At a cabinet meeting on 24 March 1968 Nasser justified to his ministers the much-criticized assignment of army officers to civilian and diplomatic posts as unavoidable, because of 'security incidents' in the army. 'It is always important', Nasser said, 'to make correct calculations in regard to the army and the general opinion in the armed forces must be satisfied. We should not forget that he who wants to strike at the regime will do it through the army.' (Abd al-Majid Farid, 'Nasser's Secret Files', weekly series, *23rd July*, no. 24, 13 Aug. 1979).

7. According to the minister of higher education in 1968, Dr Abd al-Wahab al-Burullusi, Nasser's inner cabinet (including ministers with a university background, together with the minister of the interior, the Intelligence chief and others) had regular meetings in September 'shortly before the start of the academic year to discuss the political situation and its likely effect on university students'. (*Rose al-Youssef*, 29 Sept. 1975).

8. Speeches of President Sadat, *al-Akhbar*, 31 Jan. 1977 and *al-Ahram*, 6 Sept. 1981.

9. Interview.

10. In Musa Sabri, *Documents of the October War*, 1st edn (Modern Egyptian Bureau, Cairo, 1974) (in Arabic), p. 116.

11. *Al-Ahram*, 1 March 1968.

12. In their coverage of the student events in Egypt in 1972, William Dullforce and Richard Johns of the *Financial Times* wrote: 'More serious concern must centre around the army, particularly the 70,000 graduates who have joined or been conscripted since the June War of 1967. In the officer corps, they already have formed a significant pressure group. President Sadat sent General Sadek to talk to the troops at the Canal front over the weekend and is expected to do the same himself in the next few days. Now that the lid is off, he can take no risks.' (*Financial Times*, 26 Jan. 1972). There was also a rumour at the time that it was

General Sadek who prompted President Sadat to take the decision to end the student sit-in by police action, to avoid the general's threat to use the army for this purpose.

13. Ghali Shukri, *Counter-Revolution in Egypt* (Dar al-Tali'a, Beirut, 1978) (in Arabic), p. 109.

14. Ibid. See also Mustafa Kamel al-Sayyid, *Society and Politics in Egypt, 1952–1981* (Arab Future House, Cairo, 1983) (in Arabic), pp. 30 and 46.

15. Defending itself against the criticism that it was biased towards students, one of the Marxist organizations explained:

'Our intimate relationship with the student movement is due to the following considerations:

—Its paramount political importance, since it does not concentrate on syndicalist and economic demands but directs almost all its energies to the national question and the question of democratic rights and liberties.

—The direct and effective role it was thus playing, a role which the workers' movement was not fulfilling, in its fierce political resistance to the line of the ruling class power in resolving the national question . . .

—In so doing it had a direct mission to awaken the working class and other popular classes to national issues, in association with democratic liberties. It is a movement that does not confine its political stance within the boundaries of the university.

—The student movement is based in the transitional setting of university study and its potential exceeds resistance to the national crisis and awakening of the people to wider scale contributions, because the elements trained within it move after graduation to work in different sectors and among different classes of society, carrying with them their coherent attitudes towards the grave problems of the country . . . ' (*The Egyptian Communist*, no. 11 (July 1976)).

The same group urged its activists to pay more attention to students living in university hostels who were drawn mainly from the poorer strata of the peasantry. In a further report it warned: 'Because of the weakness of our activity in their ranks and because of the effect of the urban climate on them, they tend to become alienated and susceptible to religious societies.' (A Report on the Urgent Tasks of the Student Movement in Egypt. In A Group of Egyptian Militants, *The New National Democratic Movement in Egypt—An Analysis and Documentation* (Ibn Khaldun Publishing House, Beirut, 1973) (in Arabic), p. 84). Since this period, this susceptibility has become even more marked, with the dominance of Muslim fundamentalism among student activists.

16. Students were praised by state officials as 'the knowledgeable vanguard of the nation', the 'ammunition of the future', the 'confidants of the country', and the like. (See, for example, report on a parliamentary discussion, *al-Ahram*, 28 and 29 Feb. 1968). In the cases of those who sympathized with the movement, the treatment was even more exaggerated. The dean of the Engineers Union blithely suggested that: 'Parliament and the ASU Central Committee do not represent the nation as much as the students represent it.' (Minutes of the Meeting between the ASU Secretary-General and Representatives of Professional Unions, 1972. In *The Student Uprising in Egypt, January 1972* (Ibn Khaldun House, Beirut, 1972) (in Arabic), p. 117.)

17. In 1968 Heikal wrote, 'After long and detailed discussions with the young men I felt they were entitled to a deeper and more understanding approach. In brief, I felt they needed clearer facts in their hands rather than louder slogans

banging in their ears.' (*Al-Ahram*, 1 March 1968). Dr Abul-Magd, in turn, claimed that he tried, along with others, to deal with the student events of 1972–73 'in a political manner aimed at preserving students' right to self-expression and organization as a vital necessity that justifies the toleration of some excesses as a price for the achievement of that aim'. (Interview).

18. In Uthman, *Secrets*, p. 28.

19. Muhammad Abd al-Salam, *Rough Years—Memoirs of a Public Prosecutor*, 2nd edn (Dar al-Shorouk, Cairo, May 1975) (in Arabic), p. 126. The following extracts are drawn from a student declaration issued in the course of the uprising of January 1972:

LET EVERYBODY UNDERSTAND THAT:

When university students speak, the following points should be taken into consideration:

First: University students are the vanguard of society, and the people most capable of analysing matters and knowing the country's interests.

Second: University students are not the adherents of any specific group, but they are the purest and the most honourable stratum representing the Alliance of People's Forces.

Third: University students are not motivated by personal aspirations, are not ambitious for cheap gains, and do not aspire to belong to a higher class. They are concerned first and foremost with the country's interests.

Fourth: University students are balanced and thinking young men who are capable of analysing matters objectively and without anger or fanaticism.

Fifth: University students feel that they are the guardians of the interests of the people . . . (In *Student Uprising in Egypt*, pp. 73–4).

This declaration was issued by the Committee of Cultural and Political Activities in Ain Shams Union and reflected a point of view sympathetic to Nasser's government and may have been formulated by the Secretary of the Committee, Muhammad Ahmad Haseeb. However, it also reflects the wider self-understanding of average students.

20. The Security Memorandum and the Prosecution Interrogation of the First Defendant, Case No. 902 for the Year 1972.

21. Uthman, *Secrets*, p. 162.

22. In a survey conducted by Dr Sayyid Oweis in 1975 it was revealed that only 33 per cent of the students in the universities and higher institutes possessed a private library. They gave their hobbies as: 36.8 per cent reading novels and stories, 9.2 per cent theatre and 5.2 per cent fine arts. (Sayyid Oweis, 'Egyptian Youth and Culture', *al-Ahram*, 7 Dec. 1981).

Postscript

1. Ahmad Raslan, 'At the Beginning of Academic Year No. 75', *al-Musawwar*, 7 October 1983; 'Egyptian Universities in the New Year', *al-Shabab al-'Arabi*, 17 October 1983.

2. *Al-Ahali*, 29 August 1984.

3. In a survey of students at the Cairo University Faculty of Arts, a number of propositions about the teaching staff were affirmed by the following percentages

of students: teachers fulfil their obligations in the best manner, 16.6%; teachers fulfil their social duties to students, 12.6%; teachers are anxious to render services to students, 13.2%; some teachers are too strict with students, 59.6%; some teachers are aloof from students, 59.4%. See Saad Ibrahim Gama, *Youth and Political Participation*, al-Thakafa House for Publication and Distribution, Cairo 1984 (in Arabic), p. 137.

4. Muhammad Amir, 'The University and Its Problems in a Rapidly Changing World', *al-Ahram al-Iqtisadi*, 19 December 1983.

5. Mana Sirag, 'A Journey of Hope in the Hearts of Egyptian Youth', *Sabah al-Khair*, 2 February 1978. See also Fatma Yusif, 'The Egyptian Girl Student: Problems and Frustrated Dreams', *Awraq*, no. 12, June–July 1984.

6. Saad Ibrahim Gama, p. 129.

7. Iman Munir, 'Youth and the Media (summary of a survey carried out by Alexandria University)', *al-Shabab wa 'Ulum al-Mustaqbal*, July 1983.

8. For example, there were gatherings and strikes at a number of university faculties and higher institutes: the Faculty of Economics and Politics, the Technical Institute of Commerce, the Telecommunication Institute, the Institute of Cooperation Studies, the Institute of Physical Education for Girls, and the Institute of Physical Therapy.

9. In an interview with *al-Ahali* (29 September 1982), Omar Talmasani, the *de facto* leader of the Brotherhood, stated: 'Al-Nabawi Ismail [the interior minister] used to contact me in 1978 and 1979 whenever events occurred at the universities. He would receive me warmly in his office and say, "the Engineering Faculty is out of hand, the Medical Faculty is out of hand. I see you are a kind man. For God's sake meet the students and calm them down." '

10. See the defence of the activists of the Islamic Society, especially that of Abdel Manem Abu'l-Futauh, a former president of Cairo University Student Union, in which he cited incidents in which he had shown solidarity with his opponents (sponsoring lawyers to defend them, for example) and democratic attitudes in dealing with them (such as allowing them to issue wall posters and to address meetings). 'Dialogue With the Muslim Youth', *al-Shaab*, 27 March 1984.

11. *Al-Akhbar*, 31 January 1977.

12. *Al-Akhbar*, 2 February 1977. This meeting is of special significance. Although it was attended only by the Union representatives, who were not necessarily the most active in the movement, they confronted the president with a relatively firm attitude unprecedented in similar meetings with representatives of other elite groups and organizations. This caused Sadat to be very nervous in a live broadcast, which contributed to the decline of his popularity and even caused him to be ridiculed for an outburst during the meeting in which he repeatedly interrupted one student speaker.

13. An example is the Union of Democratic Egyptian Youth (UDEY), a leftist organization created in 1978 by members of the unofficial Egyptian delegation to the Eleventh International Festival of Youth and Students, held in Havana. The UDEY student section is now the member organization representing Egypt in the International Union of Students, a position formerly held by the official Student Union.

14. Shortly before the Mansoura strike the Egyptian Commission for Liberties, made up of representatives of the opposition parties and professional unions, issued a statement calling for the abolition of Presidential Decree no. 265/1979 (the Union constitution), which it considered 'unconstitutional, undemocratic, and a legalization of flagrant aggression against the freedom of student patriotic

activity; it is based on fear and mistrust of the students.' (*Al-Ahali*, 9 December 1983).

15. S.I. Gama, pp. 145 and 147.

16. Fayiz Zayid *et al.*, 'Why Do Youth Not Participate in Political Activity?', *Sawt al-Shabab*, 1 April 1984.

Index